Solidarity in Practice

Cross-border solidarity has captured the interest and imagination of scholars, activists, and a range of political actors in such contested areas as the US–Mexico border and Guantánamo Bay. Chandra Russo examines how justice-seeking solidarity drives activist communities contesting US torture, militarism, and immigration policies. Through compelling and fresh ethnographic accounts, Russo follows these activists as they engage in unusual and high-risk forms of activism (fasting, pilgrimage, civil disobedience). She explores their ideas of solidarity and witnessing, which are central to how the activists explain their activities. This book adds to our understanding of solidarity activism under new global arrangements and illuminates the features of movement activity that deepen activists' commitment by helping their lives feel more humane, just, and meaningful. Based on participant observation, interviews, surveys, and hundreds of courtroom statements, Russo develops a new theorization of solidarity that will take a central place in social movement studies.

Chandra Russo is an Assistant Professor of Sociology at Colgate University, where she teaches courses in social movements, activism, and anti-racism. Before earning her PhD from the University of California, Santa Barbara, she spent several years working on immigrant justice issues in New York State, Central Mexico, and Colorado. Her research and writing on these matters has been published in numerous venues, including *Mobilization, Race & Class, Interface*, and the *Denver Post*.

Cambridge Studies in Contentious Politics

BOOKS IN THE SERIES

(*continued after index*)

Solidarity in Practice

Moral Protest and the US Security State

CHANDRA RUSSO
Colgate University, New York

CAMBRIDGE
UNIVERSITY PRESS

University Printing House, Cambridge CB2 8BS, United Kingdom

One Liberty Plaza, 20th Floor, New York, NY 10006, USA

477 Williamstown Road, Port Melbourne, VIC 3207, Australia

314–321, 3rd Floor, Plot 3, Splendor Forum, Jasola District Centre, New Delhi – 110025, India

79 Anson Road, #06-04/06, Singapore 079906

Cambridge University Press is part of the University of Cambridge.

It furthers the University's mission by disseminating knowledge in the pursuit of education, learning, and research at the highest international levels of excellence.

www.cambridge.org
Information on this title: www.cambridge.org/9781108473118
DOI: 10.1017/9781108596237

First published 2018

Printed in the United States of America by Sheridan Books, Inc.

A catalogue record for this publication is available from the British Library.

ISBN 978-1-108-47311-8 Hardback

ISBN 978-1-108-46099-6 Paperback

Cambridge University Press has no responsibility for the persistence or accuracy of URLs for external or third-party internet websites referred to in this publication and does not guarantee that any content on such websites is, or will remain, accurate or appropriate.

Contents

Figures

Acknowledgments

This book is most centrally indebted to the communities of struggle I have had the privilege to be a part of and to document. My dear friends on the Migrant Trail left an indelible mark on me long before I decided to pursue a PhD or to include them in this study. Over the past five years, participants with School of the Americas Watch and Witness Against Torture have also touched me in transformative and enduring ways. The kindness, hospitality, and camaraderie I found in these groups have made this project not only possible but also a joy to pursue. I hope to have offered some semblance of justice to their efforts and vision.

I am thankful to the several faculty mentors at the University of California at Santa Barbara who shepherded me through this project. Verta Taylor equipped me to enter into the scholarly conversation on social movements as no one else could have. Howard Winant pushed me toward more assertive argumentation and proved an indefatigable advocate at every turn. Avery Gordon's probing inquiries and astute observations helped me to forge ahead with clarity and enthusiasm, especially during the murkier stages of writing. George Lipsitz embraced this project with enthusiasm since its most modest inception and patiently accompanied me for the next several years, always with an uncanny sense of where the book was headed.

In moving toward publication, I am immensely grateful to Suzanne Staggenborg, who believed this book might find a home at Cambridge University Press, and Senior Editor Robert Dreesen, who agreed. Feedback from the anonymous reviewers at Cambridge University Press allowed me to further hone the book's purpose and situate it more clearly within the social movements literature. I am also thankful to series editor David S. Meyer for giving the entirety of the manuscript a meticulous and encouraging review.

As I endeavored to complete this project, I have had the great fortune of Catherine Corrigall-Brown's sage advice, kindness, and perspective. My heartfelt appreciation also goes to colleagues in the Department of Sociology and

Anthropology at Colgate University, who have provided a most nurturing environment as I put the finishing touches on this book.

Some stunning photographs enrich these pages. I am grateful to Justin Norman of Witness Against Torture and Eric O. Ledermann with the Migrant Trail Walk, who have so deftly captured the work, the struggle, and the soul of their respective groups. I also thank photojournalist Christina Felschen for images taken on the Migrant Trail Walk in 2016.

Various funding opportunities at the University of California at Santa Barbara allowed me to undertake data collection for this research. These include monies from the Department of Sociology, the Flacks Fund for the Study of Democratic Possibilities, the UC Center for New Racial Studies, the Humanities and Social Sciences Grant, the Interdisciplinary Humanities Center, and the Mendell Graduate Fellowship in Cultural Literacy. At Colgate University, grant monies from the Social Sciences Division and the Research Council allowed me to bring this project to completion.

At Cambridge University Press, more people have helped on design, copy-editing, outreach, and the daily grind than I could hope to adequately thank. They include but surely exceed: Meera Seth, Joshua Penney, Robert Judkins, Stephanie Taylor, Jackie Grant, Abirami Ulaganathan, and Indra Priyadarshini. I also thank Amron Gravett of Wildclover Book Services for her careful and diligent indexing.

While this project owes its existence to these activists, scholar-mentors, institutional support, and production team, my family gives me a continual sense of purpose, especially when our global condition appears dreary and dark. My life partner, Andy Pattison, models the best of what it means to be civically engaged, to not let perfect ideals get in the way of good works. I count his boundless talents, intellect, humor, and love among my life's greatest treasures. I am infinitely grateful that we get to walk side by side on this journey, which recently included the joyous arrival of our sweet Sabine.

I

"Not Free to Be Completely Human"

Leo stands and invites the rest of us to do the same.[1] We push back our small, plastic chairs. About forty of us rise in the circle, acknowledge each other with small nods, and join hands. Witness Against Torture has gathered at Saint Stephen's Episcopal Church in Washington DC. It is the first week of January 2014. People are now entering the fifth day of their fast. Many have bundled themselves with scarves and hats. Those wearing orange jumpsuits have packed layers of wool and down under the iconic outerwear, preparing to stand for hours in front of the White House in what is certain to be a freezing drizzle.

The room is necessarily large for all that it must accommodate. Rectangles of butcher paper scribbled with colorful notes line the back wall. There are lists of team members and their requisite tasks, words, and shapes from direct action planning. A ten-foot plastic folding table is set up for letter writing – letters for the Guantánamo detainees to be delivered through attorneys, letters for various politicians demanding due process for the prisoners. Against another wall there are props for street theater: an assortment of cardboard signs, two sets of folded military fatigues, other cardboard props. A queen-size bed sheet with a large portrait of detainee Shaker Aamer painted in black acrylics has been rolled up carefully. Against another wall are more plastic folding tables holding laptops, various electronic chargers, a camera case, and detachable lens. This is "media headquarters," where appointed photographers and those who compile the daily email to the listserv sit late into the night, quietly editing

[1] Leo is a pseudonym. Throughout this study, I intersperse the use of pseudonyms and actual names. Many activists in this study were open and even eager to have their identity shared. Due to the size of their groups, it is very difficult to render them fully anonymous, most specifically from other group members. While I have done my best to protect identities from public recognition, there are two situations in which I relinquish pseudonyms altogether. The first is when drawing upon published or otherwise public documents. The second is when a participant explicitly asked to be named.

and uploading photos and video, corresponding with allied organizations and journalists, collecting relevant media coverage. A tall stack of books constitutes the lending library. Titles range from classical tomes of the activist left to theology and political theory, as well as books written by friends of the group. The prospect of reading such dense and despairing content about US militarism, torture, Guantánamo, or the prison industrial complex without having had a proper meal in days astounds me.

Where the room snakes around toward the bathrooms and small kitchen, more folding tables have been set up with all manner of liquid nourishment: fruit and vegetable juice, a continually brewing electric coffee pot, an assortment of teas and hot cocoa, and bouillon packets. As it is now early morning, sleeping rolls and personal belongings have been locked in a storage room while the group leaves for the day.

We hold hands, a shared warmth. Leo needs no microphone; his confident Bronx accent always offers structure to the space, its tenor calm, the words clear. He issues a rallying cry before the group leaves the church and makes its way out into the city. This recitation is less rehearsed than Leo's spoken word performances, but it still reverberates as poetry.

I'm not free while racism and militarism do what they do. I'm not free to be completely human. That makes me linked to crazy oppression ... I feel really strongly that I am fighting for liberation. John Brown was not *just* fighting on behalf of slaves. Our liberation is bound up in each others'.

Leo brings the circle to a close with the famous words of Lilla Watson, an Australian aboriginal activist and artist who became well known in the 1970s: "If you have come to help me, you are wasting your time. But if you have come because your liberation is bound up with mine, then let us work together."

When Leo asks the group to stand together, he speaks to the vision of solidarity that Witness Against Torture adopts. Like the other groups in this study, Witness Against Torture holds foremost a commitment to make injustice visible and to testify to the conditions of the aggrieved. These activists engage in this practice, what I term *solidarity witness*, not solely because they oppose the state-mandated suffering of others but because they believe their own fates are intertwined with the targets of state violence. For some, this is a theological principle. For most, it is a moral commitment, a practice to produce the kind of world they wish to create.

INTRODUCTION

This study explores what it means to engage in a practice of ethical witness as an expression and instantiation of solidarity across cavernous divides of wealth and power. At the onset of the twenty-first century, global inequality and militarized social control are both targets of protest and practical challenges for social movements seeking to enact solidarity across borders (Kurasawa 2007;

FIGURE 1.1. *WAT Protester*
Photo credit: Justin Norman

3

Robinson & Barrera 2011). More specifically, contemporary US security policies have become an important focus of resistance even as they present significant obstacles to transnational solidarity (Butler 2009; Pease 2009). In the face
of these daunting realities, US residents like the members of Witness Against
Torture engage in collective resistance to the US security state by imagining and
enacting solidarity with some of those who are tortured, detained, murdered,
and exposed to life-imperiling conditions at the behest of the US government.
This study proceeds through an ethnography of three distinct but similar protest groups: (1) School of the Americas Watch, which seeks to close the military
training facility at Fort Benning, Georgia; (2) the Migrant Trail Walk, part of
the US–Mexico border justice movement; and (3) Witness Against Torture, a
grassroots effort to close the Guantánamo Bay Detention Center. Often rooted
in theologically informed cosmologies, those involved in these campaigns
understand "bearing witness" as their foremost means of standing up to state
violence and forging solidarity with those who lack the practical freedoms
to advocate for themselves. For the activists in these groups, this practice of
solidarity witness is also a means to disavow and disinvest in the systems of
dominance that show up in their own lives in complex and damaging ways.

In the face of structural violence and injustice, aggrieved communities
have long generated alternative epistemologies and decolonial practices.
Among these are what Paula Ioanide (2015) terms "epistemologies of ethical
witness" – ways of seeing, feeling, and being that expose the contradictions,
injustices, and violence of the neoliberal state. Examples of ethical witness
include the Black Radical Tradition (Robinson 1983), Borderlands epistemologies (Anzaldúa 1987), the self-determination of Palestinians in exile (Said
1992), and the Chicana/o Movement (Blackwell 2011). This project builds on
this idea of witnessing as an important form of resistance, exploring how it is
used to contest the US security state.[2] Distinct from previous scholarship, however, this study identifies the emergence of a political practice among relatively
privileged groups acting in solidarity with the aggrieved, rather than among
those conventionally thought to be the most acutely violated by US security
policies. Through this practice of "solidarity witness" social movement participants utilize resistant modes of seeing and being seen to respond to political
injustices that do not most immediately impact them.

Avery Gordon (1997) suggests that the impact of "Capitalism and State
Terror" might be understood as a "haunting," in which "structures that appear

---

[2] In terming these instances of witness, I draw from Ioanide (2015). None of the authors cited
above was centrally preoccupied with the concept of "witness" per se. In fact, there have been
limited theoretical or empirical investigations of witnessing as an organized social movement
effort (Kurasawa 2007; Givoni 2013). There is, however, a vast literature on witnessing as the
necessary but imperfect response to socially orchestrated suffering. Most of this work tends to
respond to the German Holocaust (Felman & Laub 1991; Oliver 2004; White 2004; Derwin
2012). While this important body of literature informs my own understanding of the term *witness*, it is not centrally referenced.

removed from us make their impact felt in everyday life" (19). This manner of haunting shows up in complex, riddling, and sometimes counterintuitive ways. It is destructive not only to the most directly violated but also to those who are asked not to see or feel the degradations of this system. Through engaging in solidarity witness, those who are generally thought to enjoy certain privileges along with a socially structured ignorance – white, middle-class social groups from the Global North – refuse to ignore or offer consent to conduct they deem unacceptable and indecent. Rather, they make an effort to recognize and respond to the US security state by making its violence and injustice visible and undesirable to themselves and others. Through this study, I address two central and intertwined questions. First, I ask how these movement groups imagine and enact solidarity across the divisions of power and reverberations of violence that organize today's global society. Second, I seek to better understand the political avenues available for those seeking to disrupt the status quo of the US security state.

This chapter begins by explaining how I arrived at this topic of study and briefly describes its case studies and the methodology. Next, it elaborates on the neoliberal US security state as the impetus for these campaigns and narrates a brief history of the radical pacifist lineage from which these groups emerge. It then turns to some basic parameters of solidarity witness and situates this political practice within more traditional approaches to social movement studies before previewing the chapters to come.

COMING TO THE RESEARCH

The seeds of this research project were planted during the five years I spent involved in immigrant rights activism in Poughkeepsie, New York; Zacatecas, Mexico; and Denver, Colorado between 2005 and 2010. During this time, I began to think through what it means to be in solidarity with those who are under the thumb of the state in a way that I have not directly experienced. Through my organizing experience with those who shared similar concerns and commitments, I realized that many came to their work as solidarity activists for reasons of faith or religion. Because my own orientation was decidedly secular, I was at first surprised by this. Yet I quickly found that the kinds of practices that these predominately Christian activists pursued, including pilgrimages through the desert, solemn ritual, and creative civil disobedience, were emotionally evocative and meaningful in a way that more traditional protest and policy work did not feel to me. I wanted to understand why that was. Why were these somewhat unusual forms of political expression so much more appealing, transformative really, at least by my own barometer?

My first real exposure to this kind of activism was when I joined the Migrant Trail walk in 2007. I lived in Colorado at the time and was part of a group of US citizens advocating for the rights of unauthorized immigrants. This group was loosely affiliated with Quaker traditions and had supported the Migrant Trail since its inception. I had never been to the US–Mexico border and believed the walk, as daunting as it sounded, would be an important way for me to learn more about migration policy while allowing me to connect with activists who had been doing this work for longer than I had. My first time on the Migrant Trail walk was one of the most transformative experiences I had had as an activist. In subsequent years, as I established myself in Colorado as a full-time employee of a nonprofit organization committed to immigrant rights, I returned to the Migrant Trail every May to remember and mourn the dead, reconnect with the border justice movement, and nourish myself for the social justice struggles ahead. There was something particularly sustaining about this week of action. I had completed the Migrant Trail three times when I chose to take it up as a topic of research during my first year of graduate school.

The research itself proved somewhat grueling; administering surveys and conducting multiple interviews with exhausted activists, their clothes caked with desert dirt and dust, added a level of challenge to the already difficult walk. What I was able to document and assess was well worth the effort, however, allowing me to begin to consider the importance of embodied witness to the work of solidarity activism (Russo 2014). I had stumbled upon a kind of political practice and a target of activism – which I term the US security state – to which I wanted to give more attention. In the end, I decided I would choose two more group events that were similar to the Migrant Trail in three important ways. First, the activists involved across the three groups are predominantly white, middle-class, faith-driven practitioners of nonviolence. Second, each group engages in similar tactics, including fasting, pilgrimages, civil disobedience, and ritual protest. Third, the iterations of state violence that each group contests are tied to the neoliberal US security state and its military-carceral expansions from the end of the Cold War through early Free Trade Agreements and concomitant border enforcement and into the "War on Terror" following September 11, 2001.

This project, then, proceeds through an ethnography of three activist communities, broadly from the Christian Left, that protest the racialized violence of the US security state against Latino migrants, Muslim detainees, and communities and social movements throughout Central and South America. Part of what unites these groups is their loose connection to a common lineage of radical pacifism, though this is something I discovered through the research process and not why I initially selected each case. My data collection, elaborated in the methodological appendix, has included days and sometimes weeks of participant observation with each group, forty-nine semistructured interviews with activists, fifty-four surveys, and an archive of hundreds of courtroom statements from the trials for those who have committed civil disobedience. Here is a brief overview of each case.

School of the Americas Watch

Between the early 1990s and 2015, School of the Americas (SOA) Watch activists convened every November to participate in workshops, marches, and planned civil disobedience in an effort to close the SOA, a US military training school for soldiers from South and Central America. Formed in 1990, SOA Watch has linked SOA graduates to nearly every coup and major human rights violation in Latin America since the school's inception (Nepstad 2004). The SOA was renamed the Western Hemisphere Institute for Security Cooperation (WHISC, or WHINSEC) in 2001 after grassroots pressure and public outrage about these practices led Congress to nearly defund the school. Iconic of the US security state's transnational militarism, the SOA/WHISC continues to be a site where US and Latin American elites collaborate to suppress dissent against neoliberal policies that impoverish and structurally abandon the majority of the world's populations. Lesley Gill (2004) argues that central to the SOA/WHISC's operations are pedagogies that indoctrinate Latin American soldiers in the logics of the US security state and the interests of a transnational capitalist class.

Migrant Trail Walk

During the annual Migrant Trail, approximately fifty activists spend a week walking seventy-five miles through the US–Mexico borderlands to oppose migrant deaths and the growing militarization of the border. The Migrant Trail began in 2004 to respond to ever more draconian border enforcement measures initiated by the United States in the mid-1990s that have spurred a wave of migrant fatalities that number well into the thousands. Scholars contend that the public obsession and mass investment in preventing unauthorized migration points to "a global immobility regime" wherein "surveillance and control over migrants" is undergirded by cultural politics in which affect figures centrally – "a new xenophobia as part of a modern culture of fear [and] the paradigm of suspicion" (Turner 2007: 290). Leo Chavez (2008) explains that by the logics of today's US security state, Latino immigrants, particularly those from Mexico, are treated through the frame of supposed "illegality," as if they are already criminal, illegitimate, and undeserving of social supports. David Hernandez (2005) describes this condition as "lesser citizenship" in which race and immigration status combine to render immigrant communities doubly vulnerable to incursions from the state and vigilantes.

Witness Against Torture

Witness Against Torture (WAT) formed in 2005 when twenty-five activists decided to travel to Cuba in response to the first major publicized hunger strike being undertaken by the detainees at the Guantánamo Prison. Since their return, Witness Against Torture participants convene every January in Washington DC for a week of protest, fasting, and communal living to oppose the indefinite

³ Beginning in 2016, SOA Watch changed their annual convening to the US–Mexico border at Nogales, Sonora/Arizona. A more complete account of SOA Watch follows in Chapter 2.

FIGURE 1.2. *In 2013, a few thousand SOA Watch participants gathered at the gates of Fort Benning*
Photo credit: Chandra Russo

FIGURE 1.3. In 2015, fifty-nine Migrant Trail participants completed the walk, here pictured in the Buenos Aires Refuge with Baboquivari Peak in the background
Photo credit: Eric O. Ledermann

detention and torture of the Guantánamo prisoners. Guantánamo took its current form in 2002 as a detention center for so-called enemy combatants captured in Afghanistan as part of the "War on Terror," a far-reaching foreign and domestic policy response to the attacks of September 11, 2001. Amy Kaplan (2005) argues that Guantánamo traces a long and sordid history that positions it at "the heart of the American Empire" (832; see too: Paik 2010). At this US naval base in Cuba, the earlier territorial conquests that marked US imperialism in the twentieth century have been consolidated into a key military-carceral apparatus of the current US security state. The military prison is situated in a US-occupied space in Cuba, with a history of quarantining Haitian migrants, and is now an infamous location for the indefinite detention and torture of racialized Muslim and Arab bodies.

A BRIEF NOTE ON TERMS

The groups in this study use different terms to explain what they perceive as their distinct roles in the social movement landscape. SOA Watch and Witness Against Torture, for instance, call their groups *movements*. The Migrant Trail, by contrast, understands itself as part of a larger movement, which I term *border justice*. An accompanying feature to this distinction is that whereas SOA Watch and Witness Against Torture each organizes multiple actions, gatherings, and strategies to advocate for their issue, the Migrant Trail is the most patterned and constrained, conducting one week of action, once a year. The Migrant Trail and WAT, however, are similar in that they resist the label and form of "organization," which some SOA Watch participants more readily adopt. SOA Watch, as distinct from the other two groups, has been around for more than twice as long, has hemispheric reach, and does at this time have paid staff, office spaces, and other resources.

The vast literature on movements and organizations defines these concepts in ways that do not always accord with the language used by activists. The term *movement* continues to be ill-defined, and scholars have defined a *social movement organization* as everything from a very formal group arrangement with written rules and paid staff (McCarthy & Zald 1977; Kriesi 1996) to a very loose association of people with common ideals about how society should be organized (Lofland 1996).[4] When SOA Watch and Witness Against Torture use the term *movement*, it is as a descriptor indicating political resistance with clear objectives linked to a history of similar struggles, which these groups understand to also be social movements. I suspect all three groups understand the term *organization* by the most formal definition, including paid staff,

---

[4] Hanspeter Kriesi (1996) suggests that organizations require membership criteria, written rules, and paid staff, to name but a few basic parameters for his typology. John Lofland (1996) defines movement organizations quite differently, as human groupings excluded from mainstream society that advocate for certain social arrangements on ideaslistic or moralistic grounds.

FIGURE 1.4. In 2014, Witness Against Torture participants wear the iconic clothing of Guantánamo detainees and protest in front of the National Mall in Washington DC

Photo credit: Justin Norman

written rules, and even a particular tax status. Many seem reticent to use this designation because of its often-negative connotations in the global justice activist subculture with which these groups are often aligned.[5]

Network may be the most appropriate scholarly term to explain these groups' structures, and their networked dimensions are especially evident when considering their shared lineage of radical pacifism. Borrowing from Diani and McAdam (2003), I conceptualize networks as individuals and groups that are connected by relationships of mutual trust and solidarity, forged through histories of collective action, participation in activist subcultures, and membership in other organizations.[6] To illustrate how this networked quality operates among the groups in this study, it is noteworthy that a number of those involved with the Migrant Trail and with WAT reflect on SOA Watch as the protest space in which they were first politicized, suggesting this experience propelled them to become involved in subsequent movement activities.[7] However, the activists in this book never use the term *network* to describe themselves or their movement relationships, and imposing such a term on them seems to distract from rather than illuminate the central aims of exploring the practice of solidarity witness. I therefore refer to these cases as *movement groups* (or just groups) or *campaigns*, suggesting a series of coordinated activities aimed at achieving a particular outcome.

---

[5] Scholars and activists document growing skepticism toward formal, hierarchical and often "non-profit" organizations in the work of global justice and anarchist groups as well as those that understand themselves as affiliated with radical leftist politics (McDonald 2002; Notes from Nowhere 2003; INCITE! 2009).

[6] Research demonstrates that social networks are particularly important in supporting key dimensions of the kind of activism studied in this project. Solidarity witness places central importance on personal, subjective and cultural transformations. It often includes high-risk tactics. It is grounded in what most would consider a radical critique of dominant social arrangements. Scholars suggest that networks, specifically in the form of movement "free spaces" (Polletta 1999), are uniquely poised to provide the infrastructure that activists require to pursue personal, affective and cultural aims as well as more traditionally defined political goals. Furthermore research highlights the importance of direct network ties, such as close familial, friend and organizational relationships for encouraging and supporting those engaged in high-risk activism (McAdam 1986; 1988). Lastly, social networks appear to be particularly valuable for cultivating oppositional consciousness and helping sustain activists that hold radical political views (Diani & McAdam 2003).

[7] The fact that involvement in protest catalyzed future, and often deeper, engagement with movement activity reaffirms research findings on activist networks. The personal relationships of these networks encourage people to join in collective action. Yet protest activities themselves forge new relationships between individuals and groups, impacting on personal biographies as well as the networked structure of movements more generally (Gerlach & Hine 1970; McAdam 1988; Diani 1995).

METHODOLOGY

I situate this work in a tradition of social movement ethnographers who are politically aligned with, and often themselves active within, the movements they document and analyze (Butigan 2003; Rupp & Taylor 2003; Gould 2009; Taft 2011; Van Ham 2011). While various decolonial, feminist, and post-structuralist interventions in the research enterprise suggest that scholars are always embedded in the social relations under study, with important implications for ethics, representation, and knowledge production (Luff 1999; Smith 1999; Hale 2008), my position in relation to my object of research is explicitly quite close. My relationship with these groups ranges from central and continued involvement (the Migrant Trail), to ongoing relationships (WAT), to more sporadic but continued contact with activists (School of the Americas Watch). This impacts my stance as a researcher and the data to which I have access within each group. It is also bound to show up in the way I represent each case, though I do my best to document and analyze these movement groups as evenly as possible. I do not avoid critique of the groups under study and believe their modes of internal contention to be instructive (Chapter 6). Yet at the root of their activism, these activists do espouse basic premises with which I agree. Part of the motivation for this project, then, is that akin to my research participants, I too am invested in shifting those dynamics of the US security state that I understand to be egregiously unjust as well as collectively deleterious.

It is no coincidence that in proposing a "politically committed and morally engaged" social science, Nancy Scheper-Hughes (1995) understands engaged research to be itself a form of "witness." For the scholar to be a witness, as opposed to a mere spectator, means that she must be involved, take sides, and be accountable for what she sees and fails to see. Of course, all research takes a position; the pursuit of supposed objectivity is also a political and epistemological commitment. As a witness to these witnesses and in solidarity with these solidarity activists, I commit to a certain understanding of our sociohistorical moment and use the role of scholar to expose in some small way what I perceive to be the stakes of apathy and ignorance as well as the possibilities for action.

In pursuing ethnographic methods from the stance of a witness, I appreciate João Costa Vargas's (2006) formulation of "observant participation." Distinct from the "participant observation" central to most ethnographic endeavors (Emerson, Fretz, & Shaw 1995), observant participation emphasizes participation as the central method by which the social world is interpreted. Observant participation is not just an ethical or political move, but centrally an epistemological one as well. There is more to be gleaned from active participation in the social world than from merely watching others do what they do. This dovetails well with my understanding of social movements as knowledge projects, an idea I adopt from Ron Eyerman and Andrew Jamison (1991) that is also taken up by Dylan Rodriguez (2006). The idea here is that social movements might be understood as spaces of knowledge production first and foremost. Those who refuse the status quo must create an alternative common sense. What we identify as *social movement* is itself the generation, modification, articulation, indeed *movement*, of these new ideas, identities, and modes of praxis within groups and across society. What this means for scholars, as Rodriguez (2006) aptly observes, is that social movements can be learned *from* and *with*; they are not mere social units to be empirically assessed or taken as objects of scholarly knowledge. Much of what I have to say in this book I have learned from and with these movement groups. These are ways of seeing, feeling, and knowing that centrally shape this project. I now turn to some of the central theoretical anchors for this research, beginning with the political context in which I situate the practice of solidarity witness.

THE NEOLIBERAL US SECURITY STATE

This book explores how three social movement groups seek to resist US state violence and enact solidarity with the state's targets. Group participants describe the state violence they contest using a variety of terms, including "neoliberalism," (United States) "empire and imperialism." "militarism, militarization and the military industrial complex," "systemic oppression," and "structural injustice." While this study is centrally concerned with how these groups understand and respond to state violence, I here offer a brief overview of the scholarly basis for understanding what these groups resist as aspects of a unified whole. To this end, I refer to the impetus for these group's actions as "the US security state," an amalgamation of domestic and foreign military, carceral and policing priorities that coincide with the global transition to neoliberalism. Identifying some of the main features and links between the issues that these groups contest helps to better situate their resistance.

While the state violence that the groups in this study resist begins in the aftermath of the Cold War, the US security state is a continuation as well as qualitative amplification of the military expansions that commenced several decades earlier. The end of World War II saw the rise of a new US militarism, justified by the looming threat of the Soviet Union and its transnational allies (Mills 1956; Cobb 1976). Indeed, during his final address in office in 1961, President Eisenhower famously warned that the United States was headed toward a "military-industrial complex," the rise of a permanent war economy underwritten by the state. In a world no longer organized between capitalism and communism, the US security state's militarism along with new modes of border enforcement, prison expansion, and extralegal detention are best understood within the rise of a new global order: neoliberalism. Though often understood as a shrinking of the state to enhance market efficiency, neoliberal policies do not so much reduce as redirect the nation-state's investments.

Within the United States, such redirection has been in large part toward contemporary security policies.[8]

Ruth Wilson Gilmore (1998) points to the late 1960s as a particularly auspicious moment in the transition toward the neoliberal US security state. If the 1950s are often regarded as America's "Golden Age" of wealth and prosperity, the 1960s pierced any illusion of social, political, and economic equanimity. New forms of organized resistance to social mores and political priorities coincided with looming economic crisis.[9] A burgeoning conservative effort, represented by Richard Nixon's 1968 "law and order" campaign for president, won mass support by promising to address political upheaval and economic decline, while shoring up the racial anxieties of a broad swathe of American voters (Gilmore 1998; Alexander 2010). Throughout the 1970s and 1980s, enhanced "security" meant greater investments in the policing and incarceration of communities of color and immigrants along with continued military expansion abroad (Wacquant 2009; Ioanide 2015). By the 1990s and into the present, the War on Drugs, increased enforcement at the US–Mexico border, and military intervention against a nebulous Muslim/Arab enemy became de facto policy priorities, reinstantiated and amplified by each successive US administration. While the neoliberal US security state may have been inaugurated under an ascendant Right, both major US political parties have supported the ongoing transition toward militarism and mass incarceration as the foundations of a new political and economic status quo (Giroux 2008; Hall 2011).

The "security" assured by the state is of course a chimera – a set of discourses, policies, and practices that erode the well-being of the vast majority of the global populace while promising just the opposite. Ample evidence suggests that the United States continues to become less equal, less responsive to traditional political channels, and less democratic (Duggan 2004), while engaging in ever more illiberal practices, including preemptive war, indefinite detention, and torture (Margulies 2013). Yet the discourse of security is a necessary social and political force for garnering provisional consent from the public. Imogen Tyler (2013) argues that in order for neoliberal policies to be linked to the

---

[8] While an exhaustive review of the literature on neoliberalism is beyond the scope of this study, scholarship on neoliberalism might helpfully be divided into three general approaches: Marxism, Foucauldian, and statecraft. Marxists (see: Robinson 2004; Harvey 2005) understand neoliberalism as a redistributive economy in which wealth is garnered from the poor and middle classes and pushed upward to the global capitalist elite. Foucauldians are interested in neoliberalism as a cultural project, exploring how new logics are incorporated into a collective sense of self and subjectivity (see: Brown 2005; Foucault 2008; Giroux 2011). Statecraft theorists examine the transition from social welfare to social control states (see: Wacquant 2009). The ensuing analysis draws on all three areas of study.

[9] Key elements of this crisis included profit "stagflation" and the 1973 oil crisis. For a more complete theorization of profit stagnation, see William Robinson's (2004) *A Theory of Global Capitalism*. For a useful account of the 1973 oil crisis, see Timothy Mitchel's (2011) *Carbon Democracy*.

supposed enhanced security of the many requires the cultural production of a *"state of insecurity* ... continuously fueled and orchestrated through the proliferation of fears about border controls and terror threats, as well as economic insecurity and labour precariousness" (9). Within these narratives of insecurity, the racialized figures of the illegal immigrant, the terrorist, and the criminal are mobilized to encourage a sense of defensive patriotism and implicit consent for violence against populations both at home and abroad. Interrupting such narratives is a key means by which the groups in this study seek to make their impact.

I do not wish to overstate the case for consent to neoliberalism and concomitant shifts in US policy. Certainly "security" and "law and order" rhetoric have won major political gains, and racialized fears continue to saturate punditry and popular culture. At the same time, the twenty-first century has seen wave after wave of mass rejection for the key features of neoliberal security doctrine, with protests against US military interventions abroad, anti-immigrant policies at home, the state's growing subservience to the capitalist elite, and racist policing practices. For instance, when the United States and its allies prepared for the military invasion of Iraq in 2003, millions of protesters took to the streets in what was regarded as the largest political demonstrations in human history up until that time (Tharoor 2003; Walgrave & Rucht 2010). Three years later, similarly unprecedented mobilizations took place throughout the United States as hundreds of thousands of immigrants and their allies responded to anti-immigrant policy and sentiments (Voss & Bloemraad 2011).[10] By 2011, Occupy Movements across the United States, inspired by anti-austerity and anti-authoritarian resistance efforts the world over, popularized a critique of neoliberal practices and their impact on wealth inequality with statements such as "the banks got bailed out, we got sold out" and slogans of the "99 and 1%" (Hardt & Negri 2011; Calhoun 2013). The subsequent explosive rise of the Black Lives Matter movement in 2013, albeit a continuation of a centuries-long black liberation struggle in the United States, demonstrates new levels of organized mass opposition to racist police violence (Taylor 2016).

These efforts, however, have seen limited gains. The invasion of Iraq was hardly slowed, anti-immigrant policies and rhetoric continue to gain support throughout the United States, the growing wealth gap has not been stymied, and law enforcement and civilian vigilantes continue to be acquitted for perpetuating racist violence. Part of this is the nature of social movement impacts – they are hard to measure, often diffuse, and may take years or even generations to come to fruition. Moreover, scholars convincingly suggest that neoliberalism

---

[10] The most immediate reason for these protests was the passage of HR 4437, The Border Protection, Anti-terrorism, and Illegal Immigration Control Act of 2005, estimated to cost billions of taxpayer dollars in fencing at the US–Mexico border and law enforcement resources while legally reclassifying unauthorized immigration as a criminal rather than civil offence (Voss & Bloemraad 2011).

itself is a key part of the equation. We are today in a different era than the one that saw clear, if partial, victories for collective well-being, heightened justice, and greater equality. There is mounting evidence of a continued deterioration of democratic political avenues in the neoliberal state (Duggan 2004; Harvey 2005; Giroux 2008; Wacquant 2009; Brown 2015). Earning majority consent is no longer even a pretense for this state to govern. This poses real concerns about the potential for impacting social change through traditional democratic political channels.

The groups in this study emerge from an activist tradition that has never held much faith in politics as usual. This common lineage of radical pacifism is prominent in shaping the shared tactical repertoires, political understandings, and central issues each group pursues. While a more specific account of each groups' origins follows in Chapter 2, an overview of the history and key features of radical pacifism helps to situate the practice of solidarity witness that this book explores.

RADICAL PACIFISM IN THE UNITED STATES

The groups in this study are part of a centuries-long tradition characterized by the pursuit of nonviolence at all levels of society; a cynicism toward the state, established political institutions and reformist agendas; an emphasis on direct action and civil disobedience; and a commitment to moral right above and beyond political calculus. This radical pacifist lineage originates with the Historic Peace Churches, including the Mennonites, Quakers, and Church of the Brethren. Members of these churches have long opposed military service, understanding participation in war as a violation of Christ's teaching to love one's enemies. These faith traditions adopted somewhat different strands of pacifism as nineteenth-century Mennonites and Brethren opted for passive and individualized objection to war while the Quakers pursued more active and organized resistance. The mandated US draft policies of World War I, however, pushed all three Historic Peace Churches toward a more assertive and public opposition (Nepstad 2008).

The modern US peace movement was arguably forged during the inter-war years as activist groups coalesced for long-term involvement in anti-war and anti-militarism efforts. The earliest organizations, such as the faith-based Fellowship of Reconciliation (1914) and the more secular War Resisters League (1923), were predominately white, middle class, and Protestant, though levels of religiosity varied across organizations. American popular opinion during this time largely regarded involvement in World War I as a mistake, allowing the peace movement to gain influence and support. Hitler's rise to power in the 1930s, however, fundamentally troubled the pacifist, noninterventionist, and sometimes isolationist stance that had become mainstream in secular society and among mainline Protestants (Danielson 2014). The US public came to see involvement in World War II as the only adequate response to Nazi

Germany. When in 1940 the highly influential Protestant leader and theologian Reinhold Neibuhr described the option of US nonintervention as equivalent to "moral perversity," he dealt a serious blow to radical pacifists, rendering anti-war sentiments highly unpopular across Protestant congregations (Kosek 2011; Appelbaum 2014).

With the end of World War II and the onset of the Cold War, radical pacifists took part in antinuclear efforts and played key roles in the US Civil Rights Movement and subsequent anti-war efforts. Through these campaigns, they further honed and demonstrated their unique convictions. For instance, most American peace advocates pushed for the development of international institutions, such as the United Nations, as a foremost means to assure international peace and to secure against the threat of nuclear war. Radical pacifists, however, were distrustful of such organizations, believing them to be instruments of the most powerful nation-states in bolstering regimes of imperialism and exploitation (Wittner 1984). With their skepticism toward lobbying and other more traditional political channels, radical pacifists instead pursued a range of direct actions in opposition to what they perceived as unjust laws. These included refusing to pay taxes that allow the United States to maintain a military, physical disobedience to state-mandated nuclear defense drills, and military draft resistance.

During the Civil Rights Movement, radical pacifists helped to support leaders, form organizations, and pursue nonviolent tactics. Bayard Rustin of the War Resisters League and Glenn Smiley of the Fellowship for Reconciliation worked closely with Martin Luther King Jr. to build the Southern Christian Leadership Conference. The Congress of Racial Equality, founded by radical pacifists in 1942, offered a good deal of support to the Montgomery Bus boycott of 1955 and the sit-in movement of 1960 (Branch 1989; Polletta 2002). By the mid-1960s, the relationship of pacifists with many Civil Rights activists became more fraught. Those in the Black Power movement saw armed self-defense as an important part of a larger liberation strategy. Radical pacifists on the other hand believed relinquishing nonviolent tactics for reasons of political strategy to be a betrayal of their deep moral and theological convictions (Joseph 2007).

The 1960s opened up new opportunities for radical pacifists to exert significant influence on allied activists as well as US politics more broadly. Foremost among these was Vietnam War opposition. Anti-war protests mobilized some of the largest numbers in US history, and growing public consensus against US involvement in Vietnam gave activists a sense of their political power and moral authority. A particularly important tactic in this movement was organized resistance to the military draft. While initiated by a select few radical pacifists, thousands of young men ultimately participated in organized draft resistance, risking arrest and jail time. Many would publicly burn their draft cards in church-based rituals, the symbolism of fire, blood, and biblical testimony lending moral weight to these dramatic spectacles (Foley 2003). Akin to the core features of the solidarity witness I explore in this book, the tactic of draft resistance was often animated by religious symbolism, public spectacle, and personal sacrifice.

Another early harbinger of the social movement activities this book explores was the daring anti-war activism carried out by A Quaker Action Group (AQAG) in their 1967 voyage to North Vietnam aboard the boat *Phoenix*. As it was against US law to offer any form of aid to the Vietnamese, the Quaker activists knew their journey would be swiftly halted if they advertised their intentions. In fact, Quakers' previous efforts to sail to Bikini Atoll in 1958 to protest nuclear weapons testing was halted twice, and the crew sentenced to two months in prison after the second attempt. AQAG thus planned their Vietnam trip covertly, distinguishing this action from the public civil disobedience more typical of radical pacifism. Facing opposition from many, including North Vietnamese officials and even many in the Quaker community, AQAG ultimately made a successful arrival in Haiphong with needed medical supplies. Once there, they produced a documentary film, highlighting the war-torn landscape and daily sense of terror wrought by US military actions. Akin to many practices of the solidarity witness the groups in this book pursue, the *Phoenix* voyage was an act of bodily, material, and spiritual solidarity with the Vietnamese people as well as an important witness. Quaker activists offered direct aid to the targets of warfare while exposing to themselves and others the devastating impacts of US foreign policy (Pasulka 2016; Grudzinski 2017).[11]

Other intrepid Vietnam War resisters included Catholic peace activists who, like the Quakers, are quite closely linked to the three groups in this study. For instance, Catholic priest Daniel Berrigan and his brother Philip, whose daughter Frida is a founding leader in Witness Against Torture, were the principal architects of a 1968 raid on a draft board office in Catonsville, Maryland. The Berrigan brothers along with seven others, now known as the Catonsville Nine, publicly burned six hundred draft files with napalm and were each sentenced to three years in prison for their acts of civil disobedience. The Catonsville raid was only the beginning of the Berrigan brothers' lives of daring activism. Both brothers, along with hundreds of other Catholic pacifists, would become instrumental in forging the faith-based center of 1980s antinuclear activism in the United States as well as the Central American Solidarity Movement, the latter of which receives more attention in Chapter 2 (Nepstad 2004; 2008).

I end this selective history of radical pacifism shortly before the groups in this study emerge, as it points to a few key features of an activist practice also at play in the solidarity witness repertoire. First, radical pacifists can be classified as a small and largely marginal cadre of highly committed individuals who have nevertheless been instrumental in mobilizing broad-based opposition when the political moment has been right. Second, most of the

---

[11] For a much more complex and complete account of the antecedents and aftermath of this trip, see Nicole Pasulka's (2016) excellent investigation of the history of the *Phoenix*.

activists who come out of this lineage adopt a moral stance above and beyond political calculus, though this is not to discount their serious commitment to this-worldly engagement. Francesca Polletta (2002) well describes twentieth-century radical pacifists as adopting "a utopianism that refused to withdraw from the political world" (38). Third, in their cynicism toward the state, established political institutions and reformist agendas, radical pacifists have long prioritized direct action and civil disobedience as opposed to more traditional political activities like lobbying and voting. Their high-risk tactics are often undertaken as quasi-religious ritual inflected by powerful moral symbolism. Fourth, radical pacifists have honed an expansive and intersectional analysis, in part through deep, if not always seamless, involvement with various movements for historically marginalized groups, such as engagement in the US Civil Rights Movement. They have come to understand issues such as racism, sexism, poverty, and environmental degradation as both cause and outcome of war and militarism. In line with this, they have prioritized acts of solidarity and direct witness, seeking to get physically, socially, and spiritually closer to the direct targets of the state violence they contest as well as expose these experiences to wider publics.

The activists in this study emerge from this lineage. Like those that came before them, they are a relatively small, deeply committed core who, if not always religiously inclined, pursue their moral convictions even when these appear to be unlikely to win policy change in the short term. The activists engaged in solidarity witness also maintain an expansive and complex assessment of the US security state. They link war-making and state violence to poverty and structural abandonment, understanding these as the twinned dynamics that maintain despotic forms of power. For each of the groups in this book, the issue they contest evinces the necessity of militarized social control as an instrument of corporate greed. They share an understanding of the United States as a nation-state that abuses its power on the global stage to secure the interests of a small elite while neglecting the basic material, social, and spiritual needs of everyone else. These activists understand the issue they contest as a particularly draconian node in this system and see those with whom they wish to enact solidarity as one of the most egregiously targeted populations.

SOLIDARITY WITNESS

What does that mean, to witness torture? That is terrible. We have seen the Abu Ghraib photographs. We have all witnessed torture. The question is, what does that mean? ... For us, what we have made it mean is fighting to end torture by forcing other people to witness torture by the spectacle of people in jumpsuits, by penetrating symbolically important space, by identifying and marking and testifying to the existence of the crime ... We tried to understand Witness Against Torture not as an organization, but ... as a practice and as something that nobody owns but anybody can do.

Jeremy Varon, member of WAT (Grele 2011: 70)

In this excerpt, Witness Against Torture organizer Jeremy Varon reflects on the idea of witnessing as a contest to state violence. Varon explains witnessing as a *practice*. By positing evidence of the state's atrocities – making others see the horror of torture – WAT compels the public to see what the state obscures. This is in line with Lane Van Ham (2011), who notes that for activists contesting state violence at the US–Mexico border, witness is a "seeing, encouraging others to see, and acting in certain ways because of what one sees" (128). Examining the residues of trauma from the Dirty Wars in Argentina, Diana Taylor (1997) also describes witnessing as "an involved, informed, caring, yet critical form of spectatorship" (25). These understandings of witness align with the cases in this study – indefinite detention and torture at Guantánamo, violence and abandonment at the US–Mexico border, and militarism in Latin American. In all three instances, witnessing is a means of seeing, knowing, and coming to act that aims to contest the otherwise radically limited forms of visibility, knowing, and imagination that constitute the current sociopolitical order.

The political practice that this book seeks to explore and explain is something I term *solidarity witness*. This concept emerged from participants' explanations of their aims and methods as well as what I observed and experienced during research. Many of the participants in these groups explained bearing witness as a foremost means of enacting solidarity with the state's targets by standing up to state violence. For some of the faith-driven participants in this study, to witness means to see and testify to God's will, which would be that the least among us be treated with dignity and justice. Others alluded to the legal meaning of the word *witness*. To be on the witness stand means to see and testify to the truth of a crime.

One reason to append the term *solidarity* to this practice of witnessing is due to these activists' social position. These activists are what some have termed *solidarity activists* (Sundberg 2007) in the sense that they are not directly targeted by the injustices they contest.[12] In this way, the activists in this study inhabit a movement position that is shared across issues and histories. Social movements nearly always count among their ranks those who are not directly impacted by the injustice being contested. Some examples include the participation of whites in the US Civil Rights Movement (McAdam 1988), men in feminist movements (Schacht & Ewing 2001), US citizens in the struggles of Central Americans (Smith 1996), and caste Hindus allied with Untouchables in India (Marx & Useem 1971). Because solidarity activists are not directly violated by the injustice they contest, they are generally thought to be distinct from movement beneficiaries in the fact that they enjoy a set of privileges and

---

[12] Solidarity activists – a term that I first saw used by Juanita Sundberg (2007) in her rather critical interrogation of SOA Watch – have gone by many terms in the scholarship, including "conscience constituents" (McCarthy & Zald 1977), "allies" (Myers 2008) and "privileged outsiders" (Munkres 2008). In contrast, those who are most directly impacted by the issue they contest are often termed "core activists" (Kraemer 2007) or "movement beneficiaries" (Myers 2008).

protections that movement beneficiaries do not (Kraemer 2007). This locates such activists in a liminal position, rife with opportunities as well as challenges. In the most instrumental sense, solidarity activists may be able to help disenfranchised and stigmatized groups gain access to greater material and political resources and may have an easier time appealing to mainstream audiences (McCarthy & Zald 1977; McAdam 1988). At the same time, the presence of activists who enjoy such privileges has generated a host of considerations regarding internal movement conflicts and the hijacking of agendas, disputes about tactical and strategic aims, and debate over ultimate political goals (McAdam 1988; Myers 2008). The solidarity activists in this study avoid some of the most obvious instances of these dilemmas in that they have limited direct contact with the state's targets. At the same time, these activists still navigate serious ethical and political challenges in seeking to act *with* those whom they must in many instances act *for*.

In the somewhat limited research on solidarity activists, scholars have often sought to explain *why* such activists mobilize on behalf of the aggrieved.[13] In this book, I add to our understanding of what motivates solidarity activists but also examine how they navigate the ethical and political challenges of their movement involvement. I borrow from Judith Butler (1993) in suggesting that the practice of solidarity witness is rooted in the acknowledgment that "there can be no pure opposition to power, only a redrafting of its terms from resources invariably impure" (39). All forms of power and sites of resistance are stained with histories of violence and injustice. In this sense, no facile maneuver is available to anyone, regardless of social position, as they seek to combat structural injustice and systemic violence. Moreover, the ways that privilege and oppression operate in efforts at social change are always complex as the vectors that privilege some and oppress others are diverse and vast (Cocks 1989). In some sense, the very categorization of solidarity activist might obscure as much as it illuminates (Sundberg 2007). For example, to presume all solidarity activists are identically positioned because of shared privilege vastly oversimplifies the ways in which experience and identity work. Such an observation is especially important for empirically examining what solidarity witness accomplishes as a form of subject work for the groups in this study.

In choosing the term *solidarity*, I wish to speak to more than just the position of not being directly targeted by the state. Solidarity is a sociologically rich concept that fundamentally motivates the origins of the discipline. Most sociological thinking emerged in considering the possibilities for solidarity in the face of the dramatic economic, political, and social upheavals of modern industrial capitalism and urbanization. As Fuyuki Kurasawa (2007) asks:

---

[13] Findings suggest that some of the primary motivations for solidarity activists to join movements include personal relationships with movement beneficiaries (Demerath, Marwell, & Aiken 1971; McAdam 1988); religious motivations to oppose human suffering (Smith 1996; Nepstad 2004; Summers Effler 2010); and emotional appeals in the form of "moral shocks" (Jasper 1997).

How could bonds of mutual responsibility and communal belonging, as well as shared ways of thinking and acting, be sustained in light of accelerating and seemingly irreversible processes of role differentiation, formalization and complexification of social life, individuation and normative pluralization? (158)

Today, global neoliberalism and the US security state present novel, if not wholly dissimilar, considerations. Technological advances and the time-space compressions they engender make unprecedented forms of solidarity both newly imaginable and practicable. At the same time, the social organization of neoliberalism and concomitant security societies, rife with inequality and impoverished of meaningful democracy, does a good deal to prevent such solidarities from being realized.

Of course, multiple intellectual traditions are associated with the study of solidarity, each with its own set of definitions and assumptions. In this way, the very features by which solidarity is defined and the mechanisms by which it is achieved are not settled matters. For Marx, especially in his later writings, solidarity was rooted in the material conditions that organized society. An individual's class, in the form of his relationship to the capitalist system, was the impetus for cultivating solidarity with other similarly positioned members of society. Durkheim (1893) approached solidarity quite differently, understanding it as a psychic and cultural force and tracing the evolution of solidarity from premodern to industrial societies. Durkheim suggested that while the "mechanical solidarity" of old had been rooted in sameness, kinship ties, and tradition, "organic solidarity" would be rooted in the kinds of interdependence required by new and developing social, economic, and cultural differentiation. Scholars suggest that today the kind of fearful nativism upon which the US security state depends constitutes its own mode of solidarity, a unifying force by which people come to share common beliefs and goals, even if these are predicated on exclusion, damage, and violence to entire populations (Pease 2009; Ioanide 2015).

The solidarity that the activists in this study intend and enact might be best articulated as what liberation theologists term *acompañamiento* or accompaniment. Nepstad (2004) explains that the idea of *solidarity* was transmuted from a more orthodox Marxist notion of class solidarity to that of accompaniment by social movements active in Central America during the 1980s. Today, the notion of accompaniment as a kind of solidarity across differentials of power and access has been taken up by a number of activists, scholars, and theologians (Farmer 2013; Watkins 2015). The term *accompaniment* is often associated with Archbishop Oscar Romero, who called on Salvadorans to accompany the poor. Solidarity in the sense of accompaniment means meeting the needs and supporting the agency of the most powerless and oppressed, what Archbishop Romero termed "the preferential option for the poor" (Tomlinson & Lipsitz 2013). Yet as a form of solidarity, accompaniment goes further. It requires long-term commitment, a willingness to be changed, and a fundamental epistemological reorientation. A group of Catholic activists, scholars, and priests active with the movement lineage in which the groups in this study are located, define *accompaniment* as follows:

> To deviate from other pathways for a while (and then forever), to walk with those on the margins, to be with them, to let go. Accompaniment is an idea so radical and difficult for us to comprehend that its power and significance reveal themselves to our Western and Northern minds only slowly and with great difficulty (Dennis et al. 1993, p. 21 cited in Watkins 2015: 326)

The activists in this study understand themselves as solidarity activists in this sense of being those that accompany. They are not directly targeted by the injustices they contest but seek to stand up for the targets of state violence because they are those most marginalized and degraded by a system that ultimately harms everyone.

The way these activists understand and enact being a witness is fundamentally about solidarity in this sense of accompaniment. To witness includes a reaching out and drawing close to the state's targets against the structures that socially divide while damaging, sequestering, and disappearing entire groups of people. While the closeness that that these activists seek must often be affective, cultural, and spiritual, as opposed to literal and material – as Chapters 3–5 develop at length – through witnessing these activists forge an important notion of what solidarity can mean.

SITUATING SOLIDARITY WITNESS IN MORE TRADITIONAL MOVEMENT APPROACHES

The central assertion I make in this study is that, through the practice of solidarity witness, these activists expand the sphere of politics while incubating alternative ways of feeling, knowing, and being.[14] The practice of solidarity witness provides these activists with the means to resist state violence with ever greater care, commitment, and conviction. In turn, their modes of resistance challenge our traditional assumptions and categories of political activity.

The political process and contentious politics approaches to studying social movements have long been dominant to the field and invaluable for helping us

---

[14] The idea of "expanding the sphere of politics," which is central not just to this study but to my understanding of what social movements do and how they matter, came to me through the work and counsel of George Lipsitz (2011a: 127). The origins of this concept, however, derive from Nelson Lichtenstein's (2003) important observations about how organized labor turned the shop floor into the space of politics: "The responsibilities and expectations of American citizenship – due process, free speech, the right of assembly and petition – would now find their place in factory, mill, and office. A civil society would be constructed within the very womb of the privately held enterprise" (32). The US labor movement's ambitious agenda to bring democratic principles and activities into the heart of industrial capitalism's production – the literal space of the shop floor – exemplifies how social movements can expand the sphere of politics into the most unlikely of arenas.

to better understand protest and politics (Tilly 1978; McAdam 1982; McAdam, Tarrow, & Tilly 2001; Tilly 2004). In recent decades, however, scholars have challenged these frameworks as overly narrow in their understanding of politics, society, and power (Armstrong & Bernstein 2008). The political process and contentious politics approaches have tended to understand power as being centralized in political and economic structures, valuing those movement campaigns involved in claims making on governments for clear policy change, what might be understood as "instrumental" activism.[15] This, in turn, means that campaigns not engaged in obvious claims making, such as movement efforts to change culture – to impact on shared meanings and norms, values and beliefs, emotions and subjectivities – are seen as secondary to tactics seeking "real" political outcomes. Moreover, traditional approaches to social movement analysis presume that social change efforts will be carried forth by the directly aggrieved to advance their own self-interest. This series of assumptions make the practice of solidarity witness largely unintelligible.

The activists in this study engage in practices that are frankly illogical if measured by instrumental political goals. Their pursuit of solidarity makes little sense by narrow understandings of self-interest. The practice of solidarity witness, I would nevertheless argue, evinces a deeply considered political analysis developed and honed through years of struggle. These groups have come to assess that they are situated within a systemic behemoth in which claims making on a nation-state for a given policy change no longer makes sense. Their practice of solidarity witness resists the US security state as a nexus of political and economic forces that does bodily violence to many, but they pursue these ends by seeking to upend what movement scholars might term the cultural dynamics by which this state is anchored – dominant epistemologies, solidarities, and subjectivities. When these activists imagine and enact solidarity with the most degraded, they contest the narrow notion of self-interest that not only informs traditional approaches to the study of social movements but which these groups understand as a key cultural pillar to the neoliberal order.

This is not to argue that the groups in this study intend only symbolic gesture, personal and collective transformation, and the development of internal solidarity, movement dimensions that have often been defined (or denigrated) as "expressive" (Jenkins 1983). Certainly, these groups emerge from a lineage that has chosen targets of struggle for reasons of morality and faith over and above the likelihood of political success. Yet each of the groups in this study came into being to pursue a policy change that they presumed would surely be won, and rather quickly. Activists in all three groups believed that the specific institutional injustice that they chose to contest was so egregious that even the

---

[15] Scholars have long viewed *claims making* by nonroutine means as the defining feature of social movement activity. Here, claims making is understood as a demand on an institution, generally the state, for a change in policy. Nonroutine political activity generally comes in the form of protests and strikes, as opposed to political behavior sanctioned by the state, such as voting.

most apathetic or conservative audiences would be appalled. They felt relatively assured that a shift in government policy would necessarily follow. While
this has not been the case, it is still true that each group at first pursued a fairly
instrumental approach to policy change.

SOA Watch has arguably had the greatest number of traditional political
victories, which is partly due to the group's endurance and ability to mobilize
a mass base of support at different moments over the years. Witness Against
Torture seemed to have almost won the concessions they demanded when
Guantánamo's closure appeared imminent during President Obama's first year
in office. This promise was never realized. The Migrant Trail has had no obvious policy successes regarding migrant deaths at the border.

Because of these limited institutional and policy successes, some accuse
these campaigns as being merely gestural as opposed to being political in any
real sense. It is true that many of these activists share a disdain for traditional
politics. They continue with similar strategies in the face of political stalemate.
I too am centrally interested in what these activists accomplish in a broad
sense. To focus on these groups' capacity to directly impact upon policies and
institutions, however, may arbitrarily narrow the criteria by which their efforts
are assessed. In so doing, I would suggest that the important social function
they play is occluded.

The scholarly common sense, and a preoccupation widely shared by activists, is to try to understand how, when, and why social movements succeed.
On the face of it, this seems like an obvious goal for social movement studies. Scholars and activists benefit when we can better understand the power
levers in a society, as well as the social conditions and strategic decisions that
make movements more or less able to accomplish their stated aims. We also
know that questions of success can have ramifications for activists and movement sustainability. Those who perceive themselves to be politically effective
are more likely to feel empowered, a dynamic that is important for sustaining
commitment and hence movement longevity (Jasper 1997). When movements
feel themselves to be ineffectual in the face of rampant injustice, human suffering, and acute need, it is exhausting and demoralizing and can lead to activist
despair and defection (Summers Effler 2010; Ioanide 2015).

Nevertheless, it is quite hard to measure movements' public impacts since,
as David Meyer (2003) wisely assesses, "the forces that propel people to mobilize are often the same forces responsible for social change" (31). To isolate the
effects of protest from a multitude of concurrent economic, social, and political
shifts is a formidable task. Moreover, decision makers are understandably hes-
itant to admit that their change of heart or vote was impacted by movement
activity. While "power may concede nothing without a demand," as Frederick
Douglass famously posited, power is not so likely to admit that such a demand
inspired that concession.

A second and likely more important observation for the groups in this study
is that social movements must endure regardless of the state's concessions.

Political process approaches, in particular, suggest that there are more and less opportune moments for movements to win victories, and this certainly stands to reason. Such opportunities are, however, all but impossible to predict ahead of time, and activists cannot afford to wait. They must continuously try to create new openings at every juncture. This is not idealism but necessity. History shows that every campaign win can become a movement setback. Movement losses can in turn become the very instances that galvanize a mass base to shift the balance of power. This is something that we see in the history of radical pacifism in this country. It is also empirically borne out in the trajectory of countless other movements. As Howard Winant characterizes the endless volley between racial justice movements and the state, "Winning is losing. But losing is also winning" (2004: 217).

There is also an important argument made by activists and supported by research to suggest that an overemphasis on short-term, instrumental victories may actually undercut the long-term political power of social movements. Some of the dangers of an overemphasis on efficacy in claims making include the consolidation of power among a few leaders, which can lead to movement schisms, or a shift into a service-provision model that coheres with the very social structure that activists originally intended to contest. By developing leadership among disenfranchised and devalued people over and above prioritizing more traditional notions of victory, movements can redefine what success means and build the long-term capacity necessary for enduring social impact (Payne 1995; Polletta 2002; Chun, Lipsitz, & Shin 2010).

We should also ask what it would mean for the groups in this study to "win." These activists confront some of the most entrenched social dynamics of the early twenty-first century, targeting both the symbolic and institutional pillars of global inequality and militarized social control. Even if WAT can close Guantánamo, it is unlikely to be able to eliminate all CIA black sites and extrajudicial military prisons, or the military imperialism that produces them. Even if the Migrant Trail can demilitarize the border, the dynamics of poverty and forced migration will not so soon be overcome. Even if SOA Watch can shut down one army training school, US foreign policy will still be dictated by the interests of the corporate elite at the expense of poor communities in Latin America.

The activists in this study understand this, as do some of the preeminent thinkers of our time. Immanuel Wallerstein, a leading global sociologist, has suggested that when it comes to effecting transnational justice, the practicalities and institutional arrangements might in fact be of secondary importance. He observes:

I do not think that we can define in advance the institutional structures that would result in a more democratic, more egalitarian world ... The most we can probably do is push in certain directions that we think might be helpful. (Wallerstein 2008)

This "push" is not just the means but also the ends. It is the ongoing, relentless struggle for new ways of imagining, seeing, feeling, and existing.

When the groups in this study choose to enact solidarity with the targets of the US security state's most draconian policies, they put a human face on structures of injustice beyond the scope of any feasible effort at policy change. They give a tangible and commonsense goal to a trajectory of violence that exceeds what any movement can realistically confront. They translate the dynamics of empowerment and a sense of efficacy into new realms. In some sense, the reformist demands that these groups pursue, their claims on the US government to shift policies of intervention, enforcement, torture, and detention, are a stalking horse. By pursuing tangible, transitional goals, these activists expose much larger, more intractable social structures. In this sense, the question of their ability to achieve their policy goals becomes secondary.

This is not to say that these campaigns do not have real human stakes. Every one of these activists would most likely do things differently if they knew they could be more successful in closing a prison, or an army school, or a border patrol station. They did not set out to do their work circuitously. I do not believe that they themselves believe their stated goals to be secondary insofar as lives and communities are held in the balance. Nevertheless, what I see as being primary in these groups is a political practice. Solidarity witness is a way of being and acting against global dynamics of injustice and impossible divides of power. It is a way of reckoning with legacies of privilege tied to the oppression of others while also seeking to disinvest in this privilege in meaningful ways. There is no pure or best way to be in solidarity with the targets of state violence. However, by elaborating and enacting a sense of self- and collective interest that contests the potentially apocalyptic, and certainly myopic, dominant subjectivity of US consumer capitalism and the fear-laden logics of the security state, these witnesses "push" themselves and the culture in a proactive and, I argue, important direction.

CHAPTER OVERVIEW

Having outlined the overarching dimensions to this study in this chapter, Chapter 2 introduces the three groups involved in solidarity witness in greater detail. I focus on each group's origin story, touching on key distinctions between the groups and some of the demographic complexities that emerge in seeking to categorize these solidarity activists. Chapter 3 then turns to ritual protest, which plays a formative role in the practice of solidarity witness, serving as a kind of testimony to the witness. These activists see the violence of the US security state and then stage visual events that contest dominant forms of visibility and knowledge, making the state's targets more morally proximate. Chapter 4 assesses another fundamental aspect of solidarity witness – the physicality of witness. Each of the groups under study engage in the physical demands of fasting, pilgrimage, civil disobedience, and jail time. These embodied tactics allow witnesses to see, feel, and share the realities of state violence in ways that they could not without putting their bodies into their activism in this way.

Chapter 5 draws on the discussions of ritual and embodiment to argue that the subject-work of solidarity witness has an important ascetic dimension rooted in practices of physical renunciation and sociopolitical withdrawal. Through a political asceticism, these activists prepare themselves to resist the state with enhanced conviction and fortitude while forging communities that help them stay politically committed in the face of dire odds. Chapter 6 offers a capstone to the examination of solidarity witness by turning to some of the stickier questions that these activists consider in their efforts to effect social change and enact solidarity. Conflict does arise in these communities, as it does in all social groups. I have decided to show these activists in their best practices in Chapters 3–5, without cluttering this discussion with every relevant disagreement. In Chapter 6, I turn to some of the central complications that these groups face, not to tell a tale of acrimony but to enrich the intellectual and political lessons that we can draw from solidarity witness. When the participants in these groups reflect, sometimes with skepticism and frustration, on movement decisions and experiences, they raise important questions about the meaning of solidarity and the prospects for enacting resistance under the US security state.

2

"I'm Ruined for Life!" Witnessing Empire

On Sunday, November 20, 2011, Theresa Cusimano stood at the gates of Fort Benning. In the protest to close the SOA, she would be the only person that year to commit civil disobedience, climbing a ladder over the fence separating the thousands of other protesters from the Army base. Before performing this act and submitting herself to hours of arrest, booking, and jail time, Theresa had a final opportunity to address the crowd,

I'm ruined for life! Are you? When you witness injustice, it changes you, you can't function in the world the way you did before bearing witness. I think that's what brings so many of us here today ... the human rights crimes, the unjust wars, the decades of terrorizing third world communities ... it's important we keep showing up, as pacifists, as witnesses, as community activists knocking on the doors.

(Cusimano 2011)

I was not there that day. In fact, I did not begin to research SOA Watch until two years after Theresa "crossed the line." It was then that several SOA Watch veterans recommended that I speak to Theresa. The act of civil disobedience she committed in 2011 was Theresa's second, and she paid dearly for it during her six months in prison. She became devastatingly ill due to inappropriate treatment for her celiac disease and was abused by guards as she tried to get medical help.

When I finally spoke with Theresa in early 2014, I was interested not only in why she had undertaken such a risk, but what had brought her to SOA Watch in the first place. Theresa's story began with her family. She had been raised in New York. Her family migrated from Sicily and Ireland two and three generations back. Theresa was proud of her immigrant roots. She explained that through her Catholic family and schooling, she had come to understand the importance of peace. She grew up celebrating mass in her grandmother's living room, where her uncle, a Jesuit priest, would sing horribly off key, "Peace is flowing like a river ... flowing out of you and me." These gatherings had made her want to be a Jesuit too, though her gender prohibited this. Beyond these Catholic lessons of peace, Theresa explained that she had learned the skills of critical inquiry at the dinner table, where she was encouraged to debate tough social issues with her loved ones.

Theresa's path into justice work had seemed fairly straightforward. She went to law school and ultimately found herself working with a Catholic organization advocating for pro-immigrant policy reforms in Washington, DC. This is where her journey became a bit more convoluted as she began to understand the hopeless tangle of US immigration laws. She explained to me what had happened during this time:

What I ... saw was the impossibility of ever making progress with the current immigration law as it stands. I just saw myself in this maze that no one ever gets out of. Instead of just saying for policy purposes that we hate all outsiders – which I believe at the core that's what that legislation is doing – we've just layered it and layered it and layered it over the years to make it impossible for anyone to get out [of the maze].

Theresa's experience was not unusual. When activists find themselves stymied by the system time and again, this often plants the seeds for more sustained radicalism (McAdam 1988; Fukumura and Matsuoka 2002). Many of the activists in this study turned to the core practices of solidarity witness only after their efforts to work with and through legally constituted procedures revealed these to be unworkable and illegitimate.

Finding that she could no longer stomach this policy work, Theresa decided to take what she hoped would be a less emotionally exhausting position in higher education administration. She made this transition just as the September 11, 2001, attacks occurred, however, and found she could not ignore the blatant racism and xenophobia authorized under the Bush Administration's "Global War on Terror." She continued:

Guantánamo Bay presented itself, and I felt that I could not be a silent bystander and call myself a US citizen with the atrocity that was occurring in our name. I began to look for opportunities to actually participate in non-violent civil disobedience ... It was really the images that were occurring and the US abuses in Guantánamo Bay that prompted me to join [a delegation] going to the School of the Americas.

At the time of our interview, I found it remarkable that Theresa, unaware that my study encompassed movement groups other than SOA Watch, would connect the SOA, migration policy, and Guantánamo within the first five minutes of our conversation. I was uncertain, however, why the images of Guantánamo had driven her to the gates of Fort Benning. She explained that all of these institutional injustices were linked "through a public policy that's built on fear and built on deficits." She continued:

We have had a history of allowing this abuse of power to be our US foreign policy. Guantanamo Bay is just, in my opinion, one of the more recent examples. The School of the Americas and what we enabled others to do whether it's the El Mozote massacre [perpetrated by SOA graduates in El Salvador] or any one of the coups that we helped facilitate, basically on our dime, with our weaponry, with our training, it's just another abuse of power within the unquestioned military. So for me it's the big issue of our military spending and the lack of accountability and then the fear mongering that are at the root of that. We have just allowed that violence to permeate all aspects of our culture.

For Theresa, the SOA, along with Guantánamo and US immigration policy, are three of the more visible nodes of the US security state, a form of governance defined by militarism, the manufacture of public fear, and the governmental abuse of power. Theresa has come to know these aspects of US statecraft through being a witness. Her declaration to the crowd at SOA Watch began with the subjective transformation of having witnessed injustice: "I'm ruined. I have seen things that I cannot now unsee." Her experience as a legal intern forced her to witness policies that incite suffering and are designed to fail at their purported aims. She desperately sought new avenues of dissent because the traditional political process had proven futile and corrupt. Having witnessed images of Guantánamo, she decided to trespass at Fort Benning, which led to a set of experiences in which she would witness still more of the state's violent underbelly.

Theresa is fairly typical among the activists in this study in linking militarism abroad to xenophobia and economic scarcity at home. SOA Watch, the Migrant Trail, and Witness Against Torture each respond to similar dimensions of state power, though each emerged to confront a different dimension of the US security state. While Chapter 1 offered a brief introduction to the common pacifist lineage from which these groups emerge, this chapter details the origin story of each group. After detailing each group's path to resistance, I briefly discuss key distinctions between the cases, some of the demographic particularities and complexities of this study, and each group's relationship to the aggrieved.

THE SCHOOL OF THE AMERICAS

Historical Context

The SOA, renamed the WHISC, or WHINSEC, in 2001, is an Army training school located at Fort Benning in Columbus, Georgia. Founded in Panama as the Latin American Ground School in 1946 and renamed SOA in 1963, the school was relocated to Fort Benning in 1984 when the Panamanian government retook control of the Canal Zone and surrounding areas.[1] Since its

---

[1] Lesley Gill (2004) explains that Columbus was perhaps an unusual location for the school to land, and that the US military was much more interested in relocating to cities or regions with traditionally Latino communities, such as Miami, San Antonio, or the island of Puerto Rico. Two anti-Castro Cubans, major business people in the city of Columbus, however, successfully

founding, the school has trained tens of thousands of Latin American soldiers. Its graduates include notorious human rights violators and military dictators (Nepstad 2000).

It is helpful to contextualize the SOA within a larger framework of US intervention and militarism throughout Latin America, with a particular focus on the Central American conflicts that raged throughout the second half of the twentieth century. Beginning with the Spanish conquest of Central America in 1524, a system of feudalism set the stage for widespread inequality, debilitating poverty, and continuing conflict between the landless masses and elite land owners. It is beyond the scope of this project to review with great nuance the various political and economic developments that ensued and the distinct national histories pertinent to the region.[2] Relevant to the SOA protest, however, is the advent of Liberation Theology, a Catholic interpretation of the Bible first popularized in Latin America in the 1950s, which foregrounded a faith-based commitment to ameliorating poverty and addressing the root causes of strife and social suffering. By the 1960s, numerous groups throughout the region emerged to advocate for social and economic justice, often motivated by this new theological orientation. Violent cycles of collective resistance and militarized repression arose between those seeking a more just and equitable social order and an elite land-holding class that feared what systemic overhaul would mean for their wealth and security. By the 1970s, civil wars raged in El Salvador, Guatemala, and Nicaragua.

The United States was centrally involved in these conflicts, with President Reagan's Cold War era administration seeking to eliminate what were construed as "communist threats." Leftist forces enjoyed wide support throughout much of Latin America. In order not to draw negative political attention, US intervention in the region, termed "low-intensity warfare," included backing right-wing political organizations and providing weapons to proxy armies that would defeat socialist revolutionary efforts (Nepstad 2004: 43).[3] Training for these armies and paramilitary forces often took place at the SOA. The tallies of US-backed human rights atrocities in the region during Reagan's offensive are staggering. Certainly, socialist revolutionaries were also responsible for deaths and destruction. Yet this must be considered within the larger power structure. If social divisions were rampant and broad swathes of the civilian population suffered tremendously, US involvement exacerbated these dimensions

---

lobbied to bring the SOA to Georgia under the assumption that it would provide the region with a major economic boost.

[2] Important texts that review the histories in greater detail include Smith (1996) and Grandin (2006). Diane Nelson's work on Guatemala (1999; 2009) is also noteworthy.

[3] If the intention of low-intensity intervention in Central America was in part to prevent domestic and transnational opposition, it is also true that a post-Vietnam caution guided military decisions during this era. This caution was codified in the Weinberger and later Powell Doctrine, which issued new criteria seeking to prevent overly zealous military engagements abroad (Bacevich 2009).

exponentially by providing mass amounts of aid and motivation to further the violence. The UN and Amnesty International calculate that 200,000 people were disappeared or killed in Guatemala, with over 1 million more displaced, and in El Salvador, 75,000 were disappeared or killed, with 1 million displaced (Nepstad 2004).[4]

Hundreds of North American church workers living and working in Latin America since the mid-1960s witnessed the impacts of US intervention and responded in outcry. These were largely Catholic missionaries sent to the region as part of Vatican II, an effort of the 1960s papacy intended to modernize the Church (Fitzpatrick-Behrens 2011). One of the many outcomes of Vatican II was to send thousands of North American nuns and priests to Latin America to address a shortage of native-born priests. Most took on work with the poor. North American missionaries found themselves both inspired by Liberation Theology and affronted by US-backed forms of violence and repression. As these clergy returned to the United States, they mounted a hemispheric peace and solidarity movement (Nepstad 2000).

These solidarity activists, themselves predominately white, middle-class Catholics with radical pacifist orientations, undertook various efforts to oppose US intervention in the region. They used traditional political avenues, such as demanding Congress halt US funding for covert operations. Solidarity organizations also sent educational delegations to the region so that members of the American public, especially people of faith, could observe firsthand the impact of US intervention. Delegates returned to the United States to share experiences with their congregations and to do media work and legislative outreach. The organization Witness for Peace began one of the more high-risk efforts of this movement. US volunteers were sent to Nicaragua throughout the 1980s to serve as long-term human rights observers who could document and help deter US-backed Contra attacks on civilian populations (Smith 1996). Considering these antecedents to the cases examined in this study, it is clear that the act of witnessing as an instantiation of solidarity has deep roots in communities of faith-driven activists. To stand with the targets of state violence and against the perpetrators of this violence, to see and expose what dominant political actors seek to occlude, are quintessential aspects of solidarity witness.

Another effort launched by North American solidarity activists was to aid Central American refugees. Solidarity activists first attempted to help these migrants apply for legal asylum in the United States. It quickly became evident,

---

[4] The death toll and displacement in Nicaragua during this time was significantly less with 30,000 fighters and civilians killed and 20,000 severely injured. Nevertheless, the United States was embroiled in the illegal funneling of money and weapons to the Contra militia that sought to devastate the robust infrastructure of the quite popular socialist Sandinista government. The US involvement in Nicaragua was revealed during the 1986 Iran–Contra scandal, when the United States was shown to be illegally supporting the Contras as part of a larger imbroglio that included a weapons and hostage exchange with Iran (Byrne 2014).

however, that the United States would not accept those seeking to escape Central American regimes that were backed by US intervention. For example, 97 percent of those applying for asylum in the United States from either El Salvador or Guatemala were rejected, with the US courts claiming these applications came from economic migrants as opposed to political refugees (Cunningham 1995). Solidarity activists thus entered into a years-long, massively orchestrated underground railroad of sorts that came to be called the Sanctuary Movement. Ultimately 400 organizations and thousands of individuals in the United States and Mexico, largely religious, helped to transport Central Americans to the United States where they were sheltered in churches, synagogues, and people's homes (Crittenden 1988; Coutin 1991; Cunningham 1995). Activists argued that the biblical mandate to shelter the persecuted trumped inhumane US refugee laws (Van Ham 2011). Of note, the Sanctuary Movement began in Tucson, Arizona, among the same faith-based, as well as secular, activist networks that today organize the Migrant Trail, a point that I return to later in the chapter.

The Campaign to Close the School

While many participants in Central American solidarity work were not initially cognizant of the links between the SOA and conflict in the region, the devastating assassination of El Salvadoran Archbishop Oscar Romero offered the first point of evidence. The beloved Romero had evolved from an establishment priest to a foremost proponent of Liberation Theology, advocating relentlessly for the poor and against the Salvadoran regime. Romero was murdered on March 24, 1980, one day after giving a homily beseeching the Salvadoran military to cease their violence. He was swiftly held up as a martyr for the Salvadoran struggle. Thousands marched at his funeral procession, braving bombs and sniper attacks orchestrated by the government. Romero became a hero for liberation struggles, not just in El Salvador but throughout the world (Erdozaín 1981; López Vigil 2000; Nepstad 2004).

Following Archbishop Romero's murder, the Salvadoran army continued its attacks. One of these included the fairly well-publicized, brutal killings of four North American missionary women in December of 1980, two of whom were part of the Central American solidarity movement (Nepstad 2004). Their good friend, activist Roy Bourgeois, a Vietnam veteran turned Maryknoll priest, began to look into the murders of Romero and the churchwomen. He discovered that the Salvadoran military behind both attacks had been trained on US soil, at the School of the Americas.

Over the next few years, Bourgeois planned to expose the SOA. In 1983, he undertook his first direct action at the SOA, accompanied by two friends. All three dressed in uniform and impersonated officers to get onto the base. Once inside the complex, the three located the Salvadoran barracks and upon nightfall, climbed a nearby tree with boom box in tow. From their perch, they

blasted Archbishop Romero's final homily into the night. This act of civil disobedience earned Bourgeois eighteen months in prison and gained the attention of fellow activists. Soundly linking the SOA to El Salvador's human rights
atrocities, Bourgeois had planted the seeds of SOA Watch.

The SOA would not become a central target for activists for a few more
years. On November 16, 1989, another brutal massacre thrust El Salvador and
US involvement back into the spotlight. This time, the Salvadoran Army had
assassinated six Jesuit priests along with their housekeeper and her fourteen-
year-old daughter at the University of Central America. Catholics around the
world rallied to demand accountability, and ultimately the UN undertook a
formal investigation. Among the official findings, nineteen of the twenty-six
Salvadoran officers responsible were shown to be SOA graduates.

Following the Jesuit massacre, Father Bourgeois was once again convinced
that attention had to be brought to the SOA. He traveled to Georgia to tour
the school, and soon moved into a tiny apartment across the street from Fort
Benning's main entrance. Some scholars argue that the rise of SOA Watch,
instigated by Bourgeois, was a savvy effort to salvage a movement in decline
(Gill 2004; Nepstad 2004). As various peace accords signed in the late 1980s
and early 1990s helped to reduce the most acute violence in the region, the
Central American solidarity movement began to lose momentum (Smith 1996).
When the Nicaraguan Sandinistas, who had seemed the foremost hope for left-
ist transformation in the region, lost the presidency in 1990, it was clear that
the US-backed Contras were now victorious (Nepstad 2004). The end of the
Reagan presidency in 1988, fall of the Soviet Union in 1989 and beginning of
the Gulf War in 1991, drew the American public's attention away from Latin
America and fragmented the energy of Christian leftists and US peace activists
(Gill 2004).

Bourgeois's next action at the SOA was in 1990, when he invited fellow
peace activists to join him in a thirty-five-day fast at the gates of Fort Benning.
On November 16, 1990, the one-year anniversary of the Jesuit Massacre,
Father Bourgeois along with friends Charlie and Patrick Liteky, entered the
SOA with a letter demanding the school stop training Latin American soldiers.
They splashed blood donated from the other activists on the walls and floor,
exited the building, and planted a cross in the ground. There, they awaited their
arrest. Military police shuttled them to the Columbus police station. Each was
sentenced to prison, the Litekys for nine months each and Bourgeois for fourteen months, due to his previous trespass at the school (Gill 2004).

The SOA Watch campaign now began to organize in force. Activists filed
Freedom of Information Act requests with the US government to get public
records on SOA instructors and graduates, including names, nationalities, and
dates of attendance. What activists found was a set of links that far exceeded
the already known connections between the school and El Salvador's military
criminals. It quickly became obvious that SOA graduates had been instrumental in nearly every Latin American coup and major human rights violation

since the school's inception (Koopman 2008). Alumni of the school were also linked to ongoing incidents, crimes that had occurred after the signing of the peace accords (Gill 2004). Father Bourgeois began to travel the country, telling stories of SOA victims and encouraging US citizens to contact their representatives in Congress. By 1993, the SOA Watch effort had convinced Democratic Representative Joe Kennedy from Massachusetts to introduce a bill to close the SOA. The amendment was ultimately defeated, but momentum continued to build. In 1995, SOA Watch activists once again marked the anniversary of the Jesuit massacre at Fort Benning with thirteen people walking onto the base to be arrested in protest, inaugurating the vigil and civil disobedience as an annual event.

The school finally erupted in public scandal in 1996 when the Defense Department admitted to the American public that torture and assassination techniques were part of the SOA's regular curriculum materials. Following pressure from activists as well as a growing number of members of Congress, the Pentagon released what came to be known as the "torture manuals," documents used in SOA courses that specifically named Latin American political targets as appropriate for "neutralization," or murder. A number of major national newspapers issued editorials calling for the school's closure (Gill 2004). The annual Fort Benning vigil was now drawing thousands every year and hundreds were committing acts of civil disobedience by crossing onto the military base.[5] When Congress passed a bill to withdraw the school's funding in 1999, thousands converged on Fort Benning to call for the school's immediate closure, with more than 4,000 risking arrest.[6]

At this point, the military along with other branches of the US government began to invest significant resources in combatting SOA Watch's efforts. Officials from the school traveled to Bourgeois's speaking engagements to offer counter-narratives and portray the school as a beneficent entity, though rarely with much success (Gill 2004). In 1999, the FBI also became involved in a decade-long undercover operation monitoring SOA Watch.[7] By 2001, the

[5] As one of the larger annual protest events in the country, SOA Watch's Fort Benning gathering has generated some conflicting interests that reveal the push of capitalism in a military town (Gill 2004). While the Columbus Chamber of Commerce passed a resolution supporting the SOA in the face of growing controversy, hotel and restaurant owners were not oblivious to the infusion of dollars happening every November as the protest grew in popularity. By the late 1990s, SOA Watch activists were wooed with discount hotel rooms, and Delta even offered a 10 percent discount to protesters flying into Atlanta. There is also a popular understanding in the protest crowd, who sometimes mingle with the throngs of police deployed during the vigil weekend, that officers from the relatively depressed town look forward to their annual opportunity to make overtime pay.

[6] Estimates as to the number of total protesters differ here. *New York Times* reporter Kim Severson (2010) gives the most conservative estimate of 3,000. SOA Watch's own documents suggest that it was closer to 6,000, and Nepstad's (2004) sources report that 12,000 were present.

[7] In 2012, the Partnership for Civil Justice Fund, a public interest legal organization, unearthed the documents for this operation in which FBI officials admit year after year that there is no

school had been so sullied that it was forced to rename itself the WHISC, or WHINSEC, complete with a new "human rights" curriculum and continuing public relations strategy (Gill 2004). Members of Congress continued to introduce bills and amendments to close the school, many of which nearly passed. Meanwhile, activists continued to come to the annual vigil in increasing numbers. By 2003, 10,000 made it to Fort Benning, and in 2006, there was a recorded height of 22,000 protesters (Reissiger 2006).

A few years later, however, SOA Watch did begin to lose momentum, at least as evidenced by the numbers of people attending the yearly vigil. In 2010, the number of protesters was less than 5,000 again (Severson 2010). In 2013, for the first time since the vigil's inception, no one committed civil disobedience. By 2014, SOA Watch estimated that a mere 2,500 activists were in attendance. The reasons for this are likely multiple. Father Bourgeois was officially excommunicated by the Vatican in 2008 for ordaining women. Whether in disagreement with this choice or due to a mere shift in interest, many of the Jesuit universities that used to bring buses full of students to the protest were no longer doing so, heading instead to a Washington, DC "teach-in" (Severson 2010). Some activists also mentioned their sense that the increasingly punitive policing of the vigil in the aftermath of September 11, with newly erected fencing and immediate jail time for those who cross onto the base, has dissuaded the mass civil disobedience that once brought thousands to the school. It might also be the case that after getting as close as they did to closing the SOA time and again, only to be foiled, some activists decided to put their energies elsewhere.[8]

In the face of waning mass interest in the vigil, SOA Watch has nevertheless had success with other strategies. One of these included opening SOA Watch offices in Chile and Venezuela and hiring staff from Latin American social movements. In this way, SOA Watch supported those demanding that their own governments cut ties to the SOA. Some SOA Watch activists believe this is a more responsible approach to solidarity activism: supporting the self-determination of directly targeted communities. The effort has also been quite successful. In 2004, Venezuela agreed to stop sending its military to the SOA. In 2006, Argentina and Uruguay followed suit. Bolivia did the same in 2008, and Ecuador in 2012. In 2007, Costa Rica, having no military, promised to stop sending its country's police to the SOA, though it later reversed this decision. SOA Watch activists tend to believe this was due to covert US pressure, although the then-president of Costa Rica insisted that he simply changed his mind.

---

imminent threat among the pacifist masses gathering at Fort Benning. The case was finally closed in 2009 due to a lack of "significant incidents of violence or widespread property damage" (Verheyden-Hilliard 2015).

[8] These are my own suspicions based on activist explanations and a few limited media reports (Severson 2010). As far as I can tell, these later years of SOA Watch have not been written about in academic literature.

Another change of emphasis came with the spread of events and workshops to accompany the Fort Benning gathering. Since 2010, SOA Watch has added an emphasis on contesting immigrant detention to their annual gathering, an issue that organizers see as deeply linked to the SOA and its support of Latin American militarism. The new focus has been instantiated in tactics that differ from prior years. For example, as part of the weekend vigil at Fort Benning, protesters have carpooled to Lumpkin, GA, home to one of the largest immigrant detention centers in the country and less than an hour's drive from Columbus. In 2013, after a short program in the small, economically depressed town, activists walked a mile to the immigrant prison, demanding the privately run facility be closed and that US immigration policy be changed. In 2014, of the small number of people committing civil disobedience during the weekend in Georgia, more decided to risk arrest at the immigrant prison than at the SOA itself. By 2015, the desire of SOA Watch to connect to migrant justice culminated when leaders announced that rather than convene on Fort Benning in 2016, activists would head to the US–Mexico border to contest migrant abuse and increasing militarization. This was the first time SOA Watch did not hold their annual gathering in Georgia. The decision to move the annual gathering to the border at Nogales, Sonora–Arizona was continued in 2017.

A Campaign to Confront Empire

As SOA Watch grew in numbers and influence throughout the 1990s and early 2000s, the group reached beyond its original faith base to include a new generation of activists, largely people born in the 1970s and 1980s. Gill (2004) writes that these young people grew up under the very conservative Reagan and Bush Sr. administrations that sought to erase the legacy of the various leftist movements of the 1960s. For many of these young people, the Fort Benning event was a first experience of collective action, and it had some important impacts. It challenged many of their assumptions about the basic goodness of US politics and foreign policy. Just as importantly, it brought them into contact with an older generation of veteran activists, generally Christian, many of whom had spent ample time in jail for civil disobedience. As mentioned in Chapter 1, many of the core activists involved in my other two cases – the Migrant Trail Walk and Witness Against Torture – who are today in their thirties, cite SOA Watch protests as pivotal to their political awakening. They are part of the generation that came of age during these demonstrations.

SOA Watch's expansion in size and approach has come with opportunities as well as challenges. One of these has been balancing Roman Catholic roots with a desire to appeal to a diversity of activists, a point addressed later in the chapter as a dynamic that cross-cuts all three cases. A second challenge for the campaign has had to do with framing the issue of the SOA. During the group's height in the late 1990s, supporters in Congress and even in the military itself were willing to advocate against the school as a singular atrocity that sullies the legacy of the highly esteemed US Army, a notion that also appealed to a fairly pro-military American public (Gill 2004). Many of SOA Watch's core activists, on the other hand, perceive the school differently. As veterans of other peace movements, as well as veterans of the US military, most SOA Watch activists view the school as exemplary of US militarism and imperial over-reach, rather than as a bad apple. Theresa, for instance, understood that SOA Watch is "taking on the military industrial complex at its heart [in the sense that] Fort Benning is the largest military training school in the country, if not internationally."[9]

Other SOA Watch organizers agreed that the SOA was a pillar of the US security state. Targeting the school was not about eliminating an outlier but taking on an entire system of state-sanctioned violence. Damien explained:

This one institution is emblematic of something that's a very structural necessity for US imperialism in particular. Some people refer to the SOA as a symbol. I think that the body count would kind of argue against the fact that it's symbolic. It's very concrete.

Damien contested the notion that the school is *merely* a symbolic target, noting its prominent role in securing US interests throughout the Western Hemisphere. At the same time, he recognized the potency of this one institution in speaking to larger global and historical dynamics. He continued:

[The SOA] certainly is emblematic of the necessity of the US in maintaining like the Monroe doctrine, the Doctrine of Discovery, or the Rio Treaty – all of these historical ideologies that have allowed the US to maintain dominance over the hemisphere for several centuries. The School of the Americas is one of the instrumental factors in ensuring this from a structural standpoint.

In naming the Monroe doctrine, the Doctrine of Discovery, and the Rio Treaty, Damien situates the school in a lineage of conquest, settler colonialism and various forms of regional dominance that commenced with the arrival of Columbus and have been enshrined in US law. In understanding state violence, Damien suggests that the cultural and structural are intertwined; what he calls "historical ideologies" are codified through laws and institutional practices. This analysis that the cultural and structural underpinnings of the US security state are in fact deeply entangled is of course central to how all the movement groups in this study understand what they are up against and to how they practice resistance.

As SOA Watch has chosen to hold up the SOA as an exemplar of larger global power dynamics – as opposed to an anomaly in an otherwise good system – the group has had to address some issues of scope. If the goal is to take on militarism and the US security state writ large, this encompasses many

---

[9] The veracity of the claim that the SOA is the largest military training school might be debated, but it is noteworthy that it is what protesters believe.

specific manifestations, such as urban policing, prisons, immigration, and warfare, to name but a few. Today, SOA Watch's stated intentions and the issues it encompasses have expanded far beyond the closing of the SOA, supporting struggles for greater equality in Latin America and justice for Latin American migrants headed to the United States. Beyond this, leftists across the issue spectrum attend the annual Fort Benning weekend.

Broadening the scope of the campaign has obvious challenges. Long-term SOA Watch participant Leah explained what embracing so many issues has meant for the Fort Benning protest in particular:

I think it's become a little bit less focused … the event has become more and more about all issues of justice, and in that you've seen disagreement among people … I think it's distracted from the primary focus that SOA Watch started with, which was to shut down the School of the Americas.[10]

It was likely this narrow focus that first drew many to the group. Radical pacifists of the Christian left – those who were SOA Watch's original core and play an important role in the other movement groups in this study – have chosen tactics of ethical witness throughout history without regard for efficacy. Yet most people who became active with SOA Watch thought it was a winnable campaign. Activist and regional organizer Siobhan explained that she was drawn to the campaign after hearing Bourgeois speak in the 1990s because "it seemed a targeted and winnable fight, and even though I understand that closing the School of the Americas does not change foreign policy, it would be a very great victory still."

The notion of victory is indeed complicated. The school remains, its mission largely unchanged, and the US military has proffered no admission of guilt or accountability for human rights violations committed. At the same time, SOA Watch did force the school onto its heels. Former military officials have admitted that SOA Watch and its mass appeal posed the foremost threat to the school, at least during the peak years of the campaign (Gill 2004). Today many activists and scholars agree that since the SOA itself has been so consistently under the spotlight, the most unsavory parts of its curriculum have likely been outsourced to the hundreds of other military schools that the United States maintains domestically and abroad (Gill 2004; Koopman 2008). Through their albeit limited wins at the SOA, activists confront the magnitude of the US security state of which this school is one small node. SOA Watch has perhaps gotten as far as it might in exposing this school. The continually expansive vision and changing orientation of their movement efforts may be strategic for continuing a sense of momentum and purpose.

---

[10] One of the core disagreements as explained by Leah emerged between reproductive justice advocates and other Catholic pacifists who espouse the "consistent life ethic," opposing war and the death penalty as well as abortion and assisted suicide.

THE MIGRANT TRAIL WALK

Historical Context

It is the most threatening hour of the day. At just 10 a.m., we plod on in
100-degree heat under a vicious sun. Even the desert insects have stopped their
rattling below the dry burn. I sip at my water bottle. I find it difficult to quench
my thirst without filling my belly to sloshing. My lips are chapped. My joints
ache as we continue into our fourth day. About fifty people are making this
seventy-five mile trek over the course of a week through Arizona's borderlands, following the general path taken by so many migrants forced into this
remote, brutal desert. We begin in Sasabe, Sonora, Mexico, a mile south of the
border, and head north toward Tucson, traveling just east of the Baboquivari
range and the Tohono O'odham nation. Despite the discomfort, I recognize the
immense beauty of this place – stark peaks, fierce but glorious cacti flowering
everywhere. The land is saturated with the rich history of peoples and fragile
ecosystems that have made this place home for centuries.

The Migrant Trail is one of multiple collective actions planned by the border-
justice movement to protest and end migrant deaths. The annual walk began in
2004 with about twenty participants from border justice organizations in and
around Tucson, Arizona. After years of setting out water in a futile attempt to
curb migrant deaths and having recovered far too many human remains, these
twenty wanted to experience the journey and draw public attention to the daily
reality facing migrants at the US–Mexico border. They commit to walk yearly
until the deaths stop. In migrants' decision to cross the border to the United
States, economic forces and familial ties trump walls, material or virtual. While
the most aggressive and expensive border enforcement has forced migrants
into ever more perilous crossings, thousands of deaths have proven to be no
deterrent to those facing dehumanizing poverty at home.

After being out here myself with all the comforts we are afforded as walkers,
what is surprising to me is not that people have died. It is that anyone makes
it at all. I note this as we pass abandoned backpacks along Route 286, signs of
migrants who likely survived many days in the desert only to be picked up by
border patrol (Adapted from author's field notes).

The US–Mexico border has not always been a gauntlet of death for those seeking better work opportunities or to join family members in the United States.
Indeed, when Mexico ceded territory to the United States after the US–Mexico
War of 1846–8, effectively creating the 2,000-mile land boundary that now
separates the two nations, immigration between Mexico and the United States
was largely unregulated. Xenophobic anxieties over immigration were certainly alive and well in the United States. Yet during the 1800s these were often
directed at a different kind of migrant altogether: Irish and German immigrants
fleeing famines, economic crises, and failed revolutions in Western Europe. In

contrast to those arriving by boat in the northeastern United States, Mexican nationals traversed a much more sparsely populated Southwest. Their "migration" was through a part of the United States that used to belong to Mexico, and they had a good deal of cultural overlap with local populations. Moreover, their travel by land, as opposed to boat, made it relatively affordable, easy, and safe to cross the US–Mexico border as needed (Calavita 1984; Van Ham 2011).

The establishment of the Bureau of Immigration in 1891 sought to centralize the regulation of migration into the United States, but it was not until the height of the Prohibition Era, with fears about alcohol and drug smuggling from Mexico, that the Border Patrol was formed (Musto 1999; Hernandez 2010).[11] Authorized under the 1924 Johnson–Reed Immigration Act, the Border Patrol saw meager funding along with an ill-defined mandate. With minimal training or supervision, the Border Patrol became what Kelly Lytle Hernandez (2010) terms "a sanctuary of violence." Mexican nationals and Mexican Americans living near the border, along with various other racialized groups, would face widespread abuse at the hands of agents, characterized by an erratic if often heavy-handed enforcement regime (Dunn 2009; Ewing 2014). At the same time, immigration status mattered little. Perhaps counterintuitively, the Border Patrol was not focused on restricting people from entering the country via the US–Mexico border.

Viewed from today's near national obsession with the unauthorized migration of Latino peoples to the United States, it might seem odd that Johnson–Reed, the first US policy to implement national quotas, placed no official restrictions on immigration from Mexico or Latin America. Rather, responding to xenophobic anxieties emerging at the end of World War I, quotas were intended to limit the arrival of Southern and Eastern European migrants to the country. Yet Van Ham (2011) observes that this was an economic practicality very much in line with US national chauvinism, characterized by "the enticing prospect of tapping foreigners who would toil for low wages without seeking to become part of the national community" (37). Because it was so easy for Mexican migrants to come and go, returning to their families and communities in Mexico, they were understood by many landowners, and their congressional representatives, to be an ideal workforce.[12]

---

[11] Hernandez (2010) explains that racist white southerners were one of the primary checks on the growth of a policing agency in their region, as they feared any federal response to the African American activists asking for governmental help to end a rising tide of lynchings (33).

[12] There is more complexity to this story, which if beyond the scope of this research, is well detailed by Mae Ngai (2004). Anti-Mexican sentiment was certainly alive throughout the Southwest during the first decades of the twentieth century and calls for restriction abounded, often tied to notions of preventing disease and contagion. While quota limits on Mexican immigration would not become federal policy until later in the century, US consuls in Mexico did limit the number of visas distributed to Mexican migrants beginning in 1930, effectively creating a population of US workers from Mexico with "illegal alien" status. While newly deportable because of this status, this bore little impact on how Mexican nationals were policed while crossing the border.

The United States has a sordid history of exploiting migrants in accord with the needs of the national economy with blatant disregard for the human rights of workers. The most infamous example of this might be the Chinese Exclusion Act of 1882, in which federal legislation barred ethnic Chinese from migrating to the United States after Chinese workers had performed some of the most challenging and dangerous labor to build the First Transcontinental Railroad between 1863 and 1869.[13] The treatment of Mexican workers has been similarly iniquitous. During the Great Depression, two million Mexican Americans, the vast majority of them citizens, were repatriated to Mexico so as not to compete with American-born workers.[14] Just a decade later, as the United States entered World War II, the American agricultural lobby convinced Washington that a massive labor shortage was imminent, successfully muting evidence presented by the Department of Labor that this was not the case (Ngai 2004).[15] In 1942, the United States and Mexico commenced the Bracero Program, in which more than five million Mexican nationals were contracted as temporary agricultural workers, facing the widespread abuse and exploitation characteristic of all guest worker programs (SPLC 2013). In the end, the Bracero Program was not designed to accommodate the number of Mexicans wishing to work in the United States, workers who were aggressively lured by growers seeking a cheap labor flow beyond what state policy had approved. Unauthorized migration to the United States was framed as a crisis. The federal government responded with "Operation Wetback" in 1954, a massive deportation regime that saw the widespread abuse of Mexican migrants along with Latino communities throughout the United States (Ngai 2004).

In the aftermath of the Bracero Program and Operation Wetback, immigration enforcement continued to target immigrants already living in the United States. The Border Patrol participated in rampant racial profiling, regularly stopping and searching Latinos for drugs and weapons, a practice that was

---

[13] Indeed, Hernandez (2010) observes that a decade before the inauguration of the official Border Patrol, the Immigration Service of 1904 established a small force of about seventy-five officers to patrol for and apprehend undocumented Chinese entering the United States from Mexico (36).

[14] George Sanchez (1993) explains that in these repatriation campaigns a relatively small number of Mexican nationals were actually formally deported. Instead, government policies during the Great Depression made it doubly difficult for Mexicans to find employment or receive welfare provisions. Largely demoralized and impoverished, many moved to parts of Mexico where their government frankly did not want them to go. Sanchez reports that Mexican authorities were quite upset that as much as 95 percent of those repatriated moved not to where the economic need for workers was greatest, in so-called agricultural colonies, but to the places where familial and community ties were strongest (217). This offers a partial explanation for why the Mexican government was largely supportive of the Bracero Program of the next decade.

[15] Ngai (2004) explains that the Bracero Program was a radical break in US law, which, since the end of the Civil War, had outlawed foreign contract labor, understood to be a form of slavery and the antithesis of free labor. Of course, the Alien Contract Labor Law of 1885 was also intended to uphold prohibitions against employing Chinese immigrants in the United States.

especially brutal in border cities like El Paso, Texas (Dunn 2009). Well into the 1980s, however, unauthorized migrants faced relatively few barriers to actually entering the United States through urban points of entry. The robust infrastructure of the major border cities of San Diego, El Paso, and Nogales allowed for a good degree of anonymity in crossing, and Mexican migrants followed the seasonal needs of US employers.

The passage of the 1986 Immigration Reform and Control Act (IRCA) marks an epochal shift in immigration enforcement, when the United States began what Douglas Massey and colleagues (2002) term "a new era of restrictive immigration policies and repressive border controls" (2). Passed under the Reagan Administration, IRCA is often viewed by immigration restrictionists as an "amnesty package" because it allowed for the naturalization of many undocumented immigrants residing in the United States. IRCA as well as the concomitant border policies that followed in the 1990s are perhaps better understood as part of a twinned set of ideologies ushered in during the Reagan Administration's fierce cooperation with a burgeoning neoliberal order and furthered during the Clinton years (Andreas 2009). The unrestricted mobility of capital, represented by the further integration of transnational markets, would be met with heightened restrictions on the mobility of certain populations. With IRCA, Immigration and Natural Services (INS) saw a 50 percent increase in their budget, with much of the new funds earmarked for enforcement at the border and within US workplaces (Massey et al. 2002).[16]

A new enforcement strategy at the US–Mexico border sought to close off the most well-trafficked, urban points of entry where migration had happened for over a century with relative ease. In 1993, Operation Blockade – soon renamed Operation Hold the Line – was implemented at Ciudád Juarez-El Paso. In 1994, Operation Gatekeeper was put into place at Tijuana–San Diego. These two efforts alone accounted for at least two-thirds of where undocumented migrants had previously crossed (Andreas 2009). In 1995, Operation Safeguard closed off the entry point at Nogales, Arizona, and in 1997, Operation Rio Grande targeted southern Texas (Martínez et al. 2014). The governing logic behind such operations was a "prevention by deterrence" strategy (Ewing 2014). Officials presumed that while some deaths would occur, the inevitable collateral damage would demonstrate to future crossers that unauthorized migration was often fatal and, hence, not worth the risk.

These new policies did little to reduce the flow of people. Instead, the border offensive ushered in a humanitarian catastrophe exaggerated in no small part by the near simultaneous passage of the North American Free Trade Agreement (NAFTA). Implemented in 1994, the very same year that Operations Gatekeeper

---

[16] Pursuant to the Homeland Security Act, passed in 2002 in response to the events of September 11, 2001, INS has been consolidated with various other enforcement agencies into Immigration and Customs Enforcement (ICE) and housed under the Department of Homeland Security, also established in the aftermath of September 11.

and Hold-the-Line came into effect, NAFTA liberalized trade policies between the United States and Mexico, leading to a radical restructuring of the Mexican economy. NAFTA had a devastating effect on Mexican farmers, pushing an estimated 3.5 million off their land into Mexican cities and ultimately north to the United States (Ferguson, Price, & Parks 2010). Evidence suggests that officials from all three countries involved in NAFTA – the United States, Mexico, and Canada – knew that Mexican *campesinos* in particular would be negatively impacted by the agreement and that the farmers would need to migrate for work (Magaña 2008; Nevins 2010).

The combination of new free-trade agreements with a new border-enforcement strategy spurred a wave of fatalities that continues to this day (Martínez et al. 2014).[17] Migrants have been funneled into ever more remote stretches of the Sonoran Desert, an area of rugged terrain with little rainfall and temperatures that regularly reach 120 degrees Fahrenheit during the summer. Most migrants begin their multiday journey carrying less than a gallon of water. While the death rates spike in the summer, desert temperatures also fall well below freezing during winter nights, causing hypothermia. Many drown when it does rain, as the desert washes by which unauthorized migrants often travel are also prone to flash flooding. Between 1997 and 2013, the Border Patrol recorded over 6,000 migrant deaths on the US side of the border.[18] The Migrant Trail takes place in the Tucson sector, which was the most traveled as well as the most deadly area of the border between 1998 and 2012 when the walk began. By the end of 2013, however, the Rio Grande Valley sector in Texas had supplanted Tucson for the most migrant fatalities (Martínez et al. 2014).

Due to the clandestine nature of unauthorized migration and the vast territory of the Sonoran Desert, most analysts agree that official calculations represent only a fraction of those who actually perish (Martínez et al. 2014). Nor do these numbers account for the rising death toll now occurring on the Mexican side of the border among Central American migrants (see Dominguez Villegas 2014). Indeed, one of the formative indignities of current policies is that there is no unified system for finding those who go missing. Some organizations have undertaken admirable efforts to help identify the dead. Still, there are

---

[17] Migration rates, and hence fatalities, dropped some during the 2000–1 fiscal years and again after 2006. While some scholars and policy makers claim these decreases can be linked to effective enforcement, there is at least as much evidence to suggest that such flows have responded to the economic recessions, demonstrated by the uptick after 2010 in apprehensions, deaths, and the overall movement of people across the border (Martínez et al. 2014).

[18] Referring to migrant "deaths" is something of a misnomer as Offices of Medical Examiners are actually doing forensic work on "recovered remains," which may or may not belong to a migrant who perished during the same fiscal year in which they are recovered. This further complicates the task of tallying lives lost. As Martínez et al. (2014) propose, however, "for the sake of clarity, consistency, and compassion" (258), the concept of migrant deaths is preferable nomenclature to "recovered remains."

innumerable cases of families whose loved ones departed with the intention to journey north and were never heard from again (Magaña 2008; Ferguson et al. 2010).

The Border Justice Movement

By the late 1990s, US activists and community leaders in and around Tucson became aware that migrant crossers were being funneled into the Arizona desert, where they were dying. A well-established activist community felt compelled to take action. These were individuals and organizations that had cut their teeth on various racial justice, anti-poverty and immigrant rights struggles since the end of the 1960s. Many traced their roots much earlier, to the first decades of the early twentieth century.[19] Central to this history is the 1964 formation of the Manzo Area Council, a social service agency originally funded under the auspices of President Johnson's War on Poverty. By the mid-1970s, responding to the needs of a by then majority Latino population, Manzo focused on offering legal aid, particularly to help Mexican immigrants who were filling out visa applications. By the late 1970s, however, Manzo realized that a new group of people was seeking help: Central American refugees fleeing US-backed wars in Guatemala and El Salvador. Manzo took the humanitarian crisis to area churches, birthing the Sanctuary Movement, one component of the larger Central American solidarity movement discussed earlier in this chapter. Under visible leadership from Tucson-based Quaker Jim Corbett, and from John Fife, the head pastor of Southside Presbyterian Church, where the Migrant Trail today begins, Christian congregations began transporting Central American refugees into the United States in the 1980s.

While the Manzo Area Council ultimately dissolved toward the end of the 1980s with the de-escalation of the Central American conflicts, many of its key leaders would form a new organization, Derechos Humanos, in the early 1990s. Begun as a project of the American Friends Service Committee, Derechos was a response to President Reagan's IRCA policy, which had injected new funds and created more aggressive mandates to patrol the border. Derechos spent its first decade focusing on law enforcement abuse of migrants near the border. Because of the group's close connections with local Latino and immigrant communities, Derechos witnessed firsthand the deadly consequences of the 1990s' efforts to seal the US–Mexico border and helped mobilize a community-wide response.

---

[19] Van Ham (2011) notes that one of the earliest kinds of activism in the Tucson area was rooted in the tradition of *mutualistas*, mutual aid societies from the early 1900s in which Mexican American and Mexican nationals came together in the face of rampant white racism. Mutualistas hosted cultural events, provided basic services such as life insurance for dues-paying members, and fought back against discriminatory policies of the state.

In addition to Derechos and similar to the origins of SOA Watch, which also emerged from the Central American solidarity activist network, Sanctuary Movement veterans formed many of the organizations that united to address border deaths. In the summer of 2000, the "faith-motivated effort" Humane Borders began to set up water stations in the desert. Samaritans, which also has a loosely Christian mission, was established in 2002 as a complementary project, running foot patrols on common migration paths to offer water, food, and help to those in distress. No More Deaths, launched in 2004, establishes summer-long encampments in the desert (Van Ham 2011). Borderlinks, which has mobilized US citizens through educational delegations since the Central American conflicts, continues to do similar work, now taking participants to key sites at and near the border.

The Migrant Trail Begins

By 2003, some of the Borderlinks staff began discussing their desire to do something more about the crisis in their midst. Tucker, one of the original Migrant Trail organizers, explained:

I came to Tucson at a time when you were seeing the direct impacts of a clear policy decision. And this policy decision was funneling people into these desolate areas. Lots of people in Tucson were reacting to it. It just seemed – there had to be even more.

Tucker explained that organizers wanted "to have the same impacts as a protest in the sense that it would attract people's attention, attract the media ... get the message out about what was happening." Many were compelled by the idea of doing a long walk and saw the Migrant Trail as an important protest tactic. There was already a tradition of shorter ritual – infused memorial marches being undertaken at the border. Yet the distance and remoteness of the Migrant Trail make it a bit different from these walks or other, more typical street demonstrations. For Tucker, the walk has become "a protest that I wouldn't even consider a protest. It's almost a commitment."

One of the Migrant Trail's veteran organizers is Margo Cowan, who has played a central role in Tucson activism since being hired by the Manzo Area Council in 1972. Margo also worked alongside farmworker leaders César Chavez and Dolores Huerta in California. Margo explained to me during the tenth year of the Migrant Trail in 2013, "when we started, we really didn't think we'd be walking ten years later ... I used to think that it was like a fire fight." While this might seem idealistic to some, Margo can hardly be pegged as out of touch with the workings of government policy or the legal system, with a résumé that includes serving as general counsel to congresspersons and the Tohono O'odham nation as well as having served as a Pima County's public defender for over a decade (CWU Tucson 2015). Indeed, even the most veteran of activists organizing the first Migrant Trail in 2004 sincerely believed that if the public could just learn the facts about US border policy they would be horrified. While no one presumed their trek would by itself change legislation, most saw it as part of a multipronged outcry certain to garner popular support. There was a sense that a deterrence program, which now costs billions of tax dollars annually, has led to thousands of deaths and is ineffectual at its stated aims could not remain standard operating procedure.

The human cost and obvious tragedy of migrant deaths is a central motivator for Migrant Trail organizers and an important manner of galvanizing people with different political as well as religious commitments. Yet if many organizers emphasize that the walk is "only about the deaths," as a way to honor the deceased and draw attention to an unquestionably *moral* atrocity, most participants seem to understand the loss of life in the desert as evidence of larger systems of global inequality and militarized social control. For instance, Tucker explained:

When I think of the border, it represents the neoliberal model, the scheme. It goes way deep into Mexico. It comes to a crescendoing point here [at the border] in a lot of ways. Then it goes deep into the United States, where migrants are arriving – the domestic enforcement: Secure Communities, 287(g) and police enforcing immigration law, and SB 1070 in Arizona.[20]

In the late 1990s, Tucker lived in Mexico while working with Witness for Peace, the organization focused on Nicaraguan human rights observation during the Central American solidarity movement. Witness for Peace expanded and transitioned when the movement waned, commencing US delegations to Mexico where participants would learn about the impacts of free-trade policies such as NAFTA. During this time, Tucker traveled the country, visiting states in southern Mexico that had not typically counted many migrants among the general population. Speaking to me on the 2011 Migrant Trail, Tucker recalled:

Oaxaca wasn't a traditional sending state. Nor was Chiapas. We went out to communities that are just empty, literally abandoned ... This is a phenomenon [that started] in

[20] Mathew Coleman (2012) explains Secure Communities and 287(g) as the two most significant programs in the devolution of US immigration enforcement from a federal matter to a policing priority at the city, county, and state level. 287(g) is named for a section of the 1996 federal immigration legislation, the Illegal Immigration Reform and Immigrant Responsibility Act, and authorizes local law enforcement to participate in a variety of immigration-related activities that had previously been the sole provenance of the federal government. These include investigating immigration cases, making immigration arrests, and holding immigrant detainees. While few localities initially expressed interest in using the authority granted by 287(g), Coleman reports, "The situation changed dramatically after the September 2001 attacks, specifically lawmakers' emphasis thereafter on local–federal policing partnerships as crucial to homeland security" (2012: 167). For the purposes of this discussion, Secure Communities is quite similar to 287(g), insofar as both programs authorize local law enforcement bodies to actively collaborate with federal ICE. SB 1070, passed by the Arizona legislature in 2010, deputizes law enforcement officers to enforce immigration law and was the strictest state-level anti-immigration measure in the United States at the time it became law.

the last fifteen years ... people in Mexico talk about having the right not to migrate, and that resonates with me.

Tucker's observation speaks to the regional shifts that NAFTA, as an exemplar of neoliberal restructuring, has generated. Halting the deaths at the border is certainly crucial, but allowing people to choose if, when, and how to migrate in the first place is an equally fundamental right that all should be afforded. From his experiences living and advocating for more just policies in both the United States and Mexico, Tucker understood that state efforts to seal the border cannot stem global economic dynamics but do come at an immense human cost.

This idea of militarizing the border, putting all these agents, enforcement apparatus, all this technology and what not on the border itself is ridiculous. It's not [accomplishing] even the stated goal – you look at the statistics and immigration has only gone up and up.

Like Tucker, veteran organizer Susan also understood the Migrant Trail as responding to a series of complex global and national dynamics. She explained that Arizona has become a flash point in national anti-immigrant sentiment and policy-making, where the most draconian strategies are tested and then exported. When taken in conjunction with migrant deaths on the border, Susan reflected:

It's all of those issues merging together. And I would even throw in there like the environmental issues of what's happening to the desert and everything. So a merging of many issues – the militarization, the normalization of violence and death – that's all here.

To Susan, the interlocking systems of policing and border enforcement, the devaluation of certain lives, and environmental destruction that manifest at the US–Mexico border cannot be disaggregated. Moreover, Susan suggested that, though the need to reform border policy seemed obvious to the original Migrant Trail organizers in 2004, the militarization of the border had by 2011 become one of the most normalized aspects of the current immigration system. Susan believed this was evident in the fact that key organizations in the national immigrant rights movement, those who would be assumed to be allied activists, have paid relatively minimal attention to the border in advocating for a robust set of reforms. Susan continued:

When we talk about comprehensive immigration reform, we also need to remember that border security and the militarization of the border and the border deaths are an important component of our immigration policy. We can't sacrifice the people that are dying in the desert, the people who are being forced to cross through this torturous area for pieces of immigration reform.

In this assessment, Susan points to what has become ever more apparent since the Migrant Trail's inception. SOA Watch, previously discussed, was able to leverage real political pressure to expose the SOA, nearly defund it, and halt certain countries from sending officials to the school. Witness Against Torture, which I will discuss next, also seemed to have won the effort to close Guantánamo at one point. The Migrant Trail and the border justice movement as a whole, in contrast, have never appeared to be "winning"; the objective of halting migrant deaths at the border has yet to gain the popular support or political traction necessary to make it a policy priority.

At the same time, some Migrant Trail participants believe that the current stalemate on immigration policy will not endure. These activists argue that within their lifetimes, border policy will dramatically shift. Margo, who originally thought of the Migrant Trail as a "fire fight," has a long-term vision rooted in traditional political calculus and decades of experience as an immigration activist. As she spoke to our small group during one of the afternoon circles on the 2013 walk, she was confident "all of you will see a different America. The demographic will completely rock politics as we know it now." What Margo meant by this is that the Latino vote continues to grow, and these are voters that "didn't have to get politicized," having grown up under xenophobic conditions. Margo concluded, "I see this racist era as a last gasp." If a new American public is indeed nascent, and if they are politicized in the way that Margo believes, US policy toward Latin American migrants will likely change. This may portend an alternative set of policies and goals at the US–Mexico border. Nevertheless, given that the 2016 campaign for the US presidency was waged and arguably won, in part, on rancorous anti-immigrant rhetoric and the promise to build a wall and deport millions, this hoped-for alternative at the border currently seems quite distant.

WITNESS AGAINST TORTURE

The Guantánamo Military Prison

I have been a package for 12 years now. I am a package when en route to Camp Echo, the solitary confinement wing. I am a package en route to a legal call. "The package has been picked up ... the package has been delivered."
> – detainee Shaker Aamer (2014) on being held at Guantánamo[21]

On January 11, 2002, a group of Afghani men were delivered to the military prison at Guantánamo Bay, Cuba, as the first group of captives to be held there. The spectacle of male bodies, shackled and hooded, crouching below uniformed military officials was in turn disseminated to the world. The interned men, captured abroad and flown by the US government to the prison,

---

[21] This excerpt is from a letter of Aamer's published in *The Guardian*. It became part of a script for a guerilla theater piece that Witness Against Torture performed on the streets of Washington, DC, in January 2014 which I discuss in Chapter 3. Aamer was finally released in October 2015, after being imprisoned for nearly fourteen years without charge.

inaugurated the long-standing US naval base as an indefinite holding site for "enemy combatants." This legally unprecedented category was created by the Bush Administration at the onset of the "Global War on Terror," a foreign and domestic policy response to the September 11, 2001, attacks on US soil.

Guantánamo's new function as a military prison, and the creation of a new category of war captive, "enemy combatant," were but two of the many ways that the US executive began eroding basic principles of liberal democracy during the War on Terror. Captives were held at Guantánamo without charge, marking the suspension of the writ of habeas corpus – the right of a prisoner to face his accuser in a court of law and contest the legitimacy of his detention. Habeas corpus is a principle established as early as the thirteenth-century's Magna Carta and adopted by the US framers as a fundamental bulwark against tyranny. By August of 2002, the Department of Justice's Office of Legal Counsel began issuing memos giving the US government legal authority to commit torture (Greenberg & Dratel 2005).[22] US heads of state claimed the prisoners posed the highest threat, terming them "the worst of the worst." Yet to date, only a tiny percentage has ever been alleged to be involved in "terrorist activities."[23] What is much more clear is that the US security state has engaged in a regime of racialized terror, detaining and torturing Muslim men in a manner that defies legal precedent.

Building on Edward Said's now foundational arguments, many scholars observe that the Global War on Terror depends upon deeply Orientalist assumptions that conflate Muslim, Arab, and Middle Eastern peoples into the singular category of "potential terrorists" (Volpp 2002; Bayoumi 2009). Of the 780 men who have been or continue to be held at the military prison, *all* have been Muslim and the vast majority Arab. As Avery Gordon observes, for many War on Terror detainees "captivity itself confers a legally binding judgment of pre-established criminal status" (Gordon 2010: 39). To be imprisoned is to be already criminal. Even without explicit reference to race then, the logic that there are *kinds* of subjects, bodies, and peoples who can be incarcerated indefinitely without recourse to basic legal rights and procedures depends upon racial thinking.

Colonial logics have long been a structuring force at Guantánamo. One might say that the violence of capture, slavery, and sequester have been sown in the soil. Because of its strategic location at the southeastern end of Cuba, Guantánamo was an important transit point during the Atlantic Slave Trade. By 1903, the land surrounding the Bay was secured to become what is now

---

[22] Key members of the Department of Justice, specifically Jay S. Bybee and John Yoo, issued memoranda that vastly broadened the scope as to what kinds of physical and psychological harm could be administered without being legally defined as "torture."

[23] In their analysis of the Department of Defense's own documents released in 2006 in regard to the 517 men then being held, Denbeaux et al. (2006) show that only 8 percent of the detainees were accused of being al Qaeda fighters.

the United States' oldest overseas naval base, territory that the United States obtained when it waged the US–Spain War of 1898. The United States has held the 45 square miles under "lease" now for over a century, though the Cuban people have been demanding its return since at least the 1959 Revolution, a demand that the United States has plainly refused (Ratner & Ray 2004).[24] In 1991, following the US-backed overthrow of democratically elected Haitian president Jean Bertrand Aristide, the base was used as a detention center for Haitians seeking to escape the violent regime that supplanted Aristide's. Following international law, the United States could not simply deport the refugees, so they were instead intercepted mid-voyage and held in prison-like conditions, with a special quarantine zone for those forcibly tested and found to be HIV positive (Paik 2010). Spawned through this history of conquest and violence, Guantánamo has long been central to US imperial overreach and state-sanctioned forms of transnational violence (Kaplan 2005). The prison is today paradigmatic of the US security state, marked by militarized disposses-sion, war making, and a gluttonous carceral apparatus.

The Trip to Cuba

Witness Against Torture began as a journey, an embodied response to the resistance being undertaken by the detainees at Guantánamo. In the early months of 2005, some friends convened to clean out the New York City apart-ment of their much admired and recently deceased fellow activist, Elmer Maas. Among his many acts of resistance, Maas was well known for being part of the Plowshares Eight, a Catholic pacifist group that, in a 1980 act of civil disobe-dience, had trespassed into a Pennsylvania missile facility to damage nuclear weapons components and pour blood on documents (Nepstad 2008). This act inaugurated an international nuclear disarmament movement. Those who had gathered to mourn Maas and sort his things were themselves members of the Catholic Worker Movement, living in faith-based, intentional communities in accord with the Works of Mercy. Catholic Workers simultaneously minister to the poor by offering necessary services, such as soup kitchens, while advocat-ing for systemic change to address poverty, often protesting US militarism and wars abroad. Wanting to honor Maas's memory at a moment when many had already long been organizing against war, the group began to talk about their next steps together. Matt Daloisio, one of WAT's founding members, explains of the time period, "Things were shifting in the country. This was a couple years into the Bush administration, a couple years after September 11, and it seemed like things were getting fairly bleak." The group wanted to consider a meaningful response to ever more draconian US policies against the vulnerable,

---

[24] In fact, the US Treasury sends $4,085 to Cuba each year in the form of a check. Cuba has not cashed the checks in decades, contesting what it sees as US occupation of this part of the island (Kaplan 2005; Ewing 2016).

both at home and abroad. In so doing, they committed to take the fear of consequences off the table – principally significant jail time for potential civil disobedience.

Around this time, the news broke that a massive hunger strike was underway at Guantánamo. It was the spring of 2005 and about 700 men were then being held. Matt explains that the group's central questions quickly became the following:

How do we as American citizens who feel some responsibility for what our government is doing respond to these men who – regardless of their innocence or guilt, which at this point really wasn't clear – who are using the only tool that they have, which was their own bodies to cry out? How do we respond in a way that's going to end up being heard?

In line with the radical pacifist lineage from which the groups in this study emerge, those in the Catholic Worker Movement often prioritize "being faithful over being successful," targeting society's moral shortcomings even if there is little chance of seeing policy change. This time, however, the group thought they might do both. In 2005, it did not seem so far-fetched that people of different political perspectives would agree that Guantánamo was an abomination. Matt notes that the prison seemed "outside the bounds of even mainstream American thought – that we would indefinitely detain people, that we would torture people." The group believed that, at least for the vast majority of US citizens, "this was not what they wanted America to be about."

The notion of ministering to the prisoner is a central tenet in the Works of Mercy. As part of their involvement in radical pacifist efforts, including the Plowshares movement, members of the group had spent ample time in jails and prison for their civil disobedience. They knew that happenings outside a prison had a way of making their way in, especially in the case of protest. The group decided that it had to respond to the detainees in a physical way, by taking a trip to Cuba. Even if the group would not be allowed into the prison, they hoped that the detainees would hear that US citizens had traveled to respond to the hunger strike as well as to defy their government's egregious practices of indefinite detention.

In the summer of 2005, after WAT had commenced planning the trip, a reporter at a European press event voiced concern about conditions at the prison to then-President Bush. The president responded that while the "folks being detained" were held in "humane conditions," "if you've got questions about Guantánamo, I seriously suggest you go down there and take a look" (Department of State 2005). This gave WAT members additional motivation to travel to the prison. They would explain to the public that they were heeding the administration's invitation to visit the prison, even as they suspected that they would be calling the president's bluff, revealing that Guantánamo was not in fact open for scrutiny.

The journey to Guantánamo was not without its challenges. In planning for the trip, the activists were concerned about how best to navigate their protest with Cuban authorities. As US citizens, they wished to "speak to their own government," as Frida Berrigan, another WAT organizer puts it, without putting the Cuban government into an impossible position. Group members held a long-standing affection for the vision of the Cuban left. They also wanted to stay focused on the detainees' hunger strike, without creating some sort of "international incident." In preparation for the trip, WAT actively sought permission from the Cuban government but received no response.

By the fall of 2005, the group needed to purchase their airplane tickets. While they had raised sufficient funds to support incidentals, the twenty-five who wished to make it to the prison had committed to purchase their own tickets. This was no small obligation, considering that each ticket was several hundred dollars and those purchasing them – Catholic Workers who live in intentional poverty – had minimal personal wealth. Due to a half-century travel embargo between the United States and Cuba, there were no direct flights to the island. As other US tourists had long done, the group traveled through the Santo Domingo Airport in the Dominican Republic. Once at Santo Domingo, US travelers had for decades been given the opportunity to purchase a $20 document where their visa stamps for passage into and out of Cuba would be marked. This separate document allowed US travelers to keep their passport "clean," maintaining the image of having traveled only to the Dominican Republic, and allowing them easy reentry into the United States without being accused of violating the embargo. WAT members refused this offer; they wanted their US passports to hold the Cuban stamp. Through this act of civil disobedience, they hoped the US courts would call on them to testify about their journey, though this never occurred.[25]

When the group ultimately arrived in Cuba, government officials quickly arrived to confront them. They could not undertake this protest, the activists were told, and they were threatened with deportation out of Cuba if they pressed the issue. After a day of negotiating in Santiago, though, officials agreed to a more well-humored if still aggressive management strategy. While the group traversed the island on foot, with two driving a support car with some of the group's equipment, representatives of the Cuban government escorted them. Cuban officials suggested everything from places to stay to how the protesters should frame their media message. Sometimes the group gratefully accepted help. Other times they politely refused. Most nights, without assistance from the Cuban government, the group of activists simply asked local homeowners if they could set up tents on private land and were always graciously invited to do so.

[25] When the US government later sent a letter inquiring into the group's illegal trip to Cuba, to which WAT offered an explanation for the trip as well as a complete list of names and locations for those who had participated, the group was not contacted by the government again (Brown et al. 2008).

At the end of their weeklong, fifty-mile journey, WAT members ultimately arrived at the edge of the Cuban military zone that surrounds the US Naval Base, where they were stopped. Cuban officials explained that if the group had permission from the US government, they would be allowed through Cuban military territory. Lacking this, they would not be permitted. As the group had suspected, President Bush's invitation to visit the prison issued just months earlier was not without very particular conditions. WAT opted to stay at the fence, where they camped and fasted for five days in solidarity with the hunger strikers. "We called the base every day to tell them we were there and wanting to get in," Matt noted. There were many reasons for this daily call. One was to push for the access promised by the US government. Another was to generate "chatter," as Frida Berrigan puts it, a hope that word would make it to the detainees that US citizens had heard their cry for help and were responding.

One interpretation of the journey might suggest it was an ultimately futile, if noble, effort by an idealistic micro-minority with little measurable impact. The group's hopes of making a media splash were better realized with international outlets than US news organizations. Cuban television covered the walk, as did the British Broadcasting Corporation (the BBC). Bush Administration officials gave no public reaction to it, and nothing in the disposition and administration of the prison at Guantánamo changed as a result.

A different perspective would emphasize the trip's cultural, psychic, and even spiritual benefits, for the group and, to some degree, for the prisoners as well. About a month after the trip, many of those who had traveled to Cuba were in Washington, DC, holding a vigil outside of the Department of Justice. A lawyer from a Washington, DC-based firm came over to the group, explaining that she represented some of the Guantánamo prisoners. She told them that her clients in Guantánamo wanted the group to know that when they had gone to Cuba, the prisoners had known they were there. Just as WAT had hoped, word had made it into the prison that US citizens were camping and fasting outside the gates, responding to the detainees' hunger strike. The lawyer said that the men at Guantánamo had been moved and that they wanted to express their gratitude. Aware of both the necessity and insufficiency of hope in this instance, Matt reflected, "I think having those very human connections has been profoundly important [to us], and we hope important for the men there."

Over a Decade Since

Since returning from their inaugural trip to Cuba, WAT has faced years of near-victories and crushing defeats, but has maintained an unwavering solidarity with the Guantánamo prisoners and a continued commitment to exposing the security state logics that keep the prison open. While WAT participants engage in various actions in their home communities across the country throughout the year, their most consistent and sizeable actions have taken place each January, when a group of about forty core members comes together for a week to mark the anniversary of the prison's opening. They live communally in spaces provided by area churches, fast for up to ten days in solidarity with the detained men, and engage in creative, direct actions in the nation's capital.

During their early years of organizing, WAT seemed to be building substantial political momentum. Between 2005 and the 2008 presidential elections, American public opinion shifted substantially regarding operations at Guantánamo. Witness Against Torture events were able to mobilize crowds in the thousands and occasionally tens of thousands. Guantánamo cases that were making it to the Supreme Court were being won in favor of those detained.[26] Both Senators McCain and Obama campaigned on the promise to close Guantánamo as the American public was no longer convinced that the prison was actually bolstering national security. Matt explains, "We finally had won that narrative. There was some excitement about that, and some hope."

After Obama's election, WAT planned a high-pressure effort during the first months of the new presidency, the "One Hundred Days Campaign." Six members of the group moved to Washington, DC, and lived communally in a Buddhist temple for over three months. In conjunction with supporting organizations in the area, they held daily vigils in front of the White House, undertook solidarity fasts, and helped organize educational events throughout the city. Just two days into their effort, however, Obama signed an executive order to close Guantánamo. Matt explained the sense of elation, as well as some internal confusion. Obama's plan was exactly what the group had demanded, excepting the exact time frame. "We wanted a hundred days; he said it would be closed within a year," Matt explained. He continued that the executive order was one that "in many respects we could have written ourselves. It was that good. I mean, it lacked the time frame that we wanted." The group was forced to have "a frank conversation" about whether or not to stay for the 98 remaining days.

They began to discuss what they might do next with the political momentum they had built. For if Guantánamo were closed, certainly torture, extraordinary rendition, and CIA black sites still remained, along with what the group understood to be a deeply racist domestic incarceration regime. They started talking about whether to expand their work to protest the US military base in Bagram, Afghanistan, which the *New York Times* revealed in 2005 to be linked to a pattern of torture and prisoner abuse. Similarly, the group considered

---

[26] Significant among these was *Boumediene v. Bush*, which made it to the Supreme Court in 2008, and held that prisoners at Guantánamo had a right to habeas corpus under the US Constitution. Other significant cases won on the detainees' behalf at the Supreme Court include *Rasul v. Bush* (2004), *Hamdi v. Rumsfeld* (2004), and *Hamdan v. Rumsfeld* (2006), all of which ruled that Guantánamo prisoners should be granted some aspect of the due process rules guaranteed by the US Constitution. There are a number of excellent and detailed accounts of the legal challenges to Guantánamo; see, for example: Ratner and Ray (2004), Worthington (2007), Hafetz and Denbaux (2009), and Bravin (2014).

drawing more concrete connections to the overuse of US imprisonment, racial injustice, and prisoner abuse.

The group ultimately decided to stay for the duration of those 100 days with the understanding that a year was not soon enough to close the prison. Evoking a time-honored legal maxim popularized in Dr. Martin Luther King Jr.'s *Letter from a Birmingham Jail,* the activists argued that for those being detained without charge, "justice delayed is justice denied." They emblazoned this statement on banners and signs, which they carried throughout their months of direct action. Members of the public and lawmakers began to question why they were still protesting. As they met with legislators and brought their protest into congressional confirmation hearings and other proceedings, the group was told, "Guantánamo's closed ... Obama promised to do it." Yet as the months ensued, it gradually became obvious that the administration was moving too slowly to close Guantánamo. The group's sense of confidence began to erode as the devastating truth became more obvious. The president had offered what Matt termed, "a promise and not a plan." This created a unique situation for WAT. After seeming to have won, they were forced to craft a strategy not merely in the face of implausibility, but against a concession that had been given and then taken away.

Though crestfallen, many were also unsurprised. Most assessed that Guantánamo's continuing existence speaks not to the political failings of a given president or congressional stalemate but to the structural and cultural underpinnings of the US role in the world. As WAT organizer Jeremy Varon explained while speaking to oral historian Ronald Grele in 2011:

A harsh detention regime at some level is a structural requirement given the profile of American power in the world ... if you need oil on that scale, if you need to pacify populations, if you need resource extraction from the Third World, if you need access to markets, if you need global economic dominance you are going to need, at some level, military power to enforce that. If you are going to be fighting far-flung wars against a shadowy, particulated, transnational, postmodern enemy, you are embracing a mode of conflict that is going to chew people up in systems of detention, interrogation and degradation ... The extra-legal space is a requirement of empire.

(Grele 2011: 104–5)

In this assessment, Varon suggests that the effort to close Guantánamo might be understood as a limited gain around a particular feature of US imperialism. At the same time, he was clear that the impact of closing this particular prison should not be underestimated, even if it might first appear to be "so much work for so few people." WAT activists now essentially outnumber the detainees. Nevertheless, as Varon understood it:

We're standing for one hundred and sixty-six men and we're standing for a democratic and juridical legacy that stretches back centuries and is the essence of the Enlightenment and the essence of human civilized self-governance. I think smart people understand that those are the stakes, and I think history will judge those to be the stakes as well.

WAT member Cameron agreed. To protest Guantánamo, he suggested, is to expose not just the US security state's violence but also the legal, and thus cultural, logics that underwrite it.

I think [Guantánamo is] the iconic example of the War on Terror, right? We will take people, hold them indefinitely, torture them for no reason – because this is what we can do and we've made the legal framework to be able to do it. Because of this, the whole culture of the United States shifted to make way for torture as public policy.

Akin to participants in both SOA Watch and the Migrant Trail Walk, members of Witness Against Torture are drawn to contest Guantánamo because they understand the military prison as a site where the violence of an entire global order can be witnessed and the contradictions of the US security state exposed.

In the decade since, WAT has broadened their base of participants while continuing to engage in planned actions that are as creative and daring as ever. I detail many of these in the Chapters 3–5. One of particular significance was the group's 2015 return trip to Cuba over Thanksgiving, marking the ten-year anniversary of the campaign's inaugural journey. Fourteen WAT participants once again made their way to the prison, though no longer in defiance of an international travel ban. The group camped outside of the military base and fasted in solidarity with the hunger-striking detainees (Pilkington 2015). While a few core WAT members made the return voyage, the group that went to Cuba in 2015 was also quite different from the one that made the initial voyage. As one WAT member on the second trip explained to me, "The group has changed enormously. Very very significantly, the trip had two Muslims, two Dominican-American fellows. It has grown less Christian, younger, hipper, and more media savvy." In addition to new forms of racial and religious diversity among WAT members, this young and media-savvy group put great effort into crafting and sharing stunning photos of their solidarity activism through social media. The act of solidarity witness in the digital age still includes embodied and high-risk activism but has grown to encompass the staging and diffusion of powerful visuals in new ways.

SIGNIFICANT DISTINCTIONS

Though each group traces a unique historical trajectory and set of concerns, this book tends not to focus on each case as an independent entity, with its own set of actors, initiatives, and struggles. Rather, I usually examine what these groups can collectively tell us about the political practice of solidarity witness. In this section, then, I do want to elaborate on some differences between the cases, which should allow for greater clarity in the following chapters.

One important distinction between the groups is that SOA Watch and the Migrant Trail provide an avenue for entry-level activism in a way that WAT does not. I understand entry-level activism as a political activity that can be entered into as a low-risk form of experiential education, an undertaking that is often not perceived by newcomers to be *political* at all. Participants attend in order to *learn* something, to bear witness to a different reality, and they find that in the process they are transformed, mobilized, and politicized in ways they did not expect. About a third of Migrant Trail participants in any given year are not veteran activists, and attending the weeklong journey is one of their first instances of activism. While I cannot estimate the precise number of SOA Watch vigil participants coming to the event as their first exposure to activism, I do know from informal conversations with young people at the vigil as well as interviews that the Fort Benning event serves this role for many. The experiential education emphasis at both SOA Watch and the Migrant Trail is evident in the fact that many religious and educational institutions bring delegations of people to the actions in a facilitated manner.

WAT is not quite like this. There are no delegations to the week of action in January. Everyone who lives in the church together in DC is fasting for upward of seven days. The vast majority will get arrested at some point or another. In contrast, among participants at SOA Watch, only a small group of participators committed civil disobedience, especially in the Fort Benning Vigil's final years. On the Migrant Trail, no one risks arrest and much care is taken to avoid any kind of legal trouble for the walkers. While seven days in the desert is a form of physical duress, few walk the entire Migrant Trail. Most are encouraged, and often directed, to get in a vehicle if they are feeling overly tired or hot so as to reduce the likelihood of medical emergencies. WAT participants, on the other hand, do not break their fast if they begin to feel unwell. I suspect that only in a true medical emergency would they be encouraged to give up the fast altogether.

A second point of difference between the cases has to do with scale. Over its duration, a few hundred people have participated in the Migrant Trail. Several hundreds, if not more, have participated in WAT events. Yet in both of these groups, the tradition of living together in close community over several days on an annual basis is essential. Each weeklong gathering counts only about fifty people, creating an opportunity for greater intimacy and bonding. SOA Watch, in contrast, is largely defined by mass protest, when thousands if not tens of thousands of people converge.

Both WAT and the Migrant Trail participants have been drawn to the idea of increasing their numbers to be more effective at applying political pressure and winning institutional goals. On the Migrant Trail, however, a significant impediment to increasing group size has been the limited logistical support available when participants are tens of miles away from paved roads during the first days of the walk. The Buenos Aires Wildlife Refuge, where the first half of the walk takes place, also sets a limit on how many can overnight at a given campsite. To include more people, organizers originally invited additional participants to join the second half of the walk. After a few years of this, it was clear that the incoming group generated an odd dynamic. A core of walkers had already bonded, and having tens of newcomers join the community was disruptive. Today, the public is invited to join on the final night, and there are usually tens of Tucson residents that walk the shorter, last day into the city of Tucson.[27]

While wanting to build support for their campaigns, Migrant Trail and WAT members acknowledged the benefits to the fact that their group's size has remained limited. As Susan of the Migrant Trail explained:

There's a part of me that would really love it if the Migrant Trail walk had a hundred, two hundred people. But I'm not sure that's desirable because maintaining a small group allows for some of those things to happen that wouldn't happen if it were a big group. I know the name of let's say 80% of the people that are here, and [I] have actually spoken to them. If there were more people, that'd be hard. There wouldn't be as cohesive of a group.

Matt of Witness Against Torture similarly observed of the size of his group:

At the end of the day we are a community. We've become friends and that's allowed us to expand. That's also kept us from expanding too far too. So we're a group of people that really trust each other.

The tension between mobilizing a broad-based, popular front versus prioritizing group cohesion is a common movement dilemma. In Rebecca Klatch's (2002) examination of "new left" movement groups from the 1960s, the size of a movement group was "important in shaping individual experiences, in building solidarity, and in affecting the tone and style of the organization" (192). Klatch suggests that the smaller and more marginalized a group, the greater the cohesion between activists. As groups get larger, the potential for conflicting ideologies and sectarian tendencies increases.

This difference in scale is, thus, an important way in which SOA Watch is unique among these cases. At the same time, in each of these groups, the people who come back year after year, who take the most significant risks, do the lion's share of organizing, and maintain institutional memory are in the tens. They know each other through years of activism, express a sense of deep connection, and regularly use the term "community" to refer to their respective groups. Despite the distinctions in overall size, which might otherwise suggest

---

[27] This predicament, however, remains far from resolved. In the aftermath of Trump's anti-immigrant campaign in 2016, interest in the Migrant Trail skyrocketed. While fifty or sixty people have tended to sign up for the walk in years past and have done so over the two months of registration, in April and May of 2017, more than fifty had signed up within the first thirteen hours that the walk was opened to the public. Organizers were faced with a rather fractious dilemma of whether to turn people away. Some strongly advocated to lift the agreed-upon participant cap, arguing that logistical concerns should not take priority over the walk's inclusive and expansive vision. Others feared for everything from general stress on walk organizers to increased risks of having to manage actual medical emergencies. Organizers reached a somewhat disorderly compromise but kept numbers fairly constrained. About sixty people ultimately joined the walk as tens more canceled their planned participation for various reasons.

these movement efforts be inappropriate for comparison, I still understand these three groups as being a similar set of cases.

COMPLEXITIES OF RELIGION, GENERATION, AND RACE

A common feature across these cases is each group's complex and often ambivalent form of religiosity. While it is obvious that Christianity informs each group's history and shows up in shared understandings, in the central tactics of fasting, pilgrimage, and solemn vigil, and in the symbolism present, such as crosses and rosaries, participants themselves maintain varied religious beliefs and commitments. Each group also expresses its desire to be inclusive to all regardless of religion. This locates these campaigns squarely within other nonviolent traditions that have combined religious and secular elements, such as those of Mahatma Gandhi, Martin Luther King Jr., and Cesar Chavez. For the groups in this study, religion proves both an invaluable and insufficient means for explaining solidarity witness as a political practice.

Both SOA Watch and WAT began as deeply religious endeavors, composed predominately of Roman Catholics and Catholic Workers, who understood their activism as a means of living their faith. The Migrant Trail, in contrast, was never an explicitly religious activity. While some organizers and early participants on the Migrant Trail were motivated at least in part by their Christian commitments, they were quite reflective in framing the walk itself as an ecumenical undertaking, open to all faiths as well as nonbelievers. Interestingly, as the groups have evolved, they have come to a similar place in balancing religiosity with secular appeal. SOA Watch and WAT have grown less religious and more multi-faith over the years, while the Migrant Trail has perhaps become more religious, at least in that some organizers believe the walk attracts an increasing proportion of faith-driven participants.

To the extent that we can summarize, the older activists tend to be more devout, while younger participants are more inclined to be either secular or questioning, often prompted by the politics of gender and sexuality that have led many American leftists to feel ambivalent about Christianity. Even the most faithful members of these activist communities, however, tend to be highly critical of Church bureaucracy and any strict dogma. For instance, there are many Catholics across these groups who disagree with the Church's teachings on homosexuality and women, evinced by Father Bourgeois's excommunication for ordaining women, an act that is widely supported among core SOA Watch activists. While nuns, monks, and priests are present in every community, I have never observed an instance of evangelizing or someone expressing concern for another person's largely agnostic or even atheist stance. At the same time, I have been aware of gender-nonconforming individuals being put off by the religiosity of these groups. There have also been instances in which people of color who do not identify as Christian are offended by their sense of unquestioned colonial or missionary traces in group ideology or practice.

Gill (2004) trenchantly observes that some of the conflict between older and younger activists is not so much dictated by religion but rather by different cultures of activism. Gill notes that, at least among SOA Watch, the "old guard" prioritizes solemn ritual and often highlights the spiritual or faithful elements of their protest. This can be a bit different from the more theatrical tendencies of youth culture. When SOA Watch was gaining momentum, younger participants tended to share affection for anarchist currents learned in anti-globalization protests, such as the WTO gathering in Seattle and the Zapatista Movement. This younger generation, in addition to being more secular, bristled at rules and hierarchy and was more open to the role of armed insurrection.

The complexities and shifts over time in religious orientation have other implications as well. The shared lineage in Christian pacifist communities of North America means that a majority of participants across these groups tend to be white, middle-class, and highly educated. Yet each group is, or has become, racially and ethnically diverse in important ways. SOA Watch, if initiated by white US Catholics, is today a multi-racial movement effort, including US residents who identify as black, white, First Nations, Latino, Arab, and Asian, and people from throughout Central and South America. There is also a pronounced Spanish–English bilingualism in this group's actions. Though the Migrant Trail continues to draw criticism for attracting a majority white group of walkers, people of color, especially Chicano and Latino identified individuals, have always been important organizers in the group. Like SOA Watch, Spanish–English bilingualism is a key feature of the walk. WAT, if originally white and Catholic, has attracted younger Muslims, Jews, and people of color, including those who identify as Latino, Afro-Latino, Asian, and Arab. These individuals have taken on important positions of leadership. I return to a more detailed discussion of the racial dynamics as well as contests over religiosity in each group in Chapter 6.

RELATIONSHIP TO THE AGGRIEVED

Since the concept of solidarity is central to this project, I conclude this chapter's case comparison with a brief mention of each group's relationship to the aggrieved. A relationship might be assumed to be a basic prerequisite for solidarity, which is generally taken to mean communal belonging, reciprocity, and mutual accountability (Kurasawa 2007). The state's targets are present in important ways for these groups, yet each campaign holds a somewhat distinct relationship with those on whose behalf they advocate.

SOA Watch is today an extensive struggle. In this sense, there are many contexts in which to discuss the relationships between core SOA Watch activists and those confronting US-backed violence in Latin America. I focus predominately on the effort to close the SOA. Obviously those actually murdered by SOA graduates cannot join the campaign to close the school in any literal sense. At the same time, the loved ones of those killed and tortured as well as torture survivors themselves have played a central role at the Fort Benning vigil. As SOA Watch veteran Patrick explained to me, part of the purpose of this vigil is for those who have endured state violence to be heard:

Many people come here because they've lost people in Latin America. There was a mother here yesterday on the stage. Two of her kids were killed. Her husband was killed. Her mother was killed. Her father was killed. They were killed by graduates of the School of the Americas. She comes and tells a story.

Of the three groups in this study, then, SOA Watch activists likely have the most direct link to the state's targets for whom they advocate.

As a yearly event, the Migrant Trail has a much less direct relationship to those targeted by border enforcement policy, most obviously undocumented migrants crossing the US–Mexico border. There are a handful of instances in which those who crossed the border at some point in the past have returned to participate in the Migrant Trail years after legalizing their status. Undocumented migrants, however, are unlikely to participate in the walk because of the great risk they would incur traveling through an area rife with roaming border patrol, check points, and vigilantes. At the same time, the border justice movement does centrally include undocumented activists, and most regular participants on the Migrant Trail have done significant work with undocumented people and count immigrants, regardless of status, as friends and family. As one of the Migrant Trail's leaders, Ana explained of the walk's original participants, "We were all people who had an understanding, had friends who'd crossed, had been involved in all of that."

Even with their depth of connection to undocumented migrants and a commonly held understanding of the walk as a practice of solidarity, Migrant Trail participants note that the walk itself is not an act of direct relationship. As Susan explained:

It's actually best we don't have a tangible, physical relationship with [crossing migrants] because we would draw attention. Only if they're in severe suffering would migrants actually come to us [out in the desert]. But maybe we have a spiritual connection with each other. And I would hope that when migrants see us they would understand that we are people that wish them well and are fighting for them to be able to come here legally and, um, I dunno, we're praying for them.[28]

Witness Against Torture participants also regard their group's relationship with Guantánamo detainees complexly. While crafting relationships with those indefinitely detained at an offshore prison has obvious challenges, the (albeit

---

[28] There have been a few times that migrants in distress have approached the group, though this is usually when two or three participants are parked in a support vehicle, separate from the rest of the walkers. In these instances, migrants have needed urgent help, and while Migrant Trail organizers have protocol for dealing with such situations, the walk is not intended to offer the kind of direct aid that allied groups throughout the desert do.

limited) communication between WAT activists and the prisoners through their attorneys has been key to sustaining WAT participants. Carol recalled her first fast with Witness Against Torture, when the group had received a photograph sent by a detainee through his attorney. The image was that of a blue lantern, hewn from a water bottle sanded until smooth and then painted, adorned with small pieces of cardboard and string, all held together with a bit of glue. The man who made the lantern and sent its image included a note that read, "I hope that this picture will help you to keep your spirits up."

Carol reflected on this communication:

That felt like a direct gift of ingenuity – doing the little things that were subtly keeping some sense of agency and freedom. For them to be able to make this beautiful lantern and to offer that to us felt like a really concrete connection, for them to be directly addressing [those of] us who were fasting in solidarity with them.

Carol had written a reflection during that week about her experience as a first time faster. The attorneys who had delivered to WAT the image of the lantern asked if they might have her reflection translated into Arabic so that the men at Guantánamo might read her words. In the end, there was a kind of two-way communication, the unlikely concretization of the solidarity WAT participants adamantly pursue. Carol observed, "I just feel like, wow, my words have reached them. Their words have reached me."

By developing such relationships, as structurally constrained as they might be, all of the groups under study allow themselves to be recruited by the state's targets and respond through the practice of solidarity witness. Whether the group's focus is on the training of assassins, flawed immigration policy, or indefinite detention and torture, each issue is iconic of a social structure so complex and far-reaching that no single movement could adequately confront the entirety of the system. When they contest a specific node of the US security state, where the state's violence can be dramatically witnessed and exposed, these groups make the human stakes of socially structured *insecurity* more tangible and proximate to themselves and others. In the next chapter, I begin to explore the practices of solidarity witness.

3

Ritual Protest as Testimony

The year 2014 marks the twenty-fifth anniversary of SOA Watch's protest at the gates of Fort Benning. Over a thousand gather on a chilly November morning for their Sunday vigil. The weather is less forbidding than it often has been, the rain coming in fits and starts. Many wear ponchos and galoshes. A few have thought to bring umbrellas. Children huddle near the adults; a few brave ones go stomping about in puddles when the drizzle lets up.

When I arrive, about ten people command the stage, singing and drumming. A spoken word artist offers the genealogy of how SOA Watch emerges and connects. "We gather in the non-violent tradition of Gandhi, Dr. Martin Luther King, Dorothy Day, Aung San Suu Kyi." Another poet decries corporate greed, the destruction of indigenous communities throughout Latin America, the disregard for Mother Earth and the North American "Trail of Tears."

After an hour, Father Roy Bourgeois, now seventy-six years old, takes the stage, his voice and energy strong. Bourgeois explains the significance of this anniversary, how he climbed the tree next to the Salvadoran barracks at Fort Benning decades ago and played Oscar Romero's final homily into the dark night. The crowd is silent, holding white crosses. After his brief comments, Father Bourgeois proclaims, "Let the solemn funeral procession begin!" and descends from the stage to join the seven others with whom he will lead the procession. He is flanked by torture survivors, families of SOA victims, and fellow SOA Watch organizers. They hold up pictures of the murdered Jesuits and silently, slowly, step through the crowd. Behind them walk nearly twenty participants shrouded in black, their faces painted in macabre whites and grays. These are the "mourners." Some carry long slabs covered in black fabric, representing coffins.

The rest of the protesters fall into line. The routine is familiar to most. About ten people take turns on the stage announcing the names and narrating the stories of the dead. Among those named are the SOA's victims in addition to those

FIGURE 3.1. *SOA Watch vigil at Fort Benning*, 2013
Photo credit: Chandra Russo

killed in the wars in Afghanistan and Iraq, civilians killed in US drone strikes, and black Americans killed by the police. At the end of each name, the crowd sings "¡presente!" in the same haunting tones protestors have voiced here for a quarter century. The ritual allows only an hour or so to read the names, hardly enough time to speak of all the known victims, much less the many unknown casualties. For each name and story, thousands will remain unmentioned and untold.

The protesters go around the long grassy median and up to the gates two times this year. As they end their first round, the leaders place the pictures of the murdered Jesuits on the 20-foot-high metal gate, four images on either side, "meant to resemble a funeral viewing," SOA Watch veteran and organizer, Kate, had explained to me ahead of time. The protesters behind them add the hundreds of crosses they carry.

The participants move lugubriously through the street and loop around a second time. Organizers hand out thousands of black ribbons, which protesters are invited to tie onto the gate, a token both ominous and beautiful. The ribbons are unique to the twenty-fifth anniversary and are meant to provide a striking contrast with the white crosses. "The visual impact will be riveting," Kate had observed, "like the symbols you would lay on a grave."

Upon reaching the gates in conclusion, one of the procession leaders weeps loudly, barely able to hold herself upright, overpowered by grief. Two companions huddle to offer both physical and emotional buttress, holding back tears of their own. As the procession arrives at the gates, some hang banners. Many stand intently, studying pictures of victims and names on the crosses. A few kneel in prayer. Behind them, the mourners have taken to the grass, staging a silent "die-in." Their bodies take on the awkward shapes of death, limbs askew. They lay in stillness in the wet grass, silhouettes of massacres remembered. Around this time, those who wish to climb the fence prepare to do so. This year there are two, though one crossed before the procession began. A hefty ladder is now required to conquer the chain link wall in an act that will earn trespassers swift and certain arrest (Adapted from author's field notes).

The annual vigil at Fort Benning is *the* quintessential action of SOA Watch as well as an exemplar and inventory of the kinds of ritual protest that are a key feature of solidarity witness. Through ritual protest, these activists stage culturally salient, visual events that reveal the impacts of state violence. Their ritual protest is a form of testimony to their witness. Social movement scholars note that while rituals generally serve to uphold the dominant order, activists can imbue the hegemonic traditions, symbols and narratives of ritual with subversive meaning in order to challenge injustice (Pfaff & Yang 2001; Taylor et al. 2009). Religion often provides one such array of symbols, stories and traditions that can be forged into repertoires of dissent (Smith 1991; Nepstad 2007). While informed by Christianity, the groups in this study do not limit themselves to religious scripts but also reference core American values, such as democracy and equal protection under the law, as well as the secular terms of universal humanism.

In his formative studies on religious practice, Emile Durkheim (1912) suggested that ritual plays an important social role, helping a collective to craft common meanings, generate emotional ties, and ultimately cultivate a sense of solidarity. The ritual protest of solidarity witness pursues similar ends. These activists seek to forge new frames of meaning and produce affective responses, generating a sense of moral proximity with the targets of state violence. These ritual protests are not the spontaneous practices that Durkheim observed in *The Elementary Forms of Religious Life* (1912), however. They are planned social performances infused with culturally salient and emotionally evocative appeals to the public. In this sense, such rituals are a form of political theater akin to the various modes of evocative spectacle that social movements have staged for decades (Boyd & Mitchell 2012). Yet the activists in this study design their ritual protest with a particular mood and aesthetic, one that is meditative, solemn, and quiet, making it quite different from traditional protest as well as much of the more satirical and colorful street theater used in other contemporary protest (Staggenborg & Lang 2007; Taylor et al. 2009; Haugerud 2013). This makes such performances feel more authentic to the activists involved, and many report that this form of political activism is more inviting to members of the public. Ritual protest thus offers expressive movement dimensions, comforting protesters and building group solidarity, at the same time that it allows these activists to pursue the instrumental aims of sharing an emotionally compelling message with various publics.[1]

Through ritual protest, these activists attempt to "change the balance of power by turning bystanders into upstanders" (Lipsitz 2011b: 1472–3). They do this by mobilizing public affects to resistant ends.[2] It is both popular and scholarly knowledge that simply exposing people to the fact of injustice and suffering is rarely sufficient to instigate response. There are various explanations for this. Many scholars argue that in a contemporary culture of hypervisibility, an overabundance of mediated violence can generate "cultural

---

[1] Since the formative influence of Irving Goffman, sociologists have been reasonably suspect of a clear analytic distinction between that which is socially staged and that which seems authentic. This is also true when it comes to the dynamics of political action. For a particularly nuanced approach to these questions, see Ron Eyerman's (2005) application of performance theory to the study of social movements.

[2] For an excellent discussion of the distinctions between affect and emotion, especially as it relates to political life and social movements, see Deborah Gould's (2009) *Moving Politics*. The main distinction that Gould provides is that whereas affect might be explained as a kind of energetic intensity that is experienced beyond the purview of conscious thought, naming and representation, emotion allows for the communicability of affect. Emotions are already categorized and can be articulated through language and gesture. In this transition from affect to emotion, affect must necessarily be fixed and delimited. Gould suggests that emotions "capture" affect (21).

anesthesia" (Adorno 1973; Feldman 1994), desensitizing the public to injustices and constructing a "moral habituation" (Zelizer 1998: 218) to atrocity. Others suggest that representations of suffering are just as likely to aestheticize the fact of violence, evoking what are often racialized modes of psychosexual desire in the face of atrocity (Hartman 1997; Ioanide 2015).

Indeed, in one of the most elaborate sociological studies of denial, Stanley Cohen (2001) found that the propensity to deny others' suffering is a norm, not an aberration. In the face of this reality, Cohen (2001) proposed that "emotional logic" (249) might offer a successful antidote. James Jasper (1997) has also suggested that the role of social movements is often to intervene and reorganize "patterns of affect" (107) that already exist in the social body. Activists can do this by highlighting that an injustice has occurred, evoking the relevant emotions, and targeting public response toward meaningful targets. Through ritual protest, the activists in this study seek to mobilize what Alison Jaggar (1989) terms "outlaw emotions," feeling states that resist social norms and offer an important epistemological resource for identifying and then contesting injustice.[3] By wielding recognizable traditions, in particular memorial, along with visually evocative symbolism and spaces, ritual protest serves to evoke outlaw emotions, making the impacts of state violence both visible and undesirable.

Just as emotions serve as an important epistemological resource with which these activists push against the dominant frame, so too is collective memory, the contested array of narratives available to a people in making sense of their past. Because ritual is defined as such through social repetition, it is a formative means for maintaining and shaping collective memory, what Marita Sturken (1997) would term "a technology of memory." Collective memory is an important terrain for defining moral values, political responsibilities, and social identities (Durkheim 1912; Halbwachs 1925; Schwartz 1982; Bellah et al. 1985; Griffin 2004; Olick 2007). For this reason, Kurasawa (2009) suggests that one of the key obligations of witnessing is to refuse "state-sanctioned strategies of denial and social forgetting" (104). Sturken (1997) suggests that efforts to shape collective memory or, in turn, to "organize forgetting" can say as much about a national culture's "desire and denial as it does about remembrance" (7). Collective memory is thus centrally anchored in affect and emotions. By using ritual protest to shape forms of counter-memory, the activists in this study identify remembrance itself as a mode of resistance. They push the social

---

[3] Jaggar (1989) writes about "outlaw emotions" as the provenance of the oppressed. These are emotions that are experienced as a social cost, and often individually so, by those who cannot easily abide by the status quo because of their social position. At the same time, Jaggar explains that "outlaw emotions are distinguished by their incompatibility with the dominant perceptions and values" (166). In line with subsequent theorists that examine emotions as circulating across the social body (Ahmed 2004), I am using the term "outlaw emotions" in this way – as something that movements can seek to evoke, organize, and direct.

body to reconsider its social and political obligations to history and to those that suffer at present.

A final aspect of ritual protest important to how these activists understand their practice of solidarity witness is the idea that ritual can serve as a protective guise for the political messages these activists seek to deliver. There is some empirical research on this across political settings (Pfaff & Yang 2001). The officially secular state is not supposed to concern itself with religious and cultural events in the same way as it responds to explicit acts of political dissent. In effect, under certain contexts, activists can use the tools of religious or cultural ritual to exceed the state's official political spaces, creating avenues for dissent and political analyses that would not be tolerated, or might be wholly unrecognizable, in official halls of state power. The activists in this study design their public actions with an aesthetic and mood that they believe helps hedge against the near-instinctual acrimony and frustration by which so many members of the public confront dominant US politics. Through their ritual protest, these activists report making important political statements that are not dismissed in the same way as more traditional protest activities.

This chapter elaborates the key features of ritual protest. I begin by examining the practice of public mourning as a way to contest the public emotions that villainize and abject the state's targets. I then turn to how these activists use naming and the courts to impact upon collective memory and resist dominant modes of publicity. The next section focuses on the visual scenes of ritual protest, exploring the subversive use of symbolism and culturally significant space. Finally, I explore these activists' sense that their ritual offers a protective guise for their political aims. Ultimately, I argue that ritual protest allows these activists to contest the dominant emotions as well as the organized forgetting that underpin state violence while crafting symbolically rich modes of solidarity with the direct targets of the US security state.

PUBLIC MOURNING

When we arrive in Sasabe during the early afternoon on Memorial Day Monday, it appears to be a quiet Mexican town. A few mangy dogs walk the streets, but there is hardly a townsperson in sight. The locals have taken sensible refuge from the temperature, which hovers above 100 degrees Fahrenheit.

Migrant Trail participants embark on their journey after a lunch of homemade tamales and a short ceremony in Sasabe's humble church. After a sermon, some readings and songs, we stand and walk out of the pews, snaking along for about a mile through the dust and heat. At the front of the line, participants carry three coffins each painted with a cross of blue, pink, and white. The two large coffins represent the men and women who have perished in their attempt to reach work and family in the United States. The small coffin signifies the children who have tried to cross with them.

FIGURE 3.2. *Migrant Trail participants carry coffins out of Sasabe church, 2015*
Photo credit: Eric O Ledermann

Most of us hold wooden crosses, painted in white that we selected before leaving Tucson that morning. Some of us carry a cross with a name and age scribed in black. Others carry crosses, which hold the designation "desconocido/a," signifying those discovered in the desert who could not be identified.

Pink adobes, a green painted wall, and yellow lettering offer spectacular contrast against the immaculate blue of the sky and beige of the dusty road. As I plod slowly under the unmitigated burn of the afternoon sun, I can't help but consider the beauty of such a humble landscape now transformed into the setting of inordinate hope and tragedy.

As we near the border, we approach a billboard in Spanish posted by the Mexican government warning of the dangers of the desert to potential crossers: dehydration, overheating, and death from exposure. We pass a group of young men, likely in their late teens, sitting in a cluster by the side of the road. With their small backpacks, they wait for nightfall when they will cross to the east or west of the border fence. The faith leaders in our group go to them with rosaries and blessings for their passage. This group of men is not particularly unique, though their presence is a reminder of why we are walking. Despite our rosaries and best wishes, we walk past them with heavy hearts, knowing the dangers of their journey ahead.

When we reach the border fence, we gather in a circle to drumbeats and singing, an indigenous blessing ceremony. Sara is the facilitator, and her voice breaks with tears. She speaks of her heartbreak for those who have died and will continue to die. She declares her love for each of us who walk, a love offered despite the fact that many of us are strangers to her. She then makes her way around the circle, holding a shell of burning sage and cedar in one hand and the strong feathers of an eagle in the other. Those who wish to be "smudged" in a consecration of safe passage hold out their hands, palms upward. Sara stops at every person, waving the smoke over our shoulders and feet, bowing and rising in her light cotton skirt. It is a physically demanding effort to squat and stand before each of the hundred or more people that join us for the send-off.

As we each wait our turn, many of us cradle the white crosses in our arms. We do not make this journey alone, a fact I use to ground myself as I stand with nervous belly and sweaty palms, about to confront a week away from my loved ones and creature comforts. Holding our crosses, we let the sweet-smelling smoke fall over us and bless those for whom we journey (Adapted from author's field notes).

Migrant Trail organizers explain their week-long walk as an act of remembrance, "a journey of peace to remember people, friends and family who have died, others who have crossed, and people who continue to come ... [bearing] witness to the tragedy of death and to the inhumanity in our midst" (participant packet). Dave, a social worker in his 60s who has done the walk regularly since close to its inception, compared the Migrant Trail to a funeral: "It's like a funeral procession in the sense that we do it to honor the people who have died in the land that we're walking on." Referring to the history of the US–Mexico border, he reflected on the need to mourn this "tragic piece of our country's history, that we have treated our neighbors to the South in the way we have ... first we stole their land and now we set up circumstances that encourage them to take risks that result in death." In the notion of the walk as a funeral, then, is embedded a sociopolitical analysis that understands first settler colonialism and, today, neoliberal free trade policies, as instigators of the violence that needs to be contested and the deaths that need to be mourned.

Jessie, also a long-time Migrant Trail participant, emphasized the walk as an act of remembrance, terming it "a memory walk ... a time to remember those who have died." She was careful to distinguish the Migrant Trail from the literal funeral to which Dave had compared it: "To me a funeral is a gathering of people that knew the deceased and are caring for those mostly deeply impacted by the death." While "it's not a funeral march" by Jessie's estimation, it is still an emotionally saturated memorial, "this constantly remembering people who have been there and people who have died. And for me that's part of the challenge of being there, of walking and of the emotional aspects of being out there."

The emotional remembrance that both Dave and Jessie identify is central to the walk's accomplishments. Discussing the neglect and loss of migrants crossing the US–Mexico border, Rocio Magaña (2008) argues that migrant deaths in the desert take place in "de facto exile"; because so many bodies are never found and returned to their families, the dead become "incomplete losses" (118). Efforts to recognize these deaths and remember those who have crossed are an important intervention. Magaña is building on Judith Butler's (2004) argument that state violence becomes acceptable when its victims are not understood to be "publicly grievable" (34). Akin to the invisible deaths of migrants, Butler observes that Arab victims of the "War on Terror" are made invisible insofar as they do not receive obituaries in the US media. Obituaries are typically published in print newspapers, which Benedict Anderson (1983) argues were critical for establishing the contemporary idea of a national public sphere. In the twenty-first century, when print media is no longer preeminent and publics are constituted at least as much through digital media forms, US news outlets also erase the suffering of the state's targets by maintaining a singular focus on American deaths and victimhood.[4] Through public mourning rituals, the activists in this study contest the invisibility and exile to which the state's targets are subjected, refusing the state's strategies of disappearing the fact of disappearance.

Funereal rituals have been used throughout history to contest organized and unwarranted violence, making public mourning an important political task. For instance, after the murder of fourteen-year-old black teenager Emmett Till in 1955 by white racists, his mother's choice to have an open casket funeral proffered the embodied proof of racial hatred, becoming an early turning point in the US Civil Rights movement. Collective funerals were also used during South African apartheid and the "troubles" in Northern Ireland and became a means for mass gatherings that were otherwise outlawed. This is part of the political value of the funeral; its apolitical nature can evade state repression. Funereal ritual can be understood as offering a protective guise, a point on which I elaborate at the end of this chapter.[5]

Folklorist Jack Santino (2004) terms the kind of funereal rituals that these activists undertake "performative commemoratives," memorials that maintain both grassroots origins and explicitly political aims. Performative commemoratives are not sanctioned by the state or any institutionalized religion. They are also distinct from individual funerals, encouraging the involvement of the public at large. Further, performative commemoratives seek to "renarrate controversial deaths" (cited in Van Ham 2011: 129), which the popular media and dominant discourses have constructed as immaterial or even deserved. Such rituals defy public indifference and fear-laden logics that portray the dead or

---

[4] Sunaina Maira pointed this out to me, suggesting that Benedict Anderson's work should be contextualized for a twenty-first-century media economy.

[5] Incidentally, the political work of the funeral can cut both ways as Michelle Martin-Baron (2014) shows in the case of the US military funeral, a performance that upholds "the US war machine," eliding the various forms of racial abjection that constitute current military practices, ranging from violence against foreign populations to racialized domestic recruitment practices.

disappeared as criminal others. These ritual mourning practices might also be understood as performed obituaries of a sort. They are symbolically rich dramas that catalog the dead and evoke public emotions, refusing to predicate the nation's imagined community on radical divisiveness and unseen violence.

One of the most common forms of memorial ritual used by both SOA Watch and Witness Against Torture (WAT) is the practice of a "vigil." "Vigil" evokes a sense of being watchful, remaining vigilantly awake when others sleep. To keep vigil in this case means both to be awake to state violence and to awaken the public. In the Christian Church, vigil also indicates a time of religious observance, usually marked by prayerful solemnity. Vigil combines the ideas of bearing witness with a certain faith-based framework and affective tenor. Maya, who became involved in solidarity witness through SOA Watch and is now an organizer with WAT, described the importance of vigils, distinguishing this tactic from other common forms of protest,

Vigil has a sense of gravity to it, sort of a somber peaceful word. I think of vigils at night with candles and remembrance of people who have passed away or who are suffering from something. It holds also the spiritual meaning, as opposed to like the word "demonstration" or the word "direct action" or something.

For these activists, vigils are also visual performances. In being awake to state violence, activists use vigils to make violence visible to the public. Maya continued, "When we [of WAT] say 'vigil,' we mean a very specific thing, which is that everyone puts on orange jumpsuits and black hoods and goes and stands somewhere silent for a certain amount of time." Similar to WAT's use of the term, the vigil at Fort Benning connotes a ritual practice rich with visual performances that represent the impacts of SOA violence. These activists use vigils to haunt bystanders; affect and image coalesce to expose the state's injustices.

The vigil at Fort Benning contests the state's strategies of invisibility through ritual remembrance that is emotionally evocative and, for some, religiously meaningful. Burt, a career member of the military who found out about the SOA years after he had retired from the armed forces, explained the importance of this vigil, "memorializing through solemn procession the thousands upon thousands of people who were killed [is] just a way of bringing them to [Fort Benning], not forgetting what happened to them and how and why it happened." For Burt, this "how and why" analysis is impactful precisely because it is crafted through the emotive tools of ritual as opposed to being couched in the terms of abstract rationality. He continued, "It's a very emotive way of doing it. It's not a head trip; it's a real heart trip."

Siobhan, a middle-aged woman who had been involved with SOA Watch for over a decade, offered a similar analysis, highlighting the affective nature of the memorial. "The vigil is incredibly moving, I think the first six times I went I cried," she reflected. Like Burt, Siobhan discussed the importance of refusing to forget the victims of state violence, and suggested that a religious framework was important in this regard,

There's a huge spiritual element, not particularly one religion – though again a lot of this is very Catholic based – but just the feeling that those people whose names are being called out are present in spirit, that they're not forgotten, that we're trying to speak for the murdered.

The spiritual component of the SOA Watch vigil evokes emotions, enhances a sense of gravity and importance, and offers a cultural framework in which making the absent present, at least "in spirit," is familiar and intelligible. In many funerals, religious teachings offer mourners solace as an approach to existential unknowns. In these public mourning rituals, such familiar religious frameworks are mobilized but adjusted. Rather than offering mere solace and a sense of acceptance, these activists use religious grammars to proclaim that these are not inevitable deaths. While the deceased deserve to be mourned, the circumstances of their disappearances and murders also warrant systemic change.

WHAT'S IN A NAME?

In their efforts to claim the state's targets as members of the social body, memorial rituals are also a time for these activists to name the disappeared in the public register. Naming the unseen targets of state violence is an important means to gesture to what Michael Taussig (1999) calls "*public* secret[s]," which are not so much secrets as the formative social knowledge of "*knowing what not to know*" (2, cited in Ioanide 2015). In the case of these activists, it is somewhat obvious that mass killing, structural abandonment to the point of death, and indefinite detention are repressive modes of governance. It is less evident that failing to name those impacted by such violence is itself a central buttress to the system. Efforts to reclaim words or create new ways of naming things, often used by groups that hold stigmatized social identities, are often made to look petty, silly, and arbitrary (Zola 1993; Christensen & Rizvi 1996). Yet creating new languages and lexicons is important because it is part of the work to challenge dominant modes of publicity. By naming the victims of the US security state these activists reveal how structures of domination often operate in surreptitious ways. When they integrate naming into their ritual protest, these activists mark not only the physical violence of militarism, imprisonment, and neglect but point to the erasure of this violence as a less obvious but enduring injustice.

During the solemn funeral procession at Fort Benning, a group on stage takes turns naming those killed by SOA graduates and detailing what is known about each victim. The crowd of protesters responds by singing "¡presente!" lifting their crosses to honor each person named. Akin to this ritual, walkers on the Migrant Trail regularly call out the names on their crosses while they process through the desert and along highways, similarly lifting their crosses high as they shout "¡presente!" The naming ritual is an affect-laden means to humanize the disavowed. Sara Koopman (2008) reflects on the naming of the dead at Fort Benning as a means of forging "moral proximity" (838) with the victims of state violence, explaining that "in naming we bring their suffering and loss closer to us. Named, they are no longer abstract figures, but grievable lives" (838).[6]

Of note, the politics of naming have become quite central to SOA Watch's tactics and to how the school has ultimately had to respond to public pressure. Throughout their work to close the SOA, activists have created meticulous records, documenting whom the school graduates, including each soldier and instructor's name, course, rank, country of origin, and dates of attendance. Through this collection of names, SOA Watch has been able to link the records maintained by international legal organizations and truth commissions to SOA graduates, pointing to clear linkages between the school and human rights atrocities. The SOA/WHISC was also forced to engage in the politics of naming in direct response to activists' exposure of egregious practices at the school. The "School of the Americas" renamed itself the "Western Hemisphere Institute for Security Cooperation" in 2000 and stopped releasing the names of its graduates in 2003, a decision that activists challenged and ultimately had reversed in the courts. As SOA Watch struggled for more expansive forms of remembrance and knowing through naming, the school sought to constrain these by creating competing names and narratives. The activists have captured such a dynamic quite effectively with the now oft-repeated chant, "new name, same shame."

Like SOA Watch and the Migrant Trail, Witness Against Torture names the unnamed in the public register through ritual protest. One of the more moving dramas prepared by WAT was based on a Guantánamo detainee's own critique of having his name stripped from him at the offshore military prison. In an open letter published in the *Guardian*, Shaker Aamer, a British national, explained being treated "like a number," and delivered around the detention center "like a package."

WAT member and artist, Donna, had the idea that she could paint a huge portrait of Shaker Aamer's face around which the group might organize their performance. Between their many meetings and late into the evening, Donna opened buckets of black acrylic paint and rendered Aamer's face onto a queen-size bedsheet.[7] The group planned and practiced the performance a few times

---

[6] This practice can be traced to resistance throughout Latin America during the Chilean Pinochet Regime and Argentinian Dirty War. Nepstad (2007) suggests that this practice was also used in Guatemala and El Salvador during the 1980s when protesters would recite the names of those martyred for their political activity. US missionaries who participated in these protest activities during their time in Central America introduced the practice to US activists (Coutin 1993).

[7] Using client pictures from the Center for Constitutional Rights website, a legal organization which has represented many Guantánamo prisoners, Donna painted four portraits in total. One of these was of Fahd Ghazy, whom the group would make central to their 2015 street theater skit.

in the church that served as home base for the week. Two WAT members wearing military fatigues would yell out to WAT member Saad, playing the role of Aamer, from one side of the scene. "Prisoner!" (Figure 3.3) They marched Saad, attired in the iconic orange jumpsuit and black hood, toward about fifteen others, also in orange jumpsuits, standing in a line shoulder to shoulder. The two detainees in the middle unfurled the portrait of Aamer, in front of which Saad knelt. The representation of Aamer's face was larger than life; the man meant to represent him was small and crouched in body. On either side of the portrait, WAT members held up the letters SHAKER AAMER (Figure 3.4). Once everyone was in position, a WAT member initiated a call and response. The *Guardian* letter was the script.

WAT member Carol wrote about the performance:

Saad knelt with a hood over his head to represent Shaker; two of us wore fatigues to represent guards, and patrolled the scene in chilling slow motion. We recited excerpts from Shaker Aamer … "At best, we are numbers. I worry that when I come home that my children will call for 'Daddy', and I will sit unmoving. I am two three nine. I am not sure when I will ever be anything else." When we recited those words of Shaker's, we hid the letters spelling out his name. In their place, our guards strung the number "239" around Saad's neck. He knelt with his name stripped away and his humanity concealed under a black hood. (Edited to protect the anonymity of participants)

At the end of the scene, the group mounted its collective demand, "Stop torture now! Close Guantánamo now!" They then processed away from the scene, singing an adaptation, created by Peace Poet and WAT member Luke Nephew, of Sweet Honey in the Rock's *Ella's Song*: "We who believe in freedom cannot rest / We who believe in freedom cannot rest until it comes / We gotta close Guantánamo today / We gotta close Guantánamo today, Stop Torture Now."

WAT took their performance to important sites throughout Washington, DC: both outside and within the major transportation hub of Union Station; in front of the Supreme Court; outside of the American Portrait museum, where they held their own powerful portrait of Aamer's face; and inside the Kennedy Center, a performance venue where hundreds had just attended a free gospel concert. Carol reflected on how the skit was received by the bystanders at each place that WAT performed their action, *"The volume, the visuals, and the dynamic and concise nature of the piece we had rehearsed attracted listeners, some of them recording the event with their phones."* In a technological age when the production and distribution of media is more popularized and accessible than ever before, at least through certain platforms, captivating the public through a visually and aurally striking message that can then be shared digitally was a savvy means of amplifying Aamer's message.

By dramatizing Aamer's own critique, this was a way for WAT to enact the kind of conscientious solidarity that these activists seek to create whenever possible. WAT members did not need to generate their own narrative regarding the US security state but could instead highlight the voice, analysis, and agency

FIGURE 3.3. *WAT performance of Shaker Aamer skit in front of Union Station, Washington DC, 2014*
Photo credit: Justin Norman

FIGURE 3.4. *WAT performance of Shaker Aamer skit inside Union Station, Washington, DC, 2014*
Photo credit: Justin Norman

of someone most directly impacted. Through the visual representation of both Aamer's face and name, WAT members complexly represented the lived experience of a Guantánamo prisoner. They demonstrated the process of un-naming as a means to objectify the prisoner, while maintaining that the humanity of Aamer's face, the fulcrum of the drama, could not be disappeared.[8] The story of having one's name replaced by a number evokes a powerful set of emotions and is a reference that many American audiences will associate with stories of the mistreatment of prisoners during the German Holocaust.[9] When these activists ritually name those whom the dominant culture forgets and ignores, they contest the state's multilayered strategies of dehumanization and disappearance.

THE WITNESS STAND

Many of these activists engage in civil disobedience to bring the central messages of their ritual protest from the streets into the courtroom. The idiom of *witness* takes on significance in legal settings where it is customary for citizens to swear an oath to honestly narrate what they have seen and what they know to be true. When they enter the courtroom through civil disobedience, these activists are able to "speak truth to power" in the belly of the beast. The audience in a given courtroom may be quite small or not, depending on the trial and the location, and the constraints of my data do not allow me to demonstrate how activists' testimonies impact on the public or decision makers. Nevertheless, in statements to judges, occasional juries, the media, and other bystanders, whether they be in the tens or hundreds, these activists seek to put the state itself on trial for the violence and injustice it instigates. They find one of the few avenues by which their government is forced to at least record in the official archive what is so often dismissed as unintelligible or fringe critique.

In speaking to the court, many SOA Watch participants explained their ritual protest as a way of contesting dominant modes of denial and forgetting, those that erase the realities of state violence. For instance in 2006, Donte, a nineteen-year-old Black man who had earned a prestigious scholarship to an Ivy League college only to be suspended for his activism with SOA, explained to the judge the importance of the annual protest at the gates of Fort Benning,

---

[8] Philosopher Emmanuel Levinas (1969) offers an expansive discussion of the power of the face as an affectively potent command to ethical conduct. While more recent studies in the cognitive psychology of racism might refute Levinas's core argument (see, for instance: Eberhardt et al. 2004), his proposition is that the face cannot be objectified, at least not upon first being encountered. Before one recognizes the social location of the Other, the face is experienced as pure affect. For this reason, Levinas argues, the face also serves as a barrier against violence. Simultaneously vulnerable and agentic, the face is quintessentially human; it implores, "do not kill me."

[9] For a useful discussion of how the German Holocaust came to inhabit its current role within American collective memory with important implications for how the public perceives Jews and Arabs see Novick (1999).

We all know the hideously wretched history of the School of Americas. If anything, the protests at the WHINSEC military base act as candid retellings of the brutal and bloody history of repression and human cruelty that has been happened (*sic*) at the hands of SOA graduates and continues to largely ignored (*sic*) by most Americans.

(Smith 2006)

In beginning with the words "we all know," Donte refuses to believe the state's claims to innocence or ignorance. Speaking in a court of law, he also refuses to acquit the American public for ignoring a violence that they could contest. The "candid retellings" of history staged by SOA protesters are not necessarily first exposures, but a means to disrupt a norm of erasure.

Patrick, also of SOA Watch and then twenty-one years old, termed such erasure "a case of obligatory amnesia."[10] Speaking to the same court in 2003, he assessed that for the state to charge activists who crossed onto the base as criminals required forgetting "colonial roots," the removal and extermination of "indigenous populations throughout the Americas," and a series of foreign policies that have systematically impoverished and oppressed the peoples of the hemisphere. Patrick concluded:

If these memories could present their case[,] a courtroom that thrives on an amnesia preserved in legal text would simply crumble under the pressure of justice. When we "crossed the line" onto Ft. Benning we acknowledged this fact and chose to unlock these trapped memories ourselves. Disobedience is our only democracy, our only memory, so long as the past exists only to rationalize a present world so uneven in its distribution of power and wealth.

(Lincoln 2003)

Patrick speaks cogently to the efforts of these activists to democratize the dominant archive, official forms of state memory, through acts of civil disobedience. He names a lineage of settler colonialism, racism, and US militarism, demanding the scope of the court's memory be expanded to include systematic injustices that did not originate during his own lifetime or those of his audience. He also makes an important distinction between justice and the law, identifying the legal system as a site where the denial of violence is codified.

Patrick's phrasing is also important. It offers a poetics that contests dominant notions of time and space. He says that if these memories could speak for themselves, they would remember what the law forgets. Yet they cannot speak for themselves. They are trapped somewhere else, somewhere that violence has put them. It is in the "crossing of the line" that they might be unlocked and released. The line that Patrick references might have multiple significations here. It could be the territorial line that marks where it is and is not legal for the protesters to put their bodies. It might also be the line between what can and

---

[10] There are no documents that reveal Patrick's racial identity. As opposed to Donte, whose race is discussed in various news stories and public documents, Patrick's race goes unmentioned.

cannot be said, between what can and cannot be remembered, and between life and death.

Patrick and Donte offer two examples of how these activists use ritual protest and the accompanying tactic of civil disobedience as "technologies of memory" (Sturken 1997). By mourning the forgotten and disobeying the law as a means to remember differently, these activists bring close what the dominant political culture distances. They offer both participants and audiences a different experience of the temporality and spatiality of state violence than what is authorized in the courts and other dominant political arenas. In her discussion of efforts to memorialize atrocity in contemporary Chile, Macarena Gómez-Barris (2010) observes that for those most touched by state violence, "the past continues as a source of pain in the present, where the past is experienced and conditioned as endless non-closure" (42). In staging remembrance rituals and then amplifying them through courtroom testimony, these activists challenge distances of time and place, encouraging a sense of moral proximity to the disappeared.

The courtroom is also an important site for the public naming central to the practice of solidarity witness. As the US legal system is required to maintain a rigorous archive, all statements made within a court of law enter the official record, unless the judge orders otherwise during the proceedings. By naming the unnamed in the courts, these activists use the state's own rules and regulations to ensure the state's targets enter the official archive. In her 2005 courtroom statement, SOA Watch protester Meagan, at the time a college student from the Midwest, named the two people on the crosses she had carried over the Fort Benning fence in her act of civil disobedience. She announced to the judge and bystanders, "I wish to share two names with you. They are Wiliferdo Vigil and Jesus del Cid. These are the names of two of the hundreds of civilians that were slaughtered in the town of El Mozote in El Salvador." With the limited information available to her, Meagan reminded everyone that Wiliferdo Vigil and Jesus del Cid had "families and friends and dreams," drawing out the similarities between the state's targets and those in the courtroom that day. She also offered context and magnitude to their deaths, explaining them as but two of hundreds of thousands throughout Latin America murdered by SOA graduates. She then shifted her reflection on the importance of one's name, but this time in terms of the responsibility of speaking back to a government that is meant to represent her. Meagan proclaimed, "It is for these people, the oppressed, the forsaken, the forgotten, that I choose to stand up and say 'NOT IN MY NAME' to the hypocrisy of the United States government" (Doty 2005).[11] By naming the targets of state violence, these activists defy dominant governing practices, proclaiming that it is not in their name or under their watch that the state is authorized to engage in violence.

---

[11] Meagan was sentenced to three months in prison and a $500 fine.

Similar to SOA Watch, WAT has sought to bring the names of the victims of state violence into the courtroom. In so doing, WAT participants make a particular commentary on how the US legal system has failed in the case of Guantánamo. Those held at the offshore military prison have never been named, tried, or convicted in a US court of law, the basic due process rights guaranteed by the US Constitution to any detained persons. This suspension of habeas corpus – the opportunity to challenge one's detention in court – has been identified as a dangerous erosion of the key pillars of liberal democracy, legislated in documents as old as the Magna Carta. Even those who prioritize issues of national security have convincingly argued that holding people indefinitely without charge is not just fundamentally unjust, but may exacerbate anti-American sentiment abroad. The fact that Guantánamo places due process rights in jeopardy is today a commonly held criticism among those of diverse political views (Bandow 2009; Kogelmann 2013).

In 2007, nearly hundred WAT activists wearing orange jumpsuits and black hoods entered the US Federal Court House. Once in the building, they began to read the names and stories of those currently held at Guantánamo, in some instances including reports of how the detainees had been tortured. In 2008, dressed in the same attire, they went to the Supreme Court and knelt on the steps. In both actions, WAT members intended to get arrested. Rather than carry their own identification, they gave the names of Guantánamo detainees to their arresting officers. Reflecting on these actions, Joanne explained of WAT, "They use civil disobedience in the courts in a special way that not every movement has done, bringing the names of people into the court who did not have access to the justice system." Jeremy Varon added:

What we tried to do is embed our argument in the action itself ... The idea was to symbolically give detainees the day in court that they had been denied by the system. Entering them into the system is the platform for talking about the denial of this fundamental right of habeas corpus

(Grele 2011: 78–9).

Eighty were arrested at the 2008 Supreme Court action of which thirty-one were ultimately brought to trial. On this occasion, WAT members once again staged a public event, dramatizing the reasons for their original civil disobedience. Dressed in their hallmark orange jumpsuits and black hoods, group members solemnly walked from the Supreme Court to the Federal Court House where the case would be heard. Outside of the courthouse, those facing trial knelt while various speakers addressed the crowd. One speaker noted that those being tried understood that "in five months we have gone further in the legal system than these people have gone in seven years." Some of those standing trial testified about who their detainee was, humanizing him for the audience of reporters, supporters, and other bystanders. Then one by one, those kneeling took their hoods off and laid the name of each detainee in front of what WAT members had erected as an "altar of justice," large representations of the Constitution and Magna Carta and other culturally resonant symbolism.

In telling the story of this day, Jeremy reflected, "This is a press conference, but it is theater, and people are crying. It is a spectacle." The story of the trial became front-page news in the *Washington Post*. Jeremy continued:

> The folks on trial have by now de-hooded. They are no longer detainees – they are American citizens ... The whole ceremony ends with this tableau where you see all thirty-one people. Some are Catholics with collars. They made the transition from a detainee, laid the name at the altar of justice, and now they are a citizen of the world standing up for what is right.

This action afforded WAT the opportunity to capitalize on many of the central features of ritual protest. They used remembrance and naming to evoke deep emotions. They entered the courts, shaping the public archive. They also offered forth a visual drama, effective in part because of its savvy use of symbolically significant public space and iconography, a tactical strategy that I now explore further.

VISIBILITY, SYMBOLISM, AND SPACE

The concept of visibility is central to the work of witnessing; solidarity witness aims to see and testify to the suffering of others, to preventable violence that the state obscures. Through their ritual protest, these activists enact public spectacles meant to critique the dominant forms of seeing and knowing that undergird the US security state. The moral distance between a national public and those designated as outsiders depends on affectively saturated images: visions of terrorists and racialized menaces, suffering unfortunates in distant slums, and objectified, violated bodies that evoke fear, pity, and sadistic pleasures. Such images dehumanize the targets of state violence so that they are ousted from the social body. Through ritual protest, these activists respond to these dominant visuals with culturally evocative scenes that seek to generate empathy and moral outrage in lieu of divisiveness and apathy.

In crafting visual messages of political dissent, these activists repurpose culturally significant symbols and spaces, evoking images and ideas that the public can instantly and affectively recognize. Such a strategy exemplifies Joane Nagel's (1996) concept of "turning hegemony on its head." George Lipsitz and Russell Rodríguez (2012) explain that while both aggrieved communities and social movement groups "must speak back to power within the terms and logic created by power in the first place ... they cannot evade, avoid, or ignore hegemony but they can turn it on its head" (2012: 119).[12] Ritual protest becomes a

---

[12] Joane Nagel is concerned with the tools available to aggrieved communities, in her case American Indians in the Red Power movement. Nevertheless, I would suggest that this insight is applicable to all grassroots efforts to impact political culture.

means to recast hegemonic symbols and spaces, allowing these activists to create compelling visuals that are simultaneously resonant and rebellious.

Many members of WAT explained that their use of visual aesthetics was essential for conveying emotionally powerful messages. Joanne explained that this strategy was what first attracted her to the group, referencing the 2008 Supreme Court action as iconic of WAT's ritual protests: "It was not like having a rally where you hold up protest signs. I've been to plenty of those and there's nothing wrong with that. But that's a very head thing. It's a message, and it's carried on the sign." For Joanne, the power of a visual scene was that it mobilized affective meanings already present in the collective conscience (Jasper 1997; Ahmed 2004). This created what SOA protester Burt earlier called "a heart trip" as opposed to "a head trip." Joanne continued, "The thing that captivated me about this was that it was so visual and that it captured more of the emotional or moral meaning of what was going on." The image of the action remains clear in Joanne's mind, perhaps because of the numerous photos that were taken that day: "The picture of them just kneeling and waiting with the words above the Supreme Court saying 'equality and justice for all,' it has a lot of visual power." WAT member Stuart agreed with Joanne, adding that WAT has had an enduring impact on the visual messages circulated in the media about Guantánamo. "Photos of WAT demonstrations have become stock images featured in the mainstream press. That's no accident." Time and again, the group has staged emotionally evocative, political commentary without needing to speak their message or write it on signs.

By creating new associations between otherwise familiar symbols and spaces, these activists can expose the state's contradictions. Jeremy of WAT described what he called the group's "signature aesthetic," participants dressing in orange jumpsuits and black hoods that recall the now infamous media images of prisoners kneeling in degraded positions behind the fences at Guantánamo Bay. Jeremy continued, "it is incredibly arresting to have these sad, hooded figures pass by this or that monument on some crisp Washington day" (Grele 2011: 88–9). By dressing like detainees and moving in solemn procession through the nation's most hallowed spaces, members of WAT expose the hypocrisy of the US nation-state, which is supposedly exceptional in the world for upholding the fundaments of liberal democracy while continually violating its own core values (Pease 2009).

The visual power of WAT's actions often comes from members dressing as those most violated by the state while walking past the nation's most sacred sites. SOA Watch activist Theresa Cusimano inverted this equation, but for similar effect, dressing as a member of the social elite and then exposing herself to degradation at the hands of the state. Theresa explains crossing onto Fort Benning property in her 2010 act of civil disobedience:

I climbed the fence in high-heels and a Brooks Brothers suit to just stop the stereotypes of the dreadlocks and the tree huggers, of which I am one. But just to say, "hey I'm a lawyer with credentials. I work in your world. I wear your suit. And this is still ridiculous."

In an action planned collectively with SOA Watch, Theresa leveraged the cultural markers of social status, speaking truth to power in the powerful's own attire. The act visually displayed the fact that a variety of social actors morally oppose the SOA. It also demonstrated the state's brutality. Theresa's arresting officers treated her harshly, "They hauled me off, gave me a big wedgie, dragged me till my feet bled." The manner in which she was treated confirmed to other protesters and the media present the very culture of violence and disproportionate use of force that these activists seek to highlight.

Another way that these activists use ritual protest to turn hegemony on its head is by repurposing socially significant space. One of WAT's more memorable inversions of the spaces of power was a ritual protest at one of the commanding monuments in Washington, DC. In June 2006, the US military reported the first deaths of Guantánamo detainees, suggesting that three prisoners had committed suicide (Risen & Golden 2006). In a 2010 article for *Harper's Magazine*, Scott Horton, an investigative reporter who had covered issues at Guantánamo for nearly a decade, cast doubt on the government's claims of suicide, suggesting that the detainees had been tortured to death (Horton 2010).[13] Faith explained how the group decided to undertake an action at the Capitol Rotunda in January of 2010. "One person said, 'this is what we should do. We should memorialize these men at the same place that our President was laid in a wake.'"

The Capitol Rotunda constitutes one of the foremost sacred spaces of American civil religion, a term developed by Robert Bellah (1967) to describe the series of "prophets and ... martyrs ... sacred events and sacred places ..." that build on "Biblical archetypes" but are distinctly American as opposed to Christian (18). The Rotunda is where deceased national heroes and other eminent citizens are given public viewings before burial, a ceremony known as "laying in state." Indeed, upon the domed ceiling of the Rotunda, which soars ninety-six feet in height, is painted *The Apotheosis of Washington*. As the painting title denotes, George Washington is depicted as a divine being. He sits in the heavens surrounded by important figures from classical mythology. WAT activists decided to memorialize the most degraded and ignored at a site reserved for the most honored and celebrated.

Jeremy explained:

A group went to the rotunda at the very spot where dead presidents and Rosa Parks have lain in state ... [they] put a death shroud with the name of the three guys who died in 2006, sprinkled orange flower petals on the shrouds, and got arrested.

(Grele 2011: 90)

---

[13] Horton (2010) tells us about these prisoners: "Salah Ahmed Al-Salami, from Yemen, was thirty-seven. Mani Shaman Al-Utaybi, from Saudi Arabia, was thirty. Yasser Talal Al-Zahrani, also from Saudi Arabia, was twenty-two, and had been imprisoned at Guantánamo since he was captured at the age of seventeen. None of the men had been charged with a crime, though all three had been engaged in hunger strikes to protest the conditions of their imprisonment. They were being held in a cell block, known as Alpha Block, reserved for particularly troublesome or high-value prisoners."

Jeremy reflected on how turning hegemony on its head in this way held great affective and cultural impact. "To put the death shroud of detainees possibly murdered by the US government at the epicenter of a building officially called the Temple of Liberty ... that is pretty friggin' powerful" (Grele 2011: 91). The Rotunda action epitomized Santino's (2004) understanding of the performative commemorative as re-narrating controversial deaths. Through their ritual protest at the Rotunda, WAT members highlighted spurious claims of suicide at the military prison at a central site of state power.

Sometimes activists have more leeway about how they respond to hegemony than others. While WAT's Rotunda action was a creative use of one of multiple monuments available to the group when it convenes in Washington, DC, turning hegemony on its head became the only option for SOA Watch when the military erected an imposing metal fence at the edge of Fort Benning after the September 11 attacks. Leah, who has been attending SOA Watch with her family since she was a child in the late 1990s, explained how activists have responded to the fence, transforming it into a monument to victims of the school.

The fences turn into really a giant memorial to the people who have died at the hands of soldiers educated at the School of the Americas. So there's crosses with victims' names on it. There's flowers. There's pictures. (*sic*) There's just a beautiful, incredibly moving display in memory of people who have lost their lives there because of the graduates of the school.

As a central component of their ritual protest, SOA Watch protesters repurposed a built structure of the Army, one of the more tangible exemplars of radical divisiveness that they contest, into a site of collective mourning.[14]

One of the most prevalent symbols that SOA protesters use in creating this memorial, also used by participants on the Migrant Trail, are white, wooden crosses bearing the names of the dead. These crosses come from a decades-long lineage of resistance and demonstrate the centrality of religious iconography to the strategy of turning hegemony on its head through ritual protest. Akin to Nagel (1996), James Scott (1977) argues that subaltern populations can use religious practice as a mode of subterfuge; through rituals and symbolism, "the central values of elite culture are symbolically rejected or stood on their head" (Scott 1977: 17). While such subversion is often quite latent, in certain contexts it can become explicitly mobilizing. Since Vatican II and Liberation Theology, social movements throughout Latin America have repurposed the artifacts of Catholicism (Smith 1991). The cross is one such symbol that has been reimagined and rearticulated.[15]

---

[14] Other social movements, including the peace and nuclear disarmament movement to which SOA Watch activists have many connections, have used similar tactics. For instance, the women's peace camp at Greenham Common, established in 1982, turned the fence around a British Air Force base into a central element of their protest. The women chained themselves to the fence, joined hands around the six-mile perimeter fence to "embrace the base," and decorated the fence with symbols of peace (see: Roseneil 1995).

[15] Rosa Linda Fregoso (2003) offers an instance of such resistance, examining how activists have painted crosses throughout Ciudad Juaréz, Mexico, where the murder of hundreds of women

On the Migrant Trail, the ritual of traversing the desert with crosses is a symbolic means of allowing perished migrants to finish the journey they began. As they walk from remote stretches of the desert toward the more trafficked Arizona highways and, finally, into Tucson, Migrant Trail participants hold the crosses high, announcing the presence of the disappeared in public space. Magaña (2008) argues that among the dominant images of migrants in the US–Mexico borderlands, "the politics of fear and of pity tensely meet in the imaginaries aroused by the mass-mediated depiction of migrants moving slowly, painfully, but surely, across the desert" (2008: 190–1). Magaña here is building on the work of Hannah Arendt (1963 [1990]) and, later, Luc Boltanski (2004), who argue that in the eighteenth century, a "politics of pity" developed, creating a moral gulf between those who suffer and those who do not. Central to this politics of pity is a social system – today predicated on the rapid and constant circulation of images of suffering – that encourages "fortunates" to behold those who suffer as "spectacles." The politics of pity hails bystanders to be voyeurs rather than ethical witnesses.

The Migrant Trail seeks to reduce the moral and social distance that the dominant social order encourages, replacing the politics of fear and pity with a politics of solidarity. In place of dominant images of suffering migrants, this ritual protest evokes a different visual to which Americans have grown accustomed, that of a roadside shrine (Van Ham 2011). Though carried *en masse* by a group of people on the move, rather than stationary at a given site, the carrying of crosses evokes a culturally familiar concept, a memorial to a traveler or travelers that died suddenly while on a journey. The ritual protest of walking with these crosses creates an emotionally infused scene. Migrant Trail participants reach the public with ways of seeing and understanding that contest the fear and pity that underwrite the US security state.

THE RITUAL GUISE

On a cold, wet January day in Washington, DC, the National Museum of American History was bustling with tourists. The museum, free to the public, provided an ideal refuge for the afternoon. Few who meandered through the vast atrium knew this to be an auspicious anniversary. Marking the twelfth

---

working in the maquiladoras has gone unacknowledged by the Mexican State. The painted crosses are a visual way to reclaim the space of a city, populating the landscape with symbols that declare, "we see." Fregoso (2003) explains that the crosses work as "silent witnesses" ... "speaking for justice for eyes that cannot see, for women who can no longer speak, crosses marking the threshold of existence" (29). In utilizing such crosses, protesters in Juaréz introduce what Fregoso terms "religiosity" as a potent resource on two counts. Religiosity is a culturally salient way of grappling with "the trauma of the unrepresentable: death as the ultimate other" (21). Yet this is not the bureaucratic, institutionalized religion of the official Catholic Church. Instead, religiosity becomes a grammar of resistance and a contrapuntal force to dominant ways of knowing and being, those that disappear the fact of disappearance.

FIGURE 3-5. *Migrant Trail participants carry crosses throughout the walk, placing them at the base of a tree in Tucson's Kennedy Park at the culmination of their annual journey*

Photo credit: Eric O Ledermann

year of Guantánamo's official use as a military prison, WAT members prepared to add two new "exhibits" to the museum that afternoon.

Five WAT members in hoods and orange jumpsuits entered the expansive lobby, a room with an open floor plan and few walls, flanked by staircases and balconies. The five activists stood and knelt in stress positions, unmoving in front of a wall-size installation hewn of several rows of metallic plates imaging a modernist flag. The text below was carved into the tile: "The Star Spangled Banner: The Flag that Inspired the National Anthem."

Visitors to the museum seemed not to notice the staged tableau. Then into the din of conversation began the call and response. One voice, followed by tens, declared their presence. "Ladies and Gentlemen, we ask for your attention …" Banners swiftly dropped from the balconies above, hand-painted in artful orange script, "Make Guantánamo History." Soon, nearly a hundred people from what seemed to be everywhere had joined in song. They stood at far removes of the room and in close, on staircases below and balconies above. The place felt electric. Security guards gathered in a corner, their faces stern. They seemed uncertain of how to proceed. Radios emerged, presumably to ask for backup. Or guidance.

During this time, another ten or so WAT members had infiltrated the "Price of Freedom" exhibit upstairs, a special collection that detailed the sacrifices of US military personnel during the nation's twentieth- and twenty-first-century wars. At the entrance to this exhibit, one WAT member served as a docent, handing out flyers to museum attendees. He explained the situation at the military prison and answered detailed questions that museumgoers had about Guantánamo. Others in hoods and jumpsuits had taken up statuesque positions inside the exhibit, replicating how the detainees are forced to kneel and stand. Their silent bodies intended to display "the true cost of freedom," which the group's press release explained to be "*twelve years of torture and indefinite detention as the bitter cost of the United States' misguided pursuit of 'national security'.*"

WAT members expected to be arrested for their protest. Instead they were permitted to stay until the building was closed to the public that evening. This was not a straightforward decision. The guards confiscated the dropped banners in the atrium nearly instantly, though one protester explained a moment of confusion. "No, no, you're not holding it right," the WAT activist had said to the woman in uniform who was taking the huge poster from him. She had looked at him puzzled for an instant, and then realized that he was speaking to her as if she were a "comrade." She had quickly reverted to the task at hand. The guards had also swiftly closed the Price of Freedom exhibit, funneling confused members of the public back to the song-filled atrium. Then the guards spoke with group leaders and asked for their plan. There were negotiations and ultimately an agreement. The group could stay if they maintained their current activities, not damaging property or staying past the museum's closure.[16] And

---

[16] There is no official explanation for why the protesters were allowed to stay. Some believe that there was something about the institution itself and its location. As one activist observed, "In

stay they did, for hours. While those in jumpsuits and hoods in the atrium and the upstairs exhibit remained frozen in place and silent, haunting specters of the actual detainees, others spoke with those visiting the museum, handing out flyers, answering questions, engaging in conversation.

When nearly eighty members of the group convened in their circle that evening to reflect on the day, there was a spirit of wonder, hope, and surprise. Many spoke about the conversations they had had. Some bystanders at the museum had been surprised to learn the prison was still open. Others asked WAT members for help explaining to children in strollers what the ruckus was. One activist even found herself in a lengthy conversation with the mother of a soldier. While the woman was at first antagonistic to the group's actions, the two were ultimately able to find common ground around the fact that fathers should not be indefinitely separated from their children, as the detainees at Guantánamo have been.

WAT member Madeline's words that night were particularly profound:

My reflection today is about the ugliness and the nastiness of Guantánamo and the treatment of the people being held there. And the singing has really stuck with me: the power of the voices and how it drew people and it kept people. It was incredible, beautiful, really hard for people to turn away. It's not pretty to look at people in orange jumpsuits with hoods on their heads. It feels scary, and you don't know what's going on. And that combination today was really impactful, and I think it made it much more difficult for people to dismiss.

In their efforts to dramatize what the state obscures, these activists' actions seek to disrupt but not deter. As Madeline assesses, through the use of a particular aesthetic, these activists can sometimes captivate bystanders who might otherwise turn away. This is not an aestheticized rendering of others' suffering but a means of layering the truth of state violence with the resiliency of the human spirit. In their museum action, WAT generated an invitation for dialogue with the public. Though punctuated by moments of hope, and the arresting command of artful visuals and spirit-soaring song, witnessing rituals are understandably somber, meditative, and weighty. The issues these activists raise and the stories they tell are riddled with sorrow and horror. Yet activists report that the mood of these actions seems to appeal to the public in ways that many protests do not.

Washington [DC] there's a sense of the public-ness of public institutions and that we do co-create what the museum is and ultimately co-create what America is ... I think that the people handling us understood that their first oath is to the constitution, their second oath is to the powers that be." Another activist, however, described being "blown away" by "an American institution making space for us." She continued, "People want to get arrested, and they couldn't get arrested. That's democracy right there."

FIGURE 3.6. *WAT occupies the National Museum of American History in Washington, DC, 2014. Pictured is the Atrium portion of the direct action*
Photo credit: Justin Norman

Ritual protest creates an atmosphere quite distinct from the dominant frame within which American publics are taught to think about politics. Jeremy of WAT, for instance, emphasized that WAT's ritual tactics seem to have an uncanny impact on a public often allergic to political protest. Jeremy had previously been involved in the group Billionaires for Bush, which used humor and satire to try to sway audiences against reelecting then-President Bush (Haugerud 2013). Jeremy believed the groups shared some important strategies, such as playing upon public emotions through staged theatrics and using symbolism and space to subvert dominant social scripts. The mood of these two groups could not be more different, however. The tone of Billionaires for Bush was satirical and flamboyant; WAT's actions were staid. Both engaged in public, visually compelling displays, but only WAT's could be considered solemn ritual. This seemed to have a unique impact on bystanders, suggested Jeremy. Reflecting on decades of protest experience with different groups, he observed,

We have discovered that seeing somebody in a hood affects people in particular ways. They tend not to taunt you. A solemnity comes over them. Even if they disagree with you, there is some weird respect that is accorded

(Grele 2011: 88–9).

Blake of SOA Watch similarly observed that ritual tactics, in particular "vigils," were a very effective way to appeal to bystanders. Blake did not like what she understood as more typical street protests, judging them as generally ineffective and hard to drive toward a strategic agenda. In particular, she found it nearly impossible to generate a unified message in a protest situation. She recalled an action in Atlanta that she had attended a few months prior to contest current police conduct. Some people showed up with signs that said, "fuck the police." "That's a non-starter," Blake explained to me. "Plus it's disrespectful and alienating." While Blake understood that people were angry with law enforcement, and she had been herself as well, she disagreed with the approach. "A vigil is more solemn, meditative, intentional than a demonstration," she explained to me. "And that has the strategic benefit of being able to control the mood and the message."

Maya of WAT, like Blake, was similarly appreciative that "the silent, deliberate nature of the vigils communicates a sense of discipline and intentionality." Maya noted that as distinct from other protests, "There aren't folks trying to rouse the crowd with slogans or chants, there aren't flags and competing messages and issues on signage, there aren't stragglers or wanderers or folks engaging with the public in a possibly aggressive way." She even believed that such solemnity and ritual practice allowed her to feel "safer and able to participate fully."

Harriet of WAT agreed, contrasting WAT's way of doing actions from other peace and anti-war groups she had worked with in the early 2000s. She explained that she did not like the way that many of these other groups' protests felt flippant, confrontational, or, what she termed, "sarcastic." She worried that such tactics were off-putting to bystanders because of their "preachy and self-righteous attitude," one that made little room for dialogue. She added that "the anger and the yelling of people who really just wanted to express themselves in public," while understandable, was unlikely to win popular support. The "style" of WAT's tactics was different, and to Harriet more attractive. Ritual protest felt "like a very genuine non-violent witness that could have a public impact by affecting people who saw it, in a good way. As opposed to simply offending people by yelling."

Certainly there are activists in these groups who have felt stifled by the discipline and solemnity of ritual protest, believing that bystanders might need to be "offended" out of their apathy. I return to this in Chapter 6. The fact remains, however, that those involved in these groups tend to appreciate ritual protest because they believe that it hedges against public rebuke. This is due to both mood and method. Ritual protest is silent and solemn. It is not intended to foment anger. While it may inspire moral outrage, it delivers a message in a style meant to invite bystanders in rather than turn them off. Moreover, the memorial nature of these rituals is intended to be culturally familiar even if those being mourned are unknown to most of the public. In the acknowledgment of lives lost, these activists hope that bystanders who might otherwise disagree with these campaigns' political intentions will nevertheless come to humanize the targets of state violence.

CONCLUSION

Ritual protest is a central component of solidarity witness, a means for these activists to testify to the realities of state violence. Through ritual protest, these activists pursue a mode of solidarity with the state's targets, refusing the moral distance and organized forgetting that underwrite the US security state. Those who are tortured abroad or in US military prisons, sequestered indefinitely without rights, and abandoned as they journey for survival must be ignored and dehumanized. To push against this is to demand of the state a moral accounting and to ask American publics to reconsider their response and obligations to those whom their government abandons and violates.

By using ritual protest as a form of testimony to their witness, these activists leverage the tools available to them: affect and emotion, collective memory, the courts, visually evocative symbols and spaces, and the ritual guise. These are, in some sense, "the weapons of the weak" (Scott 1987), not because they are wielded by those most acutely impacted by state violence but because a few hundred or even thousand grassroots activists seeking to take on a global security complex are not particularly powerful in any traditional sense of the political. While they do intend to target core state institutions and a broad swathe of government policies, these activists' chances for melioristic reform have appeared to be small in practice. By mobilizing affectively potent rituals as a means to pursue solidarity with the state's targets, these activists seek to craft the space for a kind of politics that would neither be tolerated nor intelligible if pursued through more traditional political venues. Their tactical repertoire thus pushes for a different political frame, contesting narrow ways of seeing, feeling, and knowing the operations of the US security state.

4

The Visceral Logics of Embodied Resistance

It is dawn on the Migrant Trail, and we are awakened by the sounds of Ozomatlí, festive beats pumping out of the sound system of Ted's pickup, one of the three support vehicles that hauls our equipment, water, and food. The vehicles are also on hand to transport those who have succumbed to the heat or their blistered feet. We have half an hour to pack away tents, sleeping bags, and whatever else we will not need until the afternoon. We hold on to the few essentials: containers for toting water, sunscreen, a hat and sunglasses, and the occasional camera. We load the trailers as quickly as possible.

Once packed, we circle up to stretch and make necessary announcements. Then we read the migrant prayer.

Creator, full of love and mercy, I want to ask you for my Migrant brothers and sisters. Have pity on them and protect them, as they suffer mistreatments and humiliations on their journeys, are labeled as dangerous, and marginalized for being foreigners. Make them be respected and valued for their dignity. Touch with Your goodness the many that see them pass. Care for their families until they return to their homes, not with broken hearts but rather with hopes fulfilled. Let it be.

The prayer reminds us of the walk's meaning. It evokes tears for some. For many still groggy after a short sleep, it is an opening to the day. We line up and set out in line to traverse our ten- to fifteen-mile daily trek.

The first three mornings we walk in the Buenos Aires Wildlife Refuge on cattle roads, terrain that is often gnarled and rocky, sometimes turning to deep sand. Occasionally a fleet of volunteers must dig out the fifteen-passenger van that has become stuck in the treacherous earth. After the refuge, we transition to stretches of isolated highway. Route 286 heads north to Three Points. The more trafficked eighty six then takes us east into Tucson.

Our campsites are diverse. We spend multiple nights in the wilderness of the Wildlife Refuge. We also stay overnight at a trailer park with running water

FIGURE 4.1. *Migrant Trail participants walk on highway 286 toward Tucson, 2016*
Photo credit: Christina Felschen

and showers; a church with delicious air-conditioning; and, on our last night, a stretch of hot asphalt speckled with broken glass that sits seven miles outside of Tucson. This final site is charmingly termed "Camp Hell" by organizers, for the way that the black ground absorbs and then radiates the sun's heat well into the evening hours. The wind at Camp Hell is usually stiff, threatening to blow over our shade tents. The effect is that of sitting in a convection oven during our final afternoon.

Throughout the week, our bodies are, in turn, challenged and pampered. We walk on tired feet in searing temperatures. We sleep little. But we are spoiled with lavish meals brought by local congregations and other allied groups. A favorite treat is the Tibetan feast on day five, complete with egg rolls provided by Tibetan monks dressed in golden robes, who occasionally walk stretches of the trail with us. Every afternoon, a new, large portion of ice is brought in to keep perishable foods fresh and our water cool. We are always conscious of our physical selves (Adapted from author's field notes).

The physical challenges of the Migrant Trail exemplify the kinds of creative, risky, and sometimes counterintuitive ways that the activists in this study use their bodies. Putting one's body into one's activism is key to the practice of solidarity witness. Each group undertakes embodied tactics that generally include some degree of physical discomfort and sacrifice. Migrant Trail participants traverse tens of miles in triple-digit temperatures; they struggle with heat exhaustion and painful blisters. School of the Americas Watch activists spend months and even years in jails and prisons for their acts of civil disobedience. Witness Against Torture protesters go without food for days and engage in the risks of civil disobedience, which often include stints in jail and sometimes prison sentences. These embodied tactics intend to acknowledge and respond to those who face the most acute manifestations of state violence. Through the physicality of their resistance, these activists seek to confront bodily the state's practices of detention, torture, and killing that remove entire groups from the political scene.

For many of these activists, being a "witness" requires a willingness to undertake certain risks and sacrifices in accordance with an unwavering commitment to their cause. As one Migrant Trail participant reminded me, the word "witness" is actually the English translation of the Greek term "martyr." While these activists' fundamental intention in enduring discomfort and physical sacrifice is to express solidarity with the aggrieved and denounce injustice, those who put their bodies on the line often report feeling more proximate to the targets of state violence and paying attention to injustice in a manner that requires the felt experience of the body. The physically demanding and sometimes high-risk elements of their witness generate new ways of seeing and knowing state violence.

FIGURE 4.2. *Nearly all Migrant Trail participants suffer from blisters as well as a host of other small injuries. In this image, participants provide basic foot care to other walkers, a luxury that migrants are not afforded* Photo credit: Christina Felschen

In this chapter, I examine the importance of embodied forms of resistance to the practice of solidarity witness. I begin by exploring the body in resistance broadly considered in order to point to some of the basic motivations for engaging in the physicality of witness. I then suggest that through embodied activism, these groups push forward a principled stance of solidarity in a few different ways. Through the embodiment of witness, these activists seek to divest from their privilege, resisting the seductions of the dominant order. They cultivate a visceral sense of closeness to the most violated. They bring their bodies to bear on sites of state violence and amplify the embodied resistance of the aggrieved. Finally, they earn politically significant credibility with various audiences, from unlikely political allies to the friends and families of the disappeared.

Through the embodiment of witness, these activists reach out to the targets of state violence in solidarity, confront the state itself in dissent, and appeal to the public with a political alternative and ethical imperative. By embodying their political intentions, these activists come to see, feel, and understand state violence in ways they could not otherwise. They share these felt experiences broadly, making the state's targets, which the dominant culture disavows, harder to ignore and hold at a moral distance.

EMBODIED RESISTANCE

Embodied resistance has figured centrally throughout history. Southern Blacks in the US Civil Rights movement exposed themselves to fire hoses and dogs. People confronting military rule from Tiananmen Square to the occupied territories of Palestine have put their bodies in front of tanks. In these instances, injury and death were possible, sometimes likely. Even in less dramatic situations, the activist body is a primary means for confronting dominance. Barbara Sutton (2007) finds that this understanding was part of the common sense among women resisting neoliberal austerity measures in Argentina in the early 2000s. These activists used the bodily idiom of *poner el cuerpo*, which roughly translates as "to put the body." Sutton explains this bodily element of political conviction:

> *poner el cuerpo* means not just to talk, think, or desire but to be really present and involved; to put the whole (embodied) being into action, to be committed to a social cause, and to assume the bodily risks, work, and demands of such a commitment.
>
> (Sutton 2007: 130)

Commitment is defined here as being willing to embody one's political and moral convictions.

The activists in this study express a similar line of thinking in adopting physically demanding practices. WAT member Faith explained that the importance of embodying one's political vision was a lesson embedded in the Catholic Worker tradition from which WAT emerged. In reference to one of the Catholic Left's preeminent pacifist leaders, Faith recalled, "Phil Berrigan once said, 'Hope is where your ass is.' You gotta put yourself in it, right? ... I guess living with integrity involves this kind of body politics."

The choice to use physically demanding tactics to confront dominance has many meanings. One of the primary reasons that the activists in this study choose such tactics is because they resemble and respond to the kinds of violence endured and the kinds of resistance enacted by the state's targets. During Witness Against Torture's 2005 trip to Cuba, Frida Berrigan considered the plight of the Guantánamo detainees on a hunger strike, asking, "What does humanity look like when our only tools for persuasion, for power, for being heard, are our own bodies?" (Brown et al. 2008: 23) At the time she, along with twenty-four other members of WAT, were camped at the gates of the military prison, fasting as an act of solidarity in response to the prisoners. Having traversed the island nation, the group was now forbidden access to the detainees. At some level, Frida's was a rhetorical question, a recognition of the dehumanization inherent in indefinite detention and torture and of the fact that the prisoners' only means for being heard was hunger striking unto death. Frida's question was also an inquiry into the nature of resistance, and the role of the body in this resistance, a consideration important for those who wish to enact solidarity with the targets of state violence.

As distinct from WAT's volitional fasting, the prisoners' hunger strike was a tactic born of necessity. The indefinitely detained have no recourse to more traditional avenues of representation and rights; their embodied protest becomes their only political tool. Elaine Scarry (1985) argues that the body in pain cannot speak, that torture works to undo the agentic subject by robbing it of language. Scarry describes the exercise of physical violence as making "the body emphatically and crushingly present" and "the voice absent" (1985: 49). When screams and groans replace articulate speech, physical violence eliminates the individual's capacity to communicate. This serves the intentions of the US security regime, wherein the targets of state violence are not meant to speak, or be heard, or be seen.

In her work on the Guantánamo Prison, Avery Gordon (2010) similarly observes that a part of imprisonment's power, and devastation, is that it eradicates the prisoner's authority to speak. As distinct from Scarry whose discussion is specific to the moment of inflicted pain, however, Gordon explores the possibilities for resistance in the context of indefinite detention, in which the pain of torture is a component of but not an exhaustive form of coercion. For the prisoner who lacks a political voice, language itself takes bodily form: "prisoners know that stripped bare, literally, your body remains the most adaptable oppositional technology when communication is utterly impossible and other weapons unavailable" (2010: 38). Exerting control over one's physical self is a last grasp at dignity that can sometimes contest and confound dominance.

Thus, while deeply concerned with the implications of a political regime that reduces people to embodied expression as their *only* possible dissent, Frida understood this mode of expression complexly observing:

I remember hearing about the hunger-striking men in Guantánamo, and coming to an awareness that this act of deprivation and suffering was their only way to be heard. All they could do was offer up their bodies. It was an act of extreme desperation, but also an act of extreme hope – that someone would answer.

(Brown et al. 2008: 23)

For those reduced to the crushing presence of their physical pain or trapped in the psychic torture of indefinite detention, embodied resistance expresses *both* desperation and hope.

If aggrieved communities have long used their bodies to speak back to power, for those activists seeking to enact solidarity with the state's targets, embodied activism becomes a way to confront the dominant power structure, which also includes navigating the stance of being a supposed beneficiary of the US security state. All efforts at resistance cannot but emerge under conditions shaped by dominance (Hall 1996). The choice to embody their dissent is one way that the activists in this study engage in a practice of "critical solidarity" (Butler 1993), rooted in owning and challenging their own role in the social structure.

There is also a religious value afforded to suffering and sacrifice that bears note here, considering that each of the communities under study has deep, if complex, religious roots. Across religious traditions, Emile Durkheim (1912) finds that pain and discomfort foster social cohesion and emotional rewards. As distinct from the imposed forms of painful violence that Scarry (1985) argues to be disintegrative, destroying the relationship between the self and its world, Ariel Glucklich (2003) calls these religious forms of volitional discomfort and suffering "integrative pain," defined as "a socially and spiritually integrative force that defines and broadens the individual's sense of identity" (2003: 34). This notion of integrative pain can help to explain why these solidarity activists would intentionally pursue discomfort. Whereas an onlooker might see blisters, headaches, hunger, and jail time as barriers to wanting to engage in collective action, such discomforts can also be both socially and spiritually powerful.[1] Further, in some strains of Christianity, the condition of suffering is tied to a particular sense of spiritual value since God, in the person of Jesus, was himself tortured and crucified. I now examine the physicality of witness as a means by which these activists engage with their privilege while seeking to divest from the seductions of the dominant order. Through physical challenges and discomforts, they find a form of political activity that is spiritually and socially integrative in a way that more traditional modes of civic engagement are not.

"I HAVE STRUGGLED TO BEND MY CRAVINGS"

The solidarity activists in this study report the impetus to confront privilege as a primary reason for undertaking embodied tactics. Barbara Sutton observes that, "*poner el cuerpo* has a sacrificial dimension" (2007: 145). For these

---

[1] These religious teachings also have material and psychological ramifications. Empirical data show that religious understandings can alleviate pain for those that experience injury and disease (Norris 2009).

activists, the sacrifice of voluntary physical discomfort is often regarded as a way to maintain one's integrity while expressing solidarity with those who are in an exponentially more dire situation. WAT member Harriet explained this in the case of fasting:

I'm sitting here in all of my comfort, and I'm going to give something up. I'm going to make myself uncomfortable, trying to express solidarity, acknowledgment that these people are right now doing a hunger strike because they're suffering.

Harriet has also been arrested multiple times for her civil disobedience, which she regarded in a similar vein:

[Risking arrest is] taking a stronger stand than it would be if I weren't putting myself on the line ... I benefit from the society [and] the government that is doing these awful things. But I am at least expressing my opposition in the strongest way I can do it.

Through such tactics, Harriet understands herself as taking a stand *with* as well as *against* her privilege. Harriet explains that, to some degree, she "benefits" from the dominant social and political system, which offers her material comforts and relative bodily security. By intentionally relinquishing such comforts, she takes the strongest stand she believes she can. Harriet is skeptical that her activism – or anyone's for that matter – can significantly shift the operations of powerful US institutions. Instead, she adopts the role of the witness with its incumbent, if modest, sacrifices. She embodies her moral opposition to the status quo with the understanding that more traditional forms of political activity do not actually work as purported. Indeed, this kind of embodied, moral activism arises in part because the "normal" avenues for political dissent in US society have proven themselves defunct.[2]

Many of these activists explained that undertaking challenging bodily tactics during political action forced them to pay attention in ways they might not otherwise. As a way of confronting their privilege, this paying attention is an important practice because of the way these activists are socially positioned as having the potential to ignore. WAT member Faith suggested that the discomfort of fasting generated, if not the crushing presence of pain described by Scarry (1985), an encumbering presence nonetheless. Faith reflected, "I'm a terrible faster. I'm hungry the whole time. For some people the hunger goes away. For me, every single day, when it comes time for mealtime, I'm hungry. My stomach is so used to it." Faith found value in this, identifying in fasting the very meaning of what it is to witness. "I think the discomfort reminds me [to] keep looking at it. It's important to bear witness, to remain aware of the suffering for those who hunger physically, but for those who hunger

---

[2] One of the more obvious examples for this point is the massive global dissent to the 2003 Iraq War, protest that went ignored by the United States and its allies. For instance, on February 15, 2003, the largest demonstration in human history saw between 10 and 15 million people from over 600 cities demonstrate against invading Iraq (Walgrave & Rucht 2010; Tharoor 2003).

for justice." The physical hunger forges a kind of awareness, forcing one to "look" at injustice, to bear witness. Fasting serves as an experiential reminder to pay attention to a mode of state violence that the dominant culture seduces the public to ignore. The idiom of "hungering for justice" is turned into a political practice, important for solidarity activists because it offers an experiential link to practices of the state that are often hidden. This embodiment, this paying attention, is a reminder to witness, to see and show what the state occludes.

Migrant Trail participant Jessie similarly described the physicality of the desert walk as a means of paying attention through a particularly physical experience:

I talk about [the Migrant Trail] as being a very physical kind of incarnation of my commitment to the border in terms of research and activism. But a time to live it through walking and through feeling as opposed to staying up late writing emails or doing advocacy or going to Washington DC. This is a very physical aspect of my commitment, and it requires that I think of all people that walk.

For Jessie, the physicality of walking "requires" her to think of all the migrants who are forced to walk; it is an embodied and emotion-infused orientation to a political cause. The language of "incarnation" suggests that Jessie interprets the embodiment of this walk in part through a Christian framework, which makes sense given that Jessie's work with the Mennonite Church is what first brought her to the Migrant Trail. As a theological principle, incarnation generally describes the process by which a spiritual being is rendered flesh, often a Christian God in the person of Jesus. Applied to the Migrant Trail, Jessie suggests that walking allows her to embody the cause of border justice, giving flesh to a moral vision, so to speak. Outside of the walk, Jessie generally pursues her activism through tasks she believes to be more mundane but politically necessary, such as sending emails and working with politicians in the nation's capital.

During her reflection at the gates of Guantánamo, Frida Berrigan echoed components of Jessie's observation, distinguishing physical tactics from more common political activities. Frida, however, is a bit more critical of traditional politics than Jessie, arguing that embodied protest tactics reveal the US state as undemocratic and inequitable. Frida writes:

As I have struggled to bend my cravings for food into cravings for justice, I am in dialogue with my body. Being dependent on the body is such an un-American predicament. Americans write letters to Congress and the editor, we write checks, we hire lobbyists and PR firms, we employ people and utilize services. We do everything we can to keep from using our bodies to make a difference. For me the whole journey has been about exploring what it means to have and use a body ... in some part – purging ourselves of privilege.

(Brown et al. 2008: 23)

In Frida's view, the bureaucratic and market-driven nature of US politics has rendered the possibilities for political participation bankrupt. This hegemonic mode of political engagement stands in stark contrast to the immediacy of political activity that these activists value and understand to be necessary. By using their bodies in lieu of their pocketbooks or access to social status, these activists introduce alternative avenues for political activity. They also presume that people can sign petitions and make campaign donations and still in no way be personally touched or impacted. They demonstrate that putting oneself (bodily and all) into the political scene, a rough paraphrase of *poner el cuerpo*, is a valuable means of political engagement. This contests the rational choice perspective that sees such activity as merely a cost. For solidarity activists, such embodied activism is both a practical and ethical engagement with dynamics of privilege. It is practical because these activists are not members of the political elite. They are not Washington insiders, and they do not have enough money to impact the system. It is ethical because such money and power are not the tools for which they strive. Instead, these groups engage in embodied tactics that both require and undercut the privileges they do have, at least in contrast to the direct targets of state violence for whom they advocate.

If these activists use their bodies to work both with and against their privilege, they are quite conscious of contextualizing theirs as a small sacrifice. The physical discomforts of solidarity witness are a mere token or gesture in the face of the *ultimate* sacrifice or suffering faced by the tortured, disappeared, and sequestered. For instance, Migrant Trail participant Jonah described the challenge of walking for days in the desert in soaring temperatures, "to show our solidarity and willingness to suffer for the people who have paid the ultimate price and I guess the *ultimate* ... suffering, just to be in solidarity with those people and to call attention to what's really going on" (my emphasis). Jonah clearly values the idea of suffering as a kind of sacrificial solidarity. Still, he is clear that it is the migrants themselves, and not Migrant Trail participants, who have undergone "the ultimate suffering." Similarly, Evelyn of WAT explained, "[fasting is] the least we can do as we consider the men stuck at Guantánamo, many of whom have done extended hunger strikes as one of the only methods they have to protest the terrible injustices they continue to suffer." WAT member Eleanor added, "At the end of the fast I'll be able to eat food again. But they're still stuck in Guantánamo. I'm privileged to be able to end the fast, and their only hope is to do a hunger strike." Both Evelyn and Eleanor are aware that whereas WAT members fast out of *choice*, the detainees are hunger striking out of *necessity*.

For many of these activists, there is a distinctly Christian framework at play here that sees God, in the person of Jesus, as having undergone the ultimate suffering. In more liberal and liberationist Christian theology, Jesus is commonly understood as having been persecuted because of his outspoken efforts on behalf of the socially marginalized and poor. Christ is the original "martyr," or Christian "witness." Those who place themselves in harm's way, or are put there by social and political forces, can be seen as Christ-like figures themselves in the sense that they are primary witnesses to the suffering of the world. This notion emerged in conversations with many of the activists in this study who came from a Christian background. For instance, SOA Watch participant and long-time Catholic Worker, Paul, like many SOA Watch protesters, used the term "martyrs" to refer to the Latin American victims of military death squads. Paul explained the rationale for using this language: "People who are murdered by the death squads are martyred for being poor. It's not necessarily that somebody was some brave political person speaking out against the injustice ... They're the martyrs of imperialism – of a policy that's unjust." In some sense, what seems a deeply religious reading of the targets of state violence might also be understood as an observation with sociological merit: those who are "martyred" by imperialism are forced to bear the most proximate witness to imperialism's violence. They see and experience the most brutal operations of a global political regime as it is inscribed on their bodies.[3]

Even if they do not refer to the targets of state violence with the lexicon of *martyr*, this sensibility was reflected in statements made by Migrant Trail participants as well as WAT members. Dennis, a deeply religious, long-term participant of the Migrant Trail, observed, "I believe that God's heart is with those that are the most outcast and so the migrants are in that category ... there's a tremendous opposition to them and not much sympathy or empathy with their situation." WAT member Eleanor also described the Guantánamo detainees as martyrs of a sort, "I feel they are political prisoners, the Muslims that are being persecuted."

Of course, many of these activists do not come to their activism from a religious tradition and do not see the directly aggrieved as Christ-like figures. These activists also find it important to distinguish between solidarity activists and the directly violated. Long-time Migrant Trail participant Alex, who had spent years working at an immigration clinic in which he heard hundreds of crossing stories, juxtaposed the Migrant Trail experience to the plight of actual migrants:

We will never know what it feels like to not be able to call the police because the police are the ones who have just stolen all of your money and raped your wife in front of

---

[3] This idea is in line with the rich literature on standpoint theory, the idea that the oppressed have the clearest access to understanding and making sense of their oppression. The notion of a privileged standpoint emerging "from below" is a germinal idea in Marx, further developed by feminist historical materialists, most famously Nancy Hartsock, who argues for "standpoint as an epistemological device," in which a feminist epistemology derives from the fact that "like the lives of proletarians according to Marxian theory, women's lives make available a particular and privileged vantage point on male supremacy" (1983: 284). Jean Comaroff and John Comaroff (2012) have more recently synthesized a similar line of argument that emerges from postcolonial and subaltern studies (Spivak 1988; Chakrabarty 2000; Mbembe 2001). The Comaroffs suggest not only that Western thought and action be understood as provincial, but that thinkers should turn to the Global South (itself a complex and contested designation) for new ways of knowing, being, and acting: "it is the south that often is the first to feel the effects of world-historical forces, the south in which radically new assemblages of capital and labor are taking shape, thus [the south that will] prefigure the future of the global north" (12).

you and beat you up. We'll never know the experience of walking through this desert in the dark with no flashlight afraid that a border patrol agent is going to jump out ... It's an annoyance to us if a border patrol helicopter flies over our camp site or if a [border patrol] truck speeds by and throws dust on us. It's not a terror.

Attentive to the structures of power and privilege that separate Migrant Trail participants from migrants, Alex acknowledged that embodying solidarity is a very different experience than being targeted by the state's violence.

While these activists undertake physically demanding tactics as small sacrifices of solidarity, they cannot approximate the extremity of violence experienced by the state's targets and do not intend such mimicry. Nevertheless, such tactics do impact upon solidarity activists, generating affective ways of knowing and seeing. In this sense embodied activism is a great teacher and can often generate the emotional resources necessary for movement sustainability, a point that I now explore further.

VISCERAL JOURNEYS, FELT SOLIDARITIES

One of the most common modes of embodied witness used by these groups is the protest pilgrimage. Activists walk through the desert in searing temperatures; violate travel embargos to get to island nations; cross onto military property; and enter into jails and prisons. The protest pilgrimage draws on the tactical lineage of nonviolent movements from Gandhi's salt march in India to the US Civil Rights movement's freedom bus rides and United Farmworker marches. These are culturally potent journeys – to the hearts of darkness, to be closer to the aggrieved, and to generating different imaginings. I use the concept of pilgrimage here a bit loosely to connote a physical journey that generates subjective, social, and sometimes spiritual impacts. By this definition, I include crossing onto military bases and entering into jails and prisons, even though these acts do not require traversing great physical distances as the concept of pilgrimage traditionally implies. Protest pilgrimage is an important mode of witnessing that allows activists to see and know with all of their senses the usually obscured sites and experiences of state violence.

One of the ways that protest pilgrimage contests the logics and optics of the US security state is by confronting rarefied state rhetoric with the immediacy and tangibility of physical experience. WAT participant Jeremy explains how within US security doctrine, the "*de facto* strategy of the state [is to] to numb people with mind-boggling legalism and policy detail that drains away the core question of whether what we're doing is right or not." The political field is structured as impenetrable to those who cannot, or choose not to, broker in such technicalities and abstractions.[4] In her book on walking, Rebecca

---

[4] The groups under study have availed themselves of very sophisticated legal and policy expertise, often working with public interest attorneys or cultivating substantial knowledge in other ways.

Solnit (2000) suggests that protest pilgrimage replaces the abstract with "the actualities of places, of sights, of actions, of sensations – of handcuffs, thorns, dust, heat, thirst" (8). These activists walk through the desert, or to prisons and military installations, many of which are geographically remote from the majority of Americans, to break through the abstractions of political jargon. By traveling to sites of state violence, witnesses bring their bodies to bear on what the state seeks to obscure, juxtaposing tangible, sense experience with the abstracted rhetorical devices of the state.

Rory, a Canadian college student participating for his first time on the Migrant Trail, reflected on walking as a means of bearing witness to a reality multiply distant from his own – geographically, climactically, and nationally:

The walking itself has taken a profound physical and almost mental and emotional toll on me ... I think it's just being out here and seeing it. Seeing the climate, seeing the people and just seeing the border patrol driving by, and, you know, they're just rounding up people, loading them up on buses and that sort of thing.

Rory's ability to *see* the realities of injustice because of the physicality of walking generates the kind of visibility that these activists hold paramount- being present to see injustice and show it to others. Rory explains that this embodied confrontation with state violence generates subjective and sociopolitical transformation.

These activists' experiences of going into jails as a result of their civil disobedience are also forms of protest pilgrimage as well as journeys of seeing. By putting themselves into the machinery of the security state, these solidarity activists see and experience realities that they might otherwise be seduced to ignore. Maya reflected on her times in jail after undertaking civil disobedience by highlighting just how much of the state's barbarism she was able to *see* through this aspect of the witnessing repertoire. She described how, "you can go in and see the inside of the prison industrial system and really see how dehumanizing it is and experience it for yourself, like really see it."

One of Maya's most impactful memories of going to jail is a story in contrasts:

I just remember being in a holding cell with all these people who I love. (*sic*) We're singing and yada, yada. It was like the Witness Against Torture cell. I remember seeing all night long this line of African-American males, like hundreds and hundreds of black men being taken through this line, being processed. And I'm seeing and experiencing that and realizing the realities of what communities of color are facing and what young black men are facing.

I do not mean to suggest that they cannot confront the state because it somehow "outsmarts" them. Rather, bringing their bodies to bear on injustice constitutes its own way of knowing (and being known).

Maya was well aware of her privilege in this regard, explaining that her race and class made it impossible to experience the prison as it operates on the bodies of those who are much more commonly incarcerated. She reflected, "I'm a white woman with an education. I'm going to be treated much differently than someone else who might enter into the prison system who doesn't look like me." Nevertheless, the purview of the prison offered an embodied sense of a reality that she could only otherwise know intellectually. She described this as "having a taste of this incredibly destructive system that holds up our society and supposedly like stops people from doing bad things."

This was a "prison witness," a term that WAT members take from their Catholic Worker roots. It allowed the group to mobilize their central method of "witnessing against torture," in this instance not at Guantánamo, but within the US interior. WAT witnessed the disproportionate incarceration of black men as one exemplar of the state's racial despotism, and the indefinite detention of Muslim bodies offshore as another, revealing the interconnectedness of dehumanizing security policies offshore and at home.

The lexicon provided by Glucklich (2003) of integrative versus disintegrative pain is useful for considering these juxtaposed engagements with the prison system. Maya's journey into jail was undertaken volitionally, with a group, to articulate a moral and political stance. While the protesters could not ensure their safety when they risked arrest, theirs was still an *integrative* confrontation with state violence. It strengthened their community of resistance and served as an embodied instantiation of commitment. At the same time, the "Witness Against Torture cell" watched a profoundly *disintegrative* process underway as the black men were funneled into the jail, each one extracted from his community to become a ward of the state. At the same time, we could understand such a rigid distinction between integrative and disintegrative experiences as eliding ways that each experience has components of both. In their submission to the state's most degraded recesses, something breaks down for these activists. They are forced to unlearn, or continue in their process of unlearning, dominant ways of seeing and understanding the state. Their attachments to the hegemonic order are further loosened. By the same token, the men being funneled into the prison may also be integrated into new solidarities with each other through the process of incarceration.

As acts of solidarity and dissent, the embodiment of witness also generates a *felt* sense of connection to the direct targets of state violence. Thomas Scheff (1979), a key scholar in the sociology of emotions, suggests that the sentient, feeling body and the emotional life of the mind are inextricably linked. We experience emotions in visceral ways, and our embodied sense of the world gives us access to emotional ways of knowing. Physically challenging and high-risk tactics have important impacts on activists, and can generate the kinds of felt, subjective experiences that lead to continuing engagement (Jasper 1997). This has a particular resonance in the case of solidarity activists, whose social position is defined in part because they have not directly experienced the oppression they contest. Daniel Myers (2008) notes that solidarity activists, whom he terms "allies," "have a *commitment*-based rather than an experience-based activist identity" (169, my emphasis). Yet commitment to a cause, especially over the long term, is not merely found; it must be forged. The ability of high-risk and physically challenging protest tactics has important value in this regard. Experiencing embodied compassion for those they cannot know personally offers a compelling commitment mechanism for solidarity activists, generating emotions and sensibilities that keep these activists engaged in a long-term political struggle (Russo 2014).

Jason of WAT, for instance, explained that his strongest motivation for fasting was that, "I wanted to feel a small amount of what the men at Guantánamo have felt. It helped to have a modicum of pain physically connecting me with the detainees." This sense experience holds a key to the psychic dynamics of solidarity witnessing. When these activists engage in physically demanding efforts that allow them to see and denounce the injustice that causes another's suffering, they also feel physically and emotionally closer to those who suffer.

While WAT members undertake fasting to generate a felt sense of connection to the detainees, on the Migrant Trail minor suffering due to heat, blisters, exhaustion, and filth can generate deep empathy for those whom participants cannot otherwise meet or learn from directly. This was certainly the case for Adelheid, a twenty-two-year-old German student. As a first-time Migrant Trail participant, Adelheid had limited experiential knowledge of injustice against migrants to complement her more intellectual interest in migration. While she had studied the US–Mexico border in a university course in her home country and was in the United States to begin an internship addressing border justice issues, Adelheid explained how her physical discomfort on the Migrant Trail helped her understand the situation of migrants in a new way:

I think I kind of got it when my feet hurt so badly and ... knowing that it's like this but just a gazillion times worse is how migrants feel at night when it's dark and hiding out, walking on bare flesh kind of ... I'm walking and hurting and I have like the words in my head like [one of the walk organizers] said, "For every step you hurt think of your brothers and sisters," while I'm walking.

Adelheid's experience well exemplifies how affect and emotions become important epistemological resources that emerge with and through the embodied practices of solidarity witness.

If Adelheid's first-time experience on the Migrant Trail helped her access a kind of compassion with which she was unfamiliar, for many of these activists, the embodied generation of compassion helps to re-instantiate commitment over the years. Even after his wealth of legal knowledge and numerous conversations with those who had themselves crossed the US–Mexico border to seek work or be with their families, Alex still understood that the Migrant Trail afforded him new levels of understanding. He explained that there were times during the Migrant Trail when he had only had two gallons of water in a day, as opposed to the three gallons participants are encouraged to drink – in stark contrast to the single gallon that most migrants bring on their multiday journeys. Alex recalled getting sick, or having a headache: "My feet would be torn up and blistered." Such moments offered Alex new ways of knowing, lessons that were affective and embodied as opposed to merely informational. He explained, "what I've learned was a lesson from experience, a lesson of getting sick and this isn't as bad as it gets. I only got like very minor cases of heat stroke, dehydration … It's a lesson that I could only learn by feeling it."

The fact that embodied tactics generate empathy and a sense of connection to those who suffer at a distance instantiates important philosophical claims about crafting solidarity across difference. A significant tradition in political theory suggests that the vulnerability of the bodily organism itself can serve as a means for social cohesion across innumerable cultural distinctions and chasms of social power (Butler 2004; Turner 2006).[5] These activists often took this assessment a step further, incorporating a sense of agency and hope into what might otherwise be a rather bleak claim: that that which unites us is our capacity to feel pain and be victimized. Rather, for witnesses, vulnerability along with resiliency were regarded as twinned dimensions of what it means to be human. As WAT member Carol observed:

Not eating for ten days forces you to examine your relationship with food and those things that keep you alive. The next step for me is examining what it is that makes me human and what it is that I share with all other human beings. Food is certainly one of them. Thinking about my vulnerability – my dependence on food – and then my resilience as well.

A piece of what helped to frame this for Carol were the poems of the Guantánamo detainees themselves, which the group reads when they come together during their weeks of action. This published collection (Falkoff 2007)

---

[5] Sociologist Bryan Turner (2006) argues that human vulnerability is a helpful starting point for considering the need for universal legal protections. He explains, "Human beings experience pain and humiliation because they are vulnerable. While humans may not share a common culture, they are bound together by the risks and perturbations that arise from their vulnerability" (9). For Turner, protection from bodily suffering and indignities stands as a normative universal that can and should then be articulated in legal form. Judith Butler (2004), if generally critical toward a legal formulation such as "human rights," espouses a similar stance nonetheless: bodily vulnerability is a unifying feature of being human. It is also that which imbricates the individual in society, as ours is "a world of beings who are, by definition, physically dependent on each other, physically vulnerable to one another" (Butler 2004: 27). An infant requires the adults around it to provide food, shelter, and other basic protections. Physical violence is deplorable because it exploits and distorts this primary social tie. Certainly the uneven distribution of physical vulnerability is a central operation of global power; we are not all alike in the sense of being equally vulnerable. However, Butler believes that human vulnerability might be considered the one condition that all humans hold in common and yet maintain separately. She argues that this might be a starting point for imagining that which can unite a human community that is still attentive to difference.

offers WAT one of only a few means to hear the prisoners' voices.[6] WAT members often describe reading these poems aloud as a means to bear witness to the detainees' otherwise distant suffering. Carol reflected on the poems: "What stood out to me from that poetry were those same themes of how vulnerable and how very resilient they are. The process of fasting to me echoed that – how all of us are vulnerable and resistant and resilient."

Tied to this notion of shared vulnerability and resilience, it is important to understand that embodied displays of solidarity do not move only in one direction, at least not in the case of WAT, which has a particular relationship with the state's targets, as noted in Chapter 2. While there have been many instances when WAT has discovered through the detainees' attorneys that their solidarity actions offered the prisoners some measure of hope and solace, the prisoners articulate solidarity toward the activists as well. In February 2012, Matt of WAT explained that only a month prior, when the group had gathered for their annual solidarity fast and week of action in Washington, DC:

> We got word that men in Guantánamo had heard about the activities in DC and were fasting in solidarity with us. There was sort of this full circle, and a real deep connection that, in some sense, has become not the ultimate goal but part of the goal in our work that has gone through some shifts over the years. One of the most important things is to maintain some sort of connection with these actual human beings; 171 of them continue to sit in a jail in Cuba.
>
> (Solis 2012: 55)

In this instance, the embodied acts of witnessing emerge as efforts to share in something that exceeds what the state can fully control. The activists and the detainees reach out for a closeness. The effort to feel viscerally proximate and to codify this through acts of embodied resistance is a political act, especially when such significant resources go into epistemologically and ontologically dividing mainstream American publics from the security state's abjected others.

The embodiment of witness allows solidarity activists to understand and respond to the realities of state violence through deeply felt physical experience. This has movement-sustaining features, generating a form of embodied compassion that can serve as a commitment mechanism for solidarity activists that otherwise lack the direct experience of the oppression they contest. At the same time, to desire and act to feel closer to the state's targets must also be understood as political. I now turn to consider how the embodied acts of bearing witness intend to generate new optics for various audiences.

---

[6] WAT's other opportunities to hear from the detainees are generally in the form of communications facilitated by the prisoners' attorneys or the rare instances in which open letters are published in the press.

ENLARGING THE OPTIC, AMPLIFYING THEIR CRIES

The embodiment of witnessing challenges narrow forms of visibility, contesting dominant ways of seeing and knowing what the state is doing. When witnesses put their bodies on the line to contest violence and feel more proximate to those with whom they seek to enact solidarity, they also challenge the collective optic. Similar to the ritual protest explored in the last chapter, the embodied tactics of pilgrimage, fasting, and civil disobedience have a performative dimension, drawing various forms of attention to the occluded elements of the US security state.

As one of its many functions, the protest pilgrimage allows witnesses to travel physically to places that might be difficult to see – to the border region, the School of the Americas, and the Guantánamo prison where the government is able to veil or hide state violence. By going bodily to the literal and symbolic sites where this violence is authorized and enacted, these activists draw public attention to state secrets. Jeremy noted the importance of Witness Against Torture's 2005 physical journey to the Guantánamo Prison as a way to render visible what the state obscures:

Guantánamo was not supposed to be seen. It is a legal black hole, far away, you cannot get there, we cannot know the prisoners' names, you do not know what is going on inside. They have these ridiculous tours for congress people and journalists, but it is pure propaganda. The War on Terror has a huge dimension of invisibility to it, and part of the fight against it is to see what cannot, should not and must not be seen. They [WAT] physically went to Guantánamo to behold the place.

(Grele 2011: 69–70)

Jeremy underscores not only how WAT's journey made state violence visible but also how the activists' efforts cut through modes of false visibility: the state's carefully orchestrated and sanitized visits to the prison made available only to approved visitors.

In her reflections as both a geographer and long-time participant in SOA Watch's Fort Benning vigil, Sara Koopman (2008) explains a dynamic similar to the one Jeremy articulates. Every year during the anti-SOA protest, the military training school would offer tours meant to showcase SOA/WHISC's institutional respectability. Key to this tour was the trumpeting of a new human rights curriculum, even if this part of the military's multiweek training is a meager eight hours in length and of questionable quality (Gill 2004). Koopman terms this effort by the school "*rights*washing" (832), a way that violence and militarism gain credence not through a complete obfuscation of power but by narrowing what is visible to the public. Building on geographer Derek Gregory's observations about Guantánamo, Koopman argues that at Fort Benning, "The military presents the school as transparent space ... [but] what the army offers is actually a constricted vision, carefully constructed so as to not show connections" (832–3). Koopman suggests that SOA Watch participants resist this

FIGURE 4.3. In 2015, ten years after their original journey to Cuba, WAT members returned to Guantánamo for a Thanksgiving fast, drawing attention to the detainees once again through their embodied witness

Photo credit: Justin Norman

narrowed vision by corporeally making their way to the military base, where they find each other and gain proximity to the school. She writes, "Our bodies, our very physical vulnerability to militarism draw counter-topographies of connection" (2008: 840). When protesters engage in civil disobedience on military property, submitting their bodies to the state through volitional arrest, they tie their own fates in some small way to the most vulnerable targets of state violence. This act of solidarity becomes a way to both see for themselves and to expose to others the state's violent practices.

SOA Watch activist Liz Deligio's statement to the court after committing civil disobedience highlights the state's use of force as both disproportionate and ethically spurious:

I handed over my body to the military officials of Ft. Benning. I crossed a line that this court and the military wishes to name a line of property, of law. I stand before you charged with criminal trespass because I stood on military property and prayed for the countless lives lost and for the humanity each soldier must sacrifice in their own hearts to be these forces of death.

(Deligio 2004)

This short statement carries a multilayered critique. By making herself vulnerable to state forces through her act of civil disobedience, Liz intends to embody her solidarity with those Latin American communities who have been terrorized by militaries also trained at the SOA. Moreover, Liz juxtaposes her own criminal charge to the state's much more draconian and violent acts, placing into question the designation of "criminal." Finally, she exposes the state's priority of upholding property law – the reason she has been brought to court – as morally impoverished, especially as contrasted to the intentions of SOA protesters who wish to respond to "countless lives lost" and "the humanity each soldier must sacrifice."

Changing the scope and mode of seeing through physical encounters need not entail the high cost of being arrested, however. Through their very bodily presence, witnesses shift the terrain of visibility. Koopman continues, "our angle of vision is on the ground, in our bodies, emotional" (2008: 836). Liz corroborates this as she concludes her court statement:

We may try to abstract these deaths, this suffering, call them collateral damage, rebels, insurgency[,] but somewhere someone bends over a grave or kneels to pray for the missing and wonders why no one ever seems to care. I am here then to care, to love, with my body.

(Deligio 2004)

When witnesses bring their bodies to bear on the way that state violence is discussed and understood, the lens is dynamically altered. "To care, to love, with my body" does not require that one cross onto the base at Fort Benning. It merely means witnesses be present, bodily, to see and denounce injustice.

A key way in which these activists seek to alter the dominant lens is by using their own bodies to amplify both the violence endured and the resistance enacted by the state's targets. For WAT participants, highlighting the Guantánamo prisoners' hunger strikes has been central to why the group engages in solidarity fasts. WAT's inaugural action was to travel to Cuba to respond physically to what the group understood as an embodied cry for help. Earlier in this chapter, Frida Berrigan considered the hope and horror of the prisoners' reliance on their bodies as a final means for political contest. Even as WAT has been painfully aware of the dire situation into which the prisoners are thrust, they have sought to hold onto an understanding of solidarity that seeks to empower and uphold the plight of the most impacted. As WAT member Cameron explained:

Good solidarity work is remembering that what we do is support [the] struggle [of the most directly impacted], take the lead from them. You're not the hero of the story, you're never the hero of a story. [Our role is to] let people know what they're doing instead of highlighting our own actions, because the reality is ... [they are] taking the real risks.

However, for the groups under study, taking guidance from the state's targets can sometimes be hard, at other times, impossible. Cameron continued:

I think it's really hard to take direction from the men in Guantánamo, for the obvious reasons. But it started from the hunger strike, right? And then people going down there and trying to respond to the hunger strike, seeing it as an act of resistance and trying to support that resistance ... Even though there's no direct relationship 'cause it's impossible, but seeing, listening, and having an eye out or having contacts with their lawyers, and trying to figure out a way to listen to their voices and take those actions.

Here, Cameron identifies the process of going to the place of violence, becoming more physically proximate, and then bearing witness – "seeing, listening ... trying to figure out a way to listen" – as one of the few modes of solidarity available to WAT. Yet WAT has also been able to use embodied tactics performatively to draw attention to the plight and resistance of the state's most violated. In these instances, WAT has used their greater access to the media, US power brokers, and other members of the public to amplify the prisoners' acts of resistance.

A particularly impactful instance of this occurred when the prospects for closing Guantánamo looked to be the bleakest yet. It was the beginning of Obama's second term, and the administration's efforts to close the military prison had gone from a guarantee to nonexistent. In March of 2013, WAT had gathered for a strategy meeting. There was a marked sense of despair among group members that Matt described as "this feeling that everything we had gained we had lost again." Things were about to change dramatically. Matt continued, "And then the hunger strike came."

The very weekend the group had come together in Chicago, the world learned of a new, massively orchestrated hunger strike at the prison. All but the most elderly detainees were refusing food and medicine. Having already come together for their preplanned gathering, the usually dispersed group of activists was able to mobilize quickly, launching a nationwide, weeklong solidarity fast; street protests across the country; calls to the White House, Department of Defense, and Military Command, all demanding the prison's closure.

The detainees' hunger strike impacted the public conversation and by many accounts was pivotal to igniting new momentum. In May of 2013, President Obama publicly recommitted to close the prison. By the end of 2013, ten detainees who had been long cleared for release were repatriated, a marked shift in policy considering that the President's first term in office had been defined by a political stalemate with Congress over the issue of Guantánamo (Worthington 2015).[7]

WAT's efforts to respond and amplify the detainees' collective action with their own bodies, in addition to more traditional forms of political engagement, exemplified the group's ethos of solidarity. Matt remarked:

We remind ourselves that the answer of how to close Guantánamo most likely will come from Guantánamo itself. I think this hunger strike has proven that to be true ... All of these things that the people we've worked with in all of these organizations have discussed and tried – the years of waiting in court and hearing grand statements by leaders of this country that have no effect – [all of these things] have failed to do what this group of over a hundred men not eating for over a hundred and twenty-five days now has done, which is to bring this issue back into the public conversation.

This is another instance in which embodied forms of resistance – here, the detainees' hunger strike amplified by WAT – reaffirms to these activists the immoral status quo of the state as well as the futility of pursuing change through traditional political avenues. The nation's courts and political leaders, as Matt put it, had not achieved in nearly a decade what the hunger strike did. This was a moment not only of doing good solidarity work, taking leadership from those most impacted, but of coming to understand embodied solidarity as a political tool where no other options had worked. The moment reignited hope that the prison would finally close, and political momentum to make

---

[7] During the summer of 2013, attorney Clifford Sloan was appointed to the State Department as the Special Envoy for Guantánamo Closure, a post that he left at the end of 2014. During his tenure, thirty-nine detainees approved for transfer were released, as opposed to only four in the two years before the 2013 hunger strike (Sloan 2015). In the first months of 2015 directly following Sloan's resignation, the flow of prisoners out of Guantánamo seemed to halt altogether as Congress considered new restrictions on releasing prisoners. By June 2015, though, there once again seemed to be forward progress. Six Yemen nationals were released to Oman, although the Obama Administration had previously refused to transfer anyone from the country of Yemen (Worthington 2015).

change was underway. Almost a year later, WAT member Jeremy reflected on this moment in time:

The hunger strike of the men at Guantánamo [in March 2013] is what brought the issue back into public consciousness in a brilliant and unexpected way. If we played any small role in amplifying their sacrifice and forcing that awareness, then we've accomplished something.

While WAT observed the importance of the detainees' hunger strike as an embodied affront to an otherwise unresponsive power structure, they also understood the stakes for the detainees as nothing less than a fight to the death. Matt was frank in this regard, noting that by the summer of 2013, "More people [had] left [the prison] in coffins than actually being charged and going through any legal process."[8] In this sense, while embodied resistance exposes the charade of "politics as usual" and offers new forms of resistance, the stakes cannot be romanticized, especially not in the case of the state's targets. As Frida asked in her indictment of the current system while the group fasted at the gates of Guantánamo in 2005, "What does it mean for humanity when our *only* political tools are our bodies?"

Solidarity activists use their bodies to pry open the space to see. They travel to obscured sites of state violence and seek to highlight the resistance of the state's targets if and when possible. At the same time, physically challenging and high-risk activism can help them to gain credibility with geographically distant and sometimes seemingly unlikely audiences, a point that I address in this next and final section.

TOUCHING OTHERS, BUILDING ALLIANCE

By putting themselves bodily into spaces and experiences of state violence that the dominant culture keeps hidden, solidarity activists emerge with compelling stories that they can then share broadly. Such demonstrations of commitment often earn these activists credibility that they might not otherwise enjoy. Sometimes this translates into having a broader impact with the public. Other times, it can help to build stronger alliances with those communities most directly impacted by US security policies. Long-term Migrant Trail participant Susan noted the importance of being physically present to the injustices of border enforcement as a means for connecting geographically distant audiences to this reality:

I'm not here in the border region, and I don't get to witness this on a daily basis. My reality in Chicago's very different. Having that interaction with the border, seeing the

---

[8] As of January 2015, nine people had died at Guantánamo, seven from apparent suicide and the other two from medical complications. Only eight had been processed through the, albeit legally questionable, Military Commissions process.

helicopters of the border patrol, the vigilantes, the crazy people with the guns – physically and emotionally and spiritually witnessing all of that and seeing the fence and taking that witness back to Chicago and telling that story is why I feel like I need to come here.

Susan explained that the physicality of this witness holds the key to its value, "It's an event. It's something that's tangible. You can talk about it." Susan was also cognizant of how her privilege functions in this regard, not only *vis á vis* crossing migrants but also in a class-stratified US public sphere. Employed at the time by an organization that paid for her travel and considered the walk to be salaried work time, Susan knew that she had a rare opportunity: "Not everyone can come here ... As a white person who has the institutional power and privilege, I feel that it is my – duty's not the right word but still comes to mind – [to use] my privilege to make social change."

Migrant Trail participant Darlene also saw her participation in the walk as a means for reaching distant audiences, not only those geographically and socially distant from the border but also groups that might seem to be unlikely political allies. Darlene only participated in the Migrant Trail once, in 2011, but held a long-term commitment to immigrant rights work both before and after her time on the walk. In correspondence shared a year and a half after she had participated, Darlene explained that in her very conservative town, "I have come to believe that my ability to relate to conservative white people, mostly religious, is where I might be able to have the most impact in terms of changing hearts and arguing a pro- immigrant position." Darlene explained that because she had participated in the walk, "people are much more apt to hear my first-hand witness to the border situation than if I hadn't participated. People see that I have an investment in immigration and am not just spouting sound bites."

Darlene's "conservative" Christian community valued the fact that Darlene would engage in the physical demands of a pilgrimage rather than partake in politically expedient and shallow speech acts, what she terms "spouting sound bites." In the Protestant church she attended, there may also be an element of the Puritan ethic at play that values hardship and sacrifice as morally righteous. Darlene gained credibility and clout because she was willing to embody her moral convictions in the face of significant discomforts.

Alexa of SOA Watch also believed that her experiences with high-risk activism afforded her a unique platform for discussing the violence of the US security state. Alexa noted how the large-scale civil disobedience of SOA Watch participants dramatized the issue in compelling ways: "It's something that really calls to the people that we're trying to share this story with ... hearing about the hundreds of people that have done all kinds of beautiful, creative actions, that is so gripping." Having been arrested twice at Fort Benning and serving six months in prison for her second trespass, Alexa now carried the SOA story through her various social networks. She explained, "I continue to work different jobs and meet new people, and talking about this kind of action has always been like, 'Wow, tell me about that. What was prison like?' It's a way to introduce the subject of the SOA and imperialism."

Alexa's experience posits a notable juxtaposition to what are often the structural impediments and stigma that others face in the aftermath of having gone to prison. Even though she is trailed by a criminal record, Alexa carries a sacrificial experience that tends to be valued by those she meets. This, of course, is in part because of her race and class privilege, a point that warrants a bit of nuance, as will be elaborated in Chapter 5. The fact that a mass of people would collectively and volitionally break the law and go to jail for a cause positions Alexa's prison time within the framework of moral principle rather than deviance, earning her audiences who are often eager to learn more.

If the embodiment and high-investment of witnessing appeals to mainstream publics who might otherwise ignore or not see the realities of state violence, risk-taking can also express solidarity and commitment to a most important audience: the state's targets and those who survive them. Some of the most meaningful moments for the groups in this study are when they are able to connect either spiritually or emotionally with the state's targets. Yet such connections can also generate more instrumental outcomes. SOA Watch participant Siobhan noted that US activists' civil disobedience at Fort Benning has played an important role in building the trust necessary for more long-term alliance building with communities in Latin America. She explained:

[Civil disobedience] has been very important because when [SOA Watch participants] go to Central and Latin America, the people are amazed that that there are individuals in the US willing to go to jail. I mean [these activists in Latin America] have no choice. They risk arrest for any kind of action. But the fact that people would intentionally put themselves in harm's way is apparently very impressive.

When those who have the privilege and practical freedoms to avoid the bodily risks of imprisonment *choose* to put themselves on the line, these expressions are often received as an ultimate expression of solidarity. These bodily and high-risk demonstrations of commitment are not just emotionally satisfying to all parties. They have been instrumental in allowing SOA Watch to work with communities throughout Latin America in demanding that these national governments stop sending armies and police forces to the SOA for training. For those who are under the thumb of violence, the knowledge that there are distant others who also resist with such a high level of conviction is heartening. In some instances, it offers psychic rewards; in others, it helps to build more lasting alliances.

CONCLUSION

Nonviolent movements throughout history have used high-risk tactics to express and instantiate commitment to a moral vision and political project.

This often entails a physicality of witnessing. For solidarity activists who have not experienced the acute state violence that they contest, embodied tactics hold a particular importance. By embodying their political commitments, these activists force themselves to pay attention to injustices that the dominant order seduces mainstream publics to ignore.

In this chapter, I suggest that embodied tactics function in four different ways for these activists. First, the physicality of their witness allows these activists to refuse the traditional political avenues offered them by a governing structure predicated on moneyed, elite interests and the rarefied rhetoric of the state. Second, through felt experience, they feel and bring close those whom a mainstream American political culture has rendered morally, socially, and politically distant. Third, embodied practices allow these groups to get closer to sites of state violence and, in some instances, to amplify the resistance of the state's targets. This is a key part of what many understand as doing "good solidarity work." Fourth, the fact of their high-risk activism at times wins these activists certain more traditionally considered social movement goals, appealing to unlikely audiences and building alliances with the survivors of state violence.

By putting their bodies into their political action, these activists render macro-political dynamics into deeply intimate experience. In so doing, they cannot but be touched. This engenders transformations. One of these is feeling closer to the aggrieved and insisting bodily that the disappeared be brought back into the public sphere from which they have been excised. Yet the transformations of witnessing go further to include all kinds of untethering from the dominant order. I now turn to the internal transformations and forms of subject work necessary for being in solidarity and for living the life of a witness.

5

Ascetic Practice and Prefigurative Community

Tracy and I sat on the curb. It was my first time traveling to Columbus, Georgia, for the SOA Watch weekend vigil. It was 2013, and on that Saturday afternoon in late November, the place felt more like a street fair than a protest. Various musical groups and spoken word artists took the stage about 200 yards down the road from where Tracy and I sat. A small crowd had gathered in front of the performers, an audience replete with tie-dyed shirts, Carhartt pants, and pins announcing various social justice causes. Behind them, lining both sides of the now blocked-off street, different organizations had set up booths – peace activists and immigrant groups next to small workers associations and progressive religious societies.

I had encountered long-time SOA Watch protester Tracy the evening before in one of the many workshops planned at the Columbus Convention Center. She graciously agreed to be interviewed. When I found her among the crowd the following day, Tracy eagerly began her story before I could get into any of the formalities of a proper interview. I had to cut her off briefly and ask to sit, where at the very least I had a chance to balance my digital recorder on a knee and shield us from friendly shouts and interruptions.

My recording of our interview opens with Tracy explaining, "I sent these little squares of origami paper in to myself before I went to prison." Tracy had crossed the line at Fort Benning eight years earlier; she was sentenced to two months in federal prison. At the time, her children were were quite young, and she had been taken to Texas, far enough from her home in Illinois that family was unable to visit. Before she was put in prison, Tracy sent herself squares of colorful origami paper. While in prison, she explains, "I started folding these colorful birds, peace cranes."

The other imprisoned women were curious about Tracy's activities:

People started coming up to me 'cause I was confined to the unit. "What are you doing?" I would tell them the story of Sadako and the thousand peace cranes and teach them how to fold cranes.

The story that Tracy told is that of Sadako Sasaki, who in 1945 was an infant in Hiroshima when the United States dropped the atomic bomb on Japan. At the age of twelve, Sadako developed leukemia. She began to fold a thousand origami cranes, inspired by a Japanese legend that such an undertaking would afford her a wish. Sadako wished to live. Although she swiftly succumbed to the cancer and was buried with her origami peace cranes, her story is today a formative legend of the transnational peace and nuclear disarmament movement. The peace crane has come to represent Sadako's plight.[1]

Tracy believed that in addition to the story and its symbolism, there was power in the colors. "In prison everything is drab, the walls, everything. And so I believe it was the color of the birds, the colorfulness. I kept folding birds, and people kept learning."

At some point, the women began to puzzle over the fate of the cranes.

We were now hiding cranes underneath our beds. You weren't supposed to have all this stuff. Some people were cutting squares out of magazines and newspapers because the paper that was for the peace cranes was getting sent back. They were denying my mail of peace cranes, of paper.

The women decided they wanted to share the peace cranes with everyone, no matter their institutional position. "They wanted to give a crane to everybody in the prison, a peace crane, and to give a peace crane to all of the staff. So it would've been about eighteen hundred birds."

The prison authorities, however, judged that the cranes posed a serious threat. This was nothing less than an origami uprising. When the warden learned that the women were planning to distribute the cranes, he intervened immediately.

Tracy explains, "He came to me and he said, 'if you hold this vigil that gives all these birds, you'll be inciting a riot, and that's punishable by five years in prison.'" Five years of prison for folding peace cranes. To Tracy, the message was clear.

What it showed me was how afraid they were of community, of building relationships, because the whole idea of prison is to keep people at each other's throat. There's one or two COs [corrections officers] for two or three hundred people on a unit. And if all those people are all united, [the COs are] afraid of being overthrown.

---

[1] The most popular telling of the story, turned into a children's book and featured in at least one film, suggests that Sadako became too weak to finish the task and died having folded about 600 cranes. By her family's account, however, Sadako folded more than 1,000 paper cranes before her death.

It is not a coincidence that the most urgent story Tracy wished to tell me was this account of folding origami peace cranes in prison. This experience testifies to one of the central undertakings of the activists in this study: forging solidarity in the face of the state's systematized divisiveness. This solidarity is both that which is imagined and enacted with the state's targets through acts of ethical witness as well as that which is enacted with each other. In their effort to take a principled stance against the US security state, these activists become *communities* in resistance.

When she told the others about what the peace cranes symbolized and showed them how to fold them, Tracy and the other women entered into a lineage of resistance, constituted through the smallest of practices yet the most ambitious forms of oppositional consciousness. Even if the power of the state portended disproportionate repression for the folding of paper cranes, the psychic rewards should not be underestimated. Developing relationships in the face of suffering generates a kind of hope. It brings little bits of color into a world of drab.

It might seem odd to call Tracy's experience in prison ascetic. She was not alone, silent, fasting, or doing anything obviously pious, at least in this instance. In this chapter, however, I suggest that Tracy's stance was indeed an ascetic political practice, and that solidarity witness includes an important ascetic dimension. It is important to remember that Tracy was in prison because of her own carefully chosen actions that adamantly renounced the dominant order at great cost to herself and her family. These actions ended her marriage. They took her away from her young children. While in prison, Tracy became ill from repeated bouts of food poisoning. She was removed from kitchen duty and began folding peace cranes to manage the boredom. Tracy had taken significant personal, bodily, financial, and social risks when she went to prison. Her act of refusing the dominant order through civil disobedience was a mode of self-discipline that led to personal and social transformations, both for the women who were with her in prison and for the SOA Watch campaign to which she returned. She worked to produce a self in relationship with others more able to resist and struggle against the state.

In the previous chapter, I examined the embodied aspects of witnessing as instantiations of solidarity, ways of feeling closer to the targets of state violence as well as performatively amplifying their plight for various audiences. I also began to point to the ways that embodied forms of resistance allow the activists in this study to divest: from their privilege, from the seductions of the dominant order, and from political avenues that have proven ineffectual and even venal. There is more to be said, however, about the high-risk and embodied practices of witnessing, in particular, the subjective and movement-building dimensions such practices acquire.

In this chapter, I turn more squarely to the subject work of solidarity witness anticipated briefly in the preceding chapters. Through their culturally potent rituals in the public sphere and through personal, *felt* journeys to be closer to the aggrieved, these activists engage in practices of embodied and sociopolitical withdrawal that craft new ways of understanding, of being and of refusing. In this sense, I understand solidarity witness as an ascetic political practice. The activists in this study undertake physical, material, and emotional sacrifices as forms of discipline that enable them to shrug off what Ken Butigan (2003) terms "the conditioning inscribed on and in the body by the social world" (28). By relinquishing certain comforts of the dominant order, they cultivate an oppositional praxis, a consciousness, and a set of actions capable of profound and long-term resistance.

In considering solidarity witness as ascetic, I borrow from Richard Valantasis (2008), who defines asceticism as the crafting of a new subjectivity:

The ascetic creates more than a basic social identity or role, an articulated self, a persona, or a personality: the ascetic constructs an entirely new agency capable of functioning in a different and resistant way to the dominant culture that defines identity, personality, and social functions from hegemonic power. (103)

For Valantasis, the concept of agency suggests a form of power, and it is precisely this power that is in play for the participants in this study. A key to this understanding is an asceticism that is both socially and politically productive. Asceticism is traditionally associated with the monastic life, which, if communal, is also solitary, silent, and centrally about piety. Solidarity witness, in contrast, is primarily oriented to this-worldly concerns and forms of human relationship.

In what follows, I begin with some key conceptual dimensions to what I am terming the ascetic political practice of solidarity witness. The chapter then proceeds with two main aims. First, I trace this ascetic practice as a personal quest that brings sometimes unexpected transformations, allows these activists to link their personal journeys to more macro social processes, and serves as a training exercise in the nonviolent ethos central to the practice of solidarity witness. I then turn to argue that this ascetic dimension is fundamentally communal. The subject work of solidarity witness aims to craft a form of collective subjectivity that starkly contrasts with what the dominant system demands. I show how prefigurative community is forged through disciplined forms of renunciation and becomes itself an ascetic practice. In turn, the psychic rewards of community offer an important source of inspiration, and sometimes solace, when tangible victories do not materialize or fall short of expectations. This experience of community is a form of transcendence, analogous to the transcendent dimension of more religiously inclined ascetic processes. It helps activists to overcome bourgeois individualism, and in this, to hedge against isolation and burnout.

Through their fasting, pilgrimage, and jail time, these activists are transformed. They learn lessons about their own roles in dominant society and prepare themselves to resist the state with enhanced conviction and commitment. They put resistant modes of solidarity into practice not only through their efforts to reach out to the targets of state violence but also through their practice of prefigurative community. This was part of what Tracy took away from her time in prison. In sharing in the practice of folding peace cranes, all involved were learning powerful lessons of human comity.

THE PARAMETERS OF ASCETIC POLITICAL PRACTICE

I have come to view the annual SOA/WHINSEC protests as very large therapeutic exercises … crossing that fence was tantamount to releasing a dark and desperate cry from within my own heart that has been forever bruised and weighted by the intensely unthinkable violence created by military institutions like WHINSEC … This doesn't mean that each of us should have walked across that fence … It demands that we each find our own way of crying out against the despair of militarism and violence.

Donte Smith, statement to the court at sentencing (Smith 2006)

When SOA Watch participant Donte Smith describes the tactics of witnessing as "therapeutic exercises," he points to something integral about social movements in general and solidarity witness as an ascetic political practice more specifically. In their efforts to change society, activists must also change themselves. This is a basic prerequisite for forging the new relationships and structures that lasting social change requires. In this way, social movements can be understood as "therapeutic," or at least involving a kind of subject work, in the interest of being ultimately subversive. Such an insight has long been proposed by those engaged in revolutionary praxis. Even Karl Marx, whose work is typically thought to be focused on class struggle and social structure as opposed to cultural and subject work, observed that workers needed a revolution not only to change their external conditions but to throw off the internalized conditioning holding them back. Through social struggle, the proletariat would be "ridding itself of all the muck of ages and become fitted to found society anew" (Marx & Engels 1845: 60).

The activists in this study, I argue, are involved in a practice of political asceticism. Their modes of self-discipline, such as fasting, pilgrimage, and jail time, renounce dominant society and craft alternative ways of seeing, knowing, and being. *Asceticism* takes its etymological roots from the Greek word *aksesis*, meaning practice or training. The ascetic engages in a set of practices in order to become more pious, ethical, or courageous (Butigan 2003). Traditionally associated with the religious life, asceticism has included relinquishing sex, food, and other bodily pleasures to maintain a primary relationship with God (Miles 1981). A number of theorists, however, have considered asceticism beyond strictly religious contexts, defining the concept more broadly as a mode of self-craft.[2] Michel Foucault (1997), for instance, proposes asceticism as "an

---

[2] Of course, Weber is central to the sociological canon when it comes to theorizing asceticism. Weber (1904) argued that the Protestant ethic, with its concomitant practices of asceticism,

exercise of the self on the self by which one attempts to develop and transform oneself, and to attain to a certain mode of being" (282). By this understanding, the ascetic is a self who, through practices of embodied discipline, becomes a different kind of person. Foucault is quite skeptical about the capacity of the social subject to escape the constraints of the dominant order in any dramatic fashion. This ascetic practice thus offers iterations of self-conduct that are ethically inclined. Sometimes the will to ethical practice leans away from the hegemonic; sometimes it leans into it.

In moving toward an understanding of ascetic political practice, I borrow from Foucault but wish to hold on to some of the more religious undertones of the term that Foucault relinquishes. The asceticism found among the groups in this study is indeed a practice of the self on the self. It includes forms of self-discipline in order to create a new kind of subjectivity in renunciation of the dominant order. Yet the ascetic practices that the activists in this study undertake are animated by religious undertones. This is so both in terms of the tactics these activists choose and the explanatory frameworks they use. Fasting, pilgrimage, and civil disobedience are practices that emerge from religious traditions even if their impact in this instance intends a political, as much as a spiritual, transformation.

The second part of the ascetic practice at play here, somewhat distinct from how asceticism is often imagined, rests in its collective and overtly sociopolitical aspects. Although monastic life has always been communal, traditional ascetics undertake a quest of piety that is largely solitary. The ascetic political practice of solidarity witness, on the other hand, is centrally organized around the pursuit of prefigurative community. As theorized by Carl Boggs (1977), prefiguration is "the embodiment, within the ongoing political practice of a movement, of those forms of social relations, decision-making, culture, and human experience that are the ultimate goal."[3] Through the enactment of prefigurative community, these activists produce a resistant mode of solidarity. They model the kinds of relationships that they wish to see in society writ large.

---

was transmuted from a focus on piety to that of economic productivity in order to serve the exigencies of the rise of industrial capitalism. My own conception of asceticism does not borrow much from Weber's, but this work bears mention as one of the first and certainly most deeply influential accounts of the social functions of asceticism.

[3] Boggs (1977) offers an important review of an entire prefigurative Marxist program that resists statist solutions, centralized control, and all forms of domination and hierarchy. This agenda, however, is part of a more traditional Marxist telos in which the ultimate goal is known. I am not suggesting that witnessing groups are part of this specific revolutionary tradition. In fact, the groups here are gesturing to a kind of movement impulse that is developed as something of a counterpoint to traditional class-based movements, especially as it takes shape in the New Left. In contrast to what Boggs presents, solidarity witness aims at something less precise, a move toward an end that cannot yet be fully formulated. Stuart Hall (1986) calls this "marxism without guarantees."

Forging prefigurative community does not necessarily contradict what asceticism can mean. Indeed, in his work on asceticism across cultures, Gavin Flood (2004) observes that "the restriction undergone in asceticism is a necessary condition for the intensification of subjectivity that transcends desire and individualism" (14). Ascetic practice instructs that in resisting one's immediate desires with intention and discipline, something more expansive or purposeful can be experienced. In the case of solidarity witness, embodied discipline allows activists to transcend narrow forms of self-interest and bourgeois individualism in pursuit of a different vision. Through their modes of ascetic practice, these activists renounce dominant forms of politics and social life. They prepare themselves bodily, psychically, socially and, for many, spiritually to better live a life of resistance. I begin this exploration with some of the elementary journeys of political asceticism.

POLITICAL ASCETICISM'S BEGINNINGS

I think spiritual practice is such an important aspect to me of being part of Witness Against Torture ... Many people in the group pray, we fast, we chant, we walk with the hoods over our heads, which is a kind of walking meditation. It's really quite incredible all the stuff that's kind of built into it ... I believe that for us as activists we really need this contemplative and reflective piece. I think it keeps us grounded in what we do.

– Faith, WAT

Faith of WAT explains some of the key aspects of what solidarity witness entails. Praying, fasting, chanting, and meditation (along with pilgrimage and jail time) are all aspects of what I am terming ascetic political practice. This is a mode of political engagement that is ritualized, often solemn, embodied and punctuated by space for reflection. For many, this mode of protest is also a deeply spiritual experience. Faith believes this is important for keeping activists conscientious of their purpose. To witness is to see clearly and actively what the state occludes.

For many of the activists in this study, however, the practice of witnessing, and certainly the transformations it engendered, took them by surprise. Forms of embodied renunciation were often experienced as very personal, physical achievements, at least initially. This has developmental specificity. Many of the formative studies of ascetic practice suggest that what ultimately becomes a sacred voyage often begins with a deeply personal and often bodily struggle. In his influential work on pilgrimage, Victor Turner (1973) explains that for the pilgrim beginning the path, "the many long miles he covers are mainly secular, everyday miles" (214). Discussing the Irish pilgrimage to Croagh Patrick, Lawrence Taylor (2007) also observes that an initial component of the journey "seems particularly open to notions of individual trial and transformation, no doubt aided by the all too vivid embodiment of the experience" (385). It is only through persistence, time, and experience that the journey takes on additional meaning.

Migrant Trail participant Dave described his first time participating in the walk in just this way. A social worker in his early sixties, Dave learned about the walk at an academic conference on migration. While he was generally disposed to helping others, he did not think of himself as an activist or as a "risk taker." Dave recalls waiting at the church in Tucson on the first day of the walk: "I was scared shitless. I really didn't know what I was doing ... that was a pretty risky thing for me. I've never been a huge risk taker. I'm kind of a stereotypic, middle class, conservative guy." While not politically conservative, Dave uses this term to describe a general lifestyle – married with children, retired after working in the school system, and regularly attending church.

Though cell phone access is limited during the first days of the walk, Dave was finally able to reach his wife on the fourth night. "I felt like I'd had this experience that I could not translate to anyone, including her. And I just began to sob on the phone." His spouse was concerned that he was sick or injured. Dave struggled to communicate the magnitude of his feelings: "[I]t was this huge experience and emotion that I didn't know much of how to explore with her." After years of participating in the walk, Dave can now more easily articulate what the Migrant Trail means to him:

The walk has become one of the central parts of my life both politically and spiritually. The experience of being on the walk is very close to what some religious people have experienced on pilgrimages, where they get away from their normal life and they re-experience their relationship both to the world as well as [to] God.

It is not uncommon for witnesses to find themselves surprised by the transformative experience of physically demanding tactics, and to struggle in explaining how a personal, physical exploration had taken on complex emotional and spiritual significance. Even after participating in the Migrant Trail for years, Molly observed, "I don't know how to talk about it ... about stuff that is buried deep, in emotions and spiritual beliefs, convictions of the heart and mind and soul." Molly went on to explain how she had come to understand the journey as both religious and humanitarian, though the former interpretation initially felt quite awkward.

For me, what it's become very personally – I use this word pilgrimage. I used it at first a little strangely, like it didn't fit well ... But I now claim that as what I do. I think it's a pilgrimage of sorts for the betterment of humanity. And then there's a whole kind of interior spiritual thing that happens for me ... It's just been perhaps one of the most transformational things I've ever done.

For Molly, the term "pilgrimage" speaks to the subjective transformation she has experienced on and through the walk, a feeling that she suggests has a decidedly spiritual dimension. At the same time, this transformation has also become profoundly political for her. "There's been an incredible growth for me spiritually and with social activism ... And I feel spurred on to my own stuff from there." As an educator, Molly has centrally incorporated migration issues in her classroom, spoken about the Migrant Trail with various student groups and her church, and has incorporated the transformations the walk has had on her into her scholarship.

Those who came from backgrounds in which ascetic practice was familiar often had an easier time speaking to the ascetic dimension of their chosen tactics. WAT member Carol, who had lived and worked with Catholic Worker communities for almost a decade and was familiar with the logics of ascetic practice, described fasting as "a sort of a centering exercise and a spiritual practice. And that practice can bring you any number of places, but it's a discipline." For activists that adopt ascetic practices, whether informed by religious motivations or not, moving away from one's daily comforts is a key element of this "discipline."

Whereas religious ascetics relinquish comforts as a way of getting closer to God, for ascetics with a social change agenda, relinquishing comforts is a way to loosen those attachments that might prevent them from becoming part of the new social order they wish to create. WAT member Joanne observed that after a week of fasting in solidarity with the hunger-striking detainees:

I came away being less attached to the idea that I always have to eat … it's liberating not to be so imprisoned by our little petty wants and needs of the day. Or you could frame it bigger, that you're not so imprisoned or attached to money or power, the things of the world that can seduce you away from a moral or ethical path.

For Joanne, abstaining from food is a first step in identifying how she is currently enmeshed in systems of dominance, how structures of "money and power" work on her subjectively, through the body as well as her psychic life. Being able to relinquish her "petty wants and needs" was, in turn, "liberating."

WAT member Faith also drew connections between the psychic, social, and spiritual benefits of fasting:

Really we are such a gluttonous society. The idea of going without food is so foreign to people. Fasting is kind of a pulling away from that, which allows me to also pull away from the norm that we are this nation that tortures. I know that I can be useful when I can be emptied of my ego, when I can be emptied of the culture that I am part of. It's a kind of emptying that also allows the Holy Spirit to move.

For Faith, the small gesture of personal sacrifice and discomfort is a way to break a chain that she sees linking herself at the most intimate level of her ego to a dominant cultural norm, that of being a "nation that tortures." Interrupting these linkages is also spiritual practice, what she describes as making space for "the Holy Spirit to move."

For the participants in this study, who understand themselves as inhabiting a social position of privilege and relative comfort, ascetic practices often reveal how the self has been forged as well as fractured by dominant social and political arrangements. I turn now to a more in-depth examination of how the ascetic journey helps activists to locate themselves within broader social and political dynamics and forge resistant subjectivities.

ASCETICISM AND THE SOCIOLOGICAL IMAGINATION

The vectors of dominance and oppression that the solidarity activists in this study protest because they are so violently exercised on the bodies of others impact upon them as well, if in very different ways. When they refuse the comforts and seductions of the dominant order, these activists come to new understandings of how their own subjectivities are shaped by those dynamics from which they seek to step away. Flood (2004) suggests that one of the defining features of ascetic subjectivity is that it "links self and cosmos, inner experience and world" (14). Often taken to be a religious or existential observation, this also has relevant implications for solidarity activists as they grapple with the complex ways in which they are implicated in dominant social relations. Valantasis (2008) suggests that through modes of self-discipline, "ascetics reveal the inner workings and effects of dominant structures" (115). For these solidarity activists, embodied challenges and high-risk activism serve as complex avenues of self-discovery and self-craft. Through ascetic practice, they develop a mode of consciousness that C. Wright Mills (1959) terms "the sociological imagination," able to link their "personal troubles" with "public issues of social structure" in ways that might not always reveal themselves so obviously.

Many of the activists in this study found that social privilege was a complex inheritance that led to its own forms of entrapment and harm. Brought up "middle class, white, suburban, well educated" by a conservative family in the Midwest, Maya's understanding of the world began to shift when she got a driver's license and was afforded greater mobility around her racially segregated city. She started asking, "How is it that I grow up in this neighborhood and go to this high school that's entirely white?" Maya explains that her teachers and family would talk about "things in the world that are 'out there and scary' – people who are different, bad people, [that] we need to stay as insulated as possible." This troubled Maya even before she had the resources to analyze its origins.

As she came to understand more, Maya felt what Kelly Kraemer (2007) suggests is common among those who discover that their own unearned privilege is predicated on others' disadvantage: "the constant, clamoring call to action ... to reject that advantage and help to redesign the social system" (27). Yet this social system is complex. In the disproportionate opportunities offered to her and others like her, Maya also identified a set of social and psychic harms: "I grew up like lots of kids in the suburbs, wanting to be the best, needing to learn how to be the best, feeling that competition. Any time I wasn't the best I was somehow broken or not good enough or wrong or something." Raised under the yoke of cutthroat individualism, Maya vacillated between feeling "broken" and confronting a sense of "emptiness or this hole."

Maya's introduction to civil disobedience as a young adult offered a different path by which she could confront the damaging modes of socialization with which she was raised. "Coming from the background that I come from, civil disobedience is an incredible way to take a risk that is seen societally as something that's like bad or wrong or silly or a waste of resources," she explains. Furthermore, high-risk activism was transformative because of the embodiment and emotions of the experience. Maya continued: "To be put in a situation where your cuffs are really tight or you feel really stressed out or you really need something and you can't get it ... those experiences of discomfort can shape us into people that are more compassionate and more understanding." This is the kind of self-craft that ascetic practice can powerfully engender.

Like Maya, Alexa of SOA Watch, found civil disobedience to be empowering, explaining high-risk activism as a confrontation with those structures of domination that had made themselves known in her life and on her body. In her decision to cross the line at Fort Benning a second time, an act which she knew would send her to prison, Alexa understood that her social privilege offered a measure of protection. She explained that as "a young, white woman from a lot of mixed but partially class-privileged background," going to prison would not be financially or legally devastating. At the time of her civil disobedience, she was attending a Quaker college where she could remain enrolled and even take a correspondence course. "It was a very supportive environment," she laughed. Alexa explained that despite these privileges, engaging in civil disobedience "was really important to me because, like a lot of women, I'm a survivor of trauma and violence." Alexa sought to reclaim her body, a body that had been victimized by a society that devalues and objectifies women, and so teaches people to victimize them. Alexa understood her social position complexly, interweaving a personal account of gendered vulnerability with the need to speak back to the US security state. "Making this statement of peace and solidarity was a way that I could use my body and my voice to enter this dialogue that we're all a part of." US intervention in Latin America is a system that Alexa believes she has a responsibility to contest because she is a US citizen. Her responsibility to combat violence was thus multiple: reclaiming a violated self while taking a stand against a hemispheric (and world-scale) violator, the US security state. The decision to get arrested was a way of simultaneously mobilizing her privilege to denounce the oppression of others while asserting agency in the face of the violence she too had faced.

Like Maya and Alexa, Migrant Trail participant Catalina also found that the process of embodying her stance against a hegemonic order offered a mechanism for reclamation, a means to both discover and position herself more firmly within her social and familial history. Among these activists, Catalina was rather uniquely positioned, since her own mother, an undocumented woman who had crossed the US–Mexico border by foot, had felt the security state directly. Catalina explained that the embodied experience of the Migrant Trail offered her a sense of greater proximity to her mother's experience:

On the third day I had to ride because I just couldn't stand the heat. I thought about my mother walking. When she got lost, when she got separated from my father, she had to walk like almost a week by herself. And I just couldn't ... I think so highly of my mother. I mean, I always have and always will. But it's just like my perspective on her has changed a lot.

A year and a half after this Migrant Trail experience, Catalina explained how coming to understand her mother's journey by approximating its physical dimensions herself was a process of self-discovery and empowerment: "The Migrant Trail for me was more about my personal growth and identity. The issues of the border were not new to me … but it was a growing step in my identity and understanding more of my roots."

As opposed to other solidarity activists, ascetic practice was not so much a means for Catalina to relinquish the seductions of the dominant order or the damaging impacts of privilege. Rather, it was a way to embody her mother's stories of crossing and, in so doing, arrive at a greater self-understanding. Nevertheless, Catalina's Migrant Trail experience exemplified Butigan's (2003) description of the asceticism of pilgrimage. For Butigan's desert protesters, the journey to the Nevada Test Site became "a place to reclaim lost or forgotten parts of oneself and one's culture, to bear witness to death and to life … a place to go *to* – temporarily leaving behind the normal routine of life – and to return *from*" (163). For Catalina, leaving the routine of her daily life to undertake the challenging walk offered a similar space for such reclamation. She returned from this journey with a deeper understanding of herself, having embodied a piece of her mother's experience.

Taken together, Maya, Alexa, and Catalina's perspectives well illustrate the complexities of responding to the dynamics of privilege and oppression that many of these activists understand to be one of their formative tasks. Feminist scholars have long observed how race, class, gender, and the other dimensions of social power intersect and rearticulate each other in complex and dynamic ways (hooks 1984; Lorde 1984; Cocks 1989; Collins 1991; Crenshaw 1991). No one is merely privileged or oppressed, and no one's experience of social life can be reduced to a single feature of her social identity. For Maya, confronting unearned privilege and its links to the oppression of others also meant untangling the psychic and social impoverishment that came with the culture of privilege in which she was raised. For Alexa, being complexly located in a series of privileges and oppressions became an impetus to act. As a supposed beneficiary of the US security state, she felt she needed to take a stand against her own government, and doing so with her body was the strongest way she could do this. By embodying her moral and political vision, she also sought to counter the gendered and sexual oppression she had experienced on and through her body as a woman victimized by sexual violence. Finally, Catalina's was a somewhat atypical journey among the activists in this study, a process of self-discovery that sought to incorporate the stories and experiences of crossing migrants into her own familial lineage.

The complexity and fluidity of social location generate important questions for those seeking to link their personal journeys to a more collective moral and political vision, to enact the sociological imagination. Social movements provide a key arena for acquiring this form of consciousness; they enable participants to see the social world in new ways and to learn about the psychic impacts of dominance. In turn, movement participants often come to inhabit a special role in society, able to share these forms of consciousness more broadly. This is what Eyerman and Jamison (1991) indicate when they argue that social movements are "knowledge projects" integral to shaping the ways of thinking of dominant society. This is also how Valantasis (2008) understands the purpose of asceticism as a form of social and political communication:

The ascetic exposes the existing power structures of the dominant society ... ascetic alterity, that is, reveals the underlying systems of identity formation and of instruments for creating social solidarity. (107)

In their ascetic journeys of self-discovery and principled renunciation, those engaged in the practices of solidarity witness reveal to themselves how the dominant social order has forged their identities. They also identify a series of alienations, embarrassments, and feelings of unease that accompany bourgeois life – what the supposed winners in the US security state are offered in exchange for their cooperation and complicity with dominance. Importantly, Valantasis here suggests that ascetic alterity is not solely about shaping a different self, but also about exposing and relinquishing the forces that create dominant modes of "social solidarity." For those in this study, those dominant forms of solidarity are the ones that are crafted by and through the US security state. These include a chauvinist nationalism that disavows and vilifies the targets of state violence. As political ascetics, the activists in this study strive to craft alternative forms of self and of solidarity in order to contest the US security state and the bourgeois values that uphold it. Before turning squarely to the collective aspects of ascetic practice, however, I discuss asceticism as a mode of political preparation for better resisting the state.

"NON-VIOLENT TRAINING MUST BE OF A DIFFERENT KIND"

SOA Watch participant Theresa Cusimano had practiced nonviolence for years. She had committed to it as a philosophy and planned for it in various protest events. Nevertheless, Theresa admits, "I doubted its importance before I was actually in prison."

While incarcerated for her civil disobedience at the gates of Fort Benning, Theresa witnessed extreme horrors. Soon after her prison stint began, Theresa's cellmate committed suicide, which Theresa attributes to the withholding of the woman's needed medications. Theresa was herself punished by prison personnel – placed in solitary confinement, denied clean water and requests for food that would not exacerbate her celiac disease. Theresa explains that the prison medic "didn't know what to do with me." He began to beat her. Theresa knew that if she attempted to defend herself, she would be guilty of assaulting a federal officer. Her rights as a prisoner were tenuous at best. "I had rights on paper, but not rights in reality. I had no witness. The truth was going to be their truth." Under this acute violence, Theresa explains, "I came outside my body and surrendered." Certainly this was an important survival mechanism, psychologically and physically. However, she also understood this as an impetus to nonviolence that maintained her integrity and, she surmises, may have also saved her life.

That is when I learned the power of nonviolence because he could have beaten me to death. He beat me as far as he did, which has done a lot of damage. But I didn't want to join in his violence.

Theresa's experience is extreme by her own estimation as well as in comparison to most of the activists with whom I spoke, who have not faced physical abuse of this magnitude and are not forced to consider their response under such circumstances. Theresa is uncertain that her civil disobedience was worth the cost to herself. She endured great violence for little tangible political impact. Yet she takes from her time in prison ethical lessons that are not dissimilar from how others reflect on their high-risk, embodied tactics:

The experience has changed me in a very radical way ... in a way that 27 years of education did not accomplish. You can read about injustice; you can work on injustice; you can be friends with people who have experienced it. When you experience it at the level I experienced it, it changes you. With change, with growth, is pain.

The concept of asceticism stems from the Greek term for training, *aksesis*. The activists in this study undertake embodied, often high-risk practices, in order to train themselves to be the kinds of participants that their movement efforts require. They embrace forms of discomfort, and occasionally extreme suffering, as part of the work of becoming an ethical witness. This is the change, growth, and pain that Theresa describes. Training is a key element of any good political practice. The activists in this study are training not only for undertaking ever more risky actions but also for the opportunity to change themselves and society, to maintain and deepen their commitments.

Building on the pacifist traditions of Gandhi and Martin Luther King Jr., these activists commit to an ethic of nonviolence, meaning they will do no harm to other beings or property. As part of this ethic, they agree to accept the legal repercussions of their civil disobedience, including complying with law enforcement officials who seek to remove or arrest them. Nevertheless, translating the ethic of nonviolent resistance into bodily practice is neither easy nor necessarily intuitive. Many remarked that it took intention and practice to enact nonviolence when the instincts of bodily self-protection take hold. During his nonviolent leadership against British Colonialism in India, Mohandas Gandhi observed, "We all know more or less what military training is like. But we have hardly ever thought that non-violent training must be of a different kind" (1940). The forms of embodied self-discipline and collective resistance undertaken by these groups are precisely this kind of training.

The encounter with law enforcement during and after civil disobedience often became one of the most challenging and meaningful moments in which to enact this ethic of nonviolence. Bodily submission to state authorities was often described as a counterintuitive embodiment – having to physically do the opposite of what one would normally choose. This is part of the logic of ascetic practice, restraining oneself from bodily desire to acquire a different kind of existence. WAT member Faith reflected on a direct action in which the group expected to be arrested but were instead physically dragged out of the way by police.

I remember my initial reaction when the cop grabbed me was to really pull away from him. I'm not used to a man putting his hands on me and was not comfortable. The natural thing for me to do was to get out of his hands, get out of his grip.

Whether this "natural" reaction was an automatic fight-or-flight response or a product of dominant socialization was unclear to her. Regardless, because she and the rest of her group had committed to be nonviolent, she resisted her impulse to escape:

I think because of the preparation with the group, and [the fact that] I was really committed to doing this action, gave me the ability to go limp and not fight it. And not run from it. That really really wasn't what I wanted to do … [but] being clear on what our intentions were, I was able to go limp in that situation and let the police officer drag me.

Succumbing in this instance was ascetic practice. Faith had trained herself in both a philosophy and set of actions. Her discipline allowed her to better resist both the state and her own inclinations.

The purpose of such actions, of course, is not to simply allow law enforcement to abuse. Activists would much prefer that they not be put in these uncomfortable and often dangerous encounters with those who wield disproportionate power. The imagery of the state exerting disproportionate force on those who are not bodily resisting, however, captured by the mainstream media and those who see the action, importantly dramatizes the state's disproportionate use of force. This is the affective logic to which nonviolent activists have long appealed: seeing law enforcement drag away peaceful dissenters is a visibly and emotionally evocative affront to the democratic ideal in which the freedom to peaceably assemble and communicate dissent are basic civic responsibilities. There is also a deeply sown belief among most practitioners of nonviolence that there is a benevolent place in every being that is touched through the nonviolent encounter. When someone exerts violence on another being who chooses not to respond in kind, the person exerting violence will be placed in a moral quandary. While most of these activists are cognizant that such a quandary can be resolved in myriad ways, often themselves quite violent, there is always the hope for some level of transformation.

In addition to its public impacts, and akin to all ascetic tactics, remaining nonviolent during direct actions reorients the self and others. Faith explained that nonviolent, high-risk tactics have been "transformative," elaborating as follows:

It requires you to dig deep into who you are and to respond in a way that is completely challenging and perhaps even counter-intuitive. It's a form of resistance that's transformative. I think that in the process of participating in nonviolent resistance that I'm changed. And I've experienced it over and over and over again.

The process of being changed, of transformation, is at the core of what an ascetic political practice intends. Through their forms of self-discipline and renunciation, these witnesses seek to transform themselves and others.

Of course, few activists begin with the level of risk undertaken by Theresa or Faith. They walk in the desert with ample support or fast for a single day. It is only over time and practice that greater risks are tackled. For instance, after a few years of what she perceived to be less risky activism, such as fasting and attending protests, Maya of WAT decided to engage in civil disobedience with a group of people she described "loving and trusting." Reflecting on having undergone arrest and time in jail, she observed, "I can look back and say I already did this, and it wasn't the end of the world. [That] allows us to act more freely in the rest of our actions." Scholars of asceticism have observed that the subjective transformations that the ascetic undergoes are often "spoken of in terms of freedom" (Flood 2004: 14). For Maya, it is through training and persistence that one comes to greater freedom in activism. This freedom is a mode of transcendence, the kind of transformative outcome that political asceticism accomplishes. In turn, ascetic political practice allows these activists to build up courage, conviction, and endurance. They train for the kind of high-stakes, collective-action scenarios that grassroots social movements often require.

Preparation for nonviolent direct action is a mode of ascetic political practice. Activists train through careful self-discipline and collective intentionality to better resist their own impulses. In so doing, many find themselves able to engage in more daring and courageous acts of political resistance. This is part of forging a new subjectivity. Importantly, this new subjectivity is not primarily individual. Maya notes that she was willing to go to jail because she had grown to love and trust members of WAT. Faith suggests that her ability to follow through bodily with the ethic of nonviolence arose from "being part of a community, having done some training, and then being clear on what our intentions were." The most important and sustaining preparatory work that the activists in this study undertake is done with and through community, a point that animates the next half of this chapter.

FIGURE 5.1. *Chantal deAlcuaz is one of the many WAT members arrested during a twenty-four-hour direct action in front of the White House in 2012*
Photo credit: Justin Norman

PREFIGURATIVE COMMUNITY AS RESISTANT SOLIDARITY

We are a group of people that come together out of a recognition that we are all connected in these very real ways and if we really want to live genuinely in this world we
need to figure out how to act out of that sense of connection realizing that our liberation therefore is also tied together. And it's a horrible context and a horrible thing to
have to do. But there is also something very beautiful that I think touches people in
particular ways in this work.

– Matt, Witness Against Torture

Matt observes that the pursuit of solidarity with the state's targets is insepa-
rable from the kind of solidarity these activists have come to forge with each
other. This is a consideration shared broadly across these groups. A sense of
solidarity among activists is important for all social movement efforts. Yet it is
particularly important for activists engaged in the practice of solidarity witness
because of their object of struggle. Draconian state violence is a moral atrocity,
certainly; it also points to the frayed social fabric beneath such a social formation. Torture, sequester, and disappearance pose indisputable evidence that
something is amiss in dominant social relations, a set of contradictions that
allow such violence to remain generally uncontested. These activists understand crafting alternative social relationships as an insistence on something
different. Envisioning, articulating, and modeling an alternative communal
existence is their foremost manner of resistance.

Asceticism is generally understood to be a solitary endeavor, a way of creating a personal relationship with God. At the same time, asceticism has traditionally been about casting off the trappings of individualism and the ego to
seek something greater than the self, what Flood (2004) terms "the transcendence of individuality" (14). As a political undertaking, the ascetic practice of
solidarity witness asks activists to relinquish bourgeois values, in particular,
liberal individualism, in order to pursue something more transformative as a
collective. Central to this is crafting prefigurative community, a resistant mode
of solidarity in which movement groups model the kinds of relationships they
wish to see in society writ large.

In examining the prefigurative politics of the New Left, Winifred Breines
(1980) argues that the idea of community itself radically challenges the hegemonic social relationships emergent under late capitalism:

There is a case to be made that community refers to a set of relationships, experiences
and institutions that have been (and continue to be) destroyed by the development of
capitalism ... The desire for connectedness, meaningful personal relationships and direct
participation ... takes on radical meaning in contemporary society. (1980: note 421)[4]

---

[4] Miranda Joseph (2002) offers a stark counter-argument about how the discourse of community
is mobilized in multiple contemporary arenas to uphold dominant forms of governance and
capitalist exploitation. Her work aptly shows how any tool that enables can also inhibit, a point
I explore further in Chapter 6.

These activists bring a lived understanding to this observation. In their efforts to do justice with and for the direct targets of state violence across cavernous divides of inequality and access, they are also attuned to the devastating impacts of an individualist bourgeois order. As Tracy and I sat on the curb at the SOA Fort Benning vigil after she had told me the story of folding origami peace cranes in prison, I asked her what the point of continuing to come to Georgia every year might be. The number of protesters had dwindled. The civil disobedience was no longer the mass undertaking it once was.

Tracy identified the prefigurative community enacted at Fort Benning as a crucial alternative to dominant social relationships. "[The vigil is about] building community. It's building relationships. In our society what keeps the oppression going is individualism. Individualism is – it's really not the truth. We really are a community, and we crave that. We crave relationships."

In explaining not just what they did, but what it was they actually *were*, activists explained that their mode of community was a foremost means to contest the dehumanization and divisiveness created through the state's acts of violence. For instance, when asked to describe Witness Against Torture, Carol explained:

The first image that comes to my mind is that it's a circle of trust ... I think it's really significant that that's there because I feel like trust is one of the things that is directly attacked by torture. People's ability to trust in humanity is destroyed when they are survivors of torture. That's one of the most difficult things to rebuild. That's what we hear from torture survivors. So the fact that here we are as a group, celebrating each other and our human ability to bond with one another and to appreciate life – that in and of itself is resistance to what we're doing to our brothers in Guantánamo.

Carol speaks of a practice of trust that contests and confounds the social relationship (de)constructed by torture. In using the concept of "a circle of trust" Carol evokes language used by organizations in the US Civil Rights Movement, even if hers is not an explicit reference. The Student Nonviolent Coordinating Committee (SNCC), for example, defined itself in a founding document as "a circle of trust, a band of sisters and brothers gathered around the possibilities of agapeic love, the beloved community" (Marsh 2004: 3). This schema locates WAT within a lineage of nonviolent resistance that understands a radical practice of solidarity as both the means and the ends of a movement effort. Dr. King explained "agapeic love" as the "recognition that all life is interrelated" (1953 [1991]: 20). This was not a personal love but a love of justice and humanity. Dr. King was not suggesting that the oppressed somehow cultivate affection for their oppressors. Rather agapeic love, and its instantiation in the notion of a beloved community, was a challenge to violence and division. Existing as a circle of trust is significant, Carol suggests, as WAT seeks to confront a regime of state terror that uses physical torture to exploit and distort the most elemental of human bonds.

Migrant Trail organizer Ted also described the community of the walk through a Civil Rights lexicon, using the idea of the "blessed community" as the synthesis of what it means to witness. For Ted, the trust of prefigurative community is located in a sense of cooperation, brotherly love, and the potential for a different kind of future:

[The Migrant Trail is] a witness, a blessed community in the sense that Martin Luther King [Jr.] talked about. It's a community that's governed by cooperation and brotherly love. It's an example of how we would like to live our lives. And it's a witness to what's going on here on the border, an exercise in solidarity with all the people that walk, and amongst ourselves all the people that care, that know about the suffering that goes on here and work to alleviate it, to change our system so that people are treated humanely, workers are free to migrate, their families aren't split up. A future where the border can be at peace again.

For Ted, the beloved community is a witness that sees what the state occludes while prefiguring alternative solidarities. Ted speaks of a practice of community that exemplifies the kinds of social relationships that Migrant Trail organizers would like to see in their lives writ large, the society they return to beyond the desert. This is a way of living that is cooperative and communal, loving and generous. It is also a way of living that is awake and aware, that knows and sees suffering, and works to change it.

Dr. King's "beloved community" depicts a radically transformed social arrangement in which the structures of power and violence that separate oppressor from oppressed are overcome. For King, the beloved community was certainly a social order in which US blacks and whites could coexist. Yet King also believed that the beloved community delivered to US society a social good that far exceeded mere questions of racial parity; it was a reimagining of the totality of social relations.[5] Ted and Carol's understandings of what their groups *are* understands the idea of witness – being present to see and expose injustice – as also an enactment of the beloved community. To witness is to exist in beloved community, says Ted. Witness Against Torture is a circle of trust, proposes Carol. Witnesses see and show injustice, but they also must deliver alternatives. Prefigurative community is one such alternative.

---

[5] Charles Marsh (2004) insists that the vision of the beloved community had theological specificity as a "realization of divine love in lived social relation … the outrageous venture of loving the other without conditions – a risk and a costly sacrifice" (2). Certainly, King was not naïve; the religious ideal of a "beloved community" also served as a strategic act of social movement framing, appealing to certain cultural structures of the mainstream in order to push for instrumental aims. Yet Marsh (2004) warns, and I think rightly so, that to only understand the religiosity of this discourse as social movement strategy might flatten a socially complex undertaking. Holding this balance of secular and religious in tension is also important in understanding solidarity witness as an ascetic practice.

PREFIGURATIVE COMMUNITY AS ASCETIC PRACTICE

Dave had lost his water bottle. In the middle of the desert on a sizzling afternoon after walking fifteen miles, the loss of a water bottle can seem like more than just a small inconvenience. Nor was this an average water bottle.

Dave explained, "I've got all the gizmos that you can get at camping stores, all that kind of crap. [This was a] high tech, fancy water bottle. You know those: the water bag that goes on your back."

Brother Adam, a Franciscan friar, learned that Dave was looking for a missing bottle, and swiftly began to rinse out one of the two he had brought for the weeklong trek. Both were used Gatorade jugs. He chose the one with the larger mouth for Dave because, as Brother Adam explained, it was the easier one to fill while walking.

Dave recalled this interaction, "This guy. He's walking in his brown robe with old sneakers and he has these two almost-to-fall-apart water bottles. And he's giving me, Mr. High Tech Camp Gear, one of his bottles."

For Dave, this was a classic instance of Brother Adam and a lesson in humility and simplicity. It also demonstrated something more. Brother Adam's rush to give what little he could was a practice in community. It exemplified the kind of social arrangements these groups seek to prefigure. Dave concluded:

> It showed me the generosity that I experience with [Brother Adam] and the generosity that I experience with a lot of people on the walk ... I want people to know that our nation is not just a nation of angry nativists who just would rather people die in the desert than make a place for them. There are people like Brother Adam who would do just about anything to save human life and to care for others.

Brother Adam's willingness to give his water bottle to Dave exemplifies prefigurative community. Through what are often small acts of kindness and generosity, these activists cultivate a mode of coexistence that resists dominant social arrangements. Certainly, as a Franciscan, Adam ascribes to a tradition that relinquishes possessions as part of its ethic and asceticism. Within the prefigurative community forged on the Migrant Trail, however, Brother Adam's is the norm for social interactions, not an aberration. Prefigurative community is central to the ascetic dimension of solidarity witness. It is both forged through embodied modes of discipline and becomes itself an experience of discipline. This community, in turn, becomes an invaluable site of *aksesis*, a place of training and subject work that leads to important transformations of self, consciousness, and political commitments.

Tucker explained that community was an inevitable outcome of the Migrant Trail:

> That community that gets established with the walk – it has to happen, right? Even with all its small conflicts or potential small conflicts. Or big conflicts maybe. But it has to be a community, you know? 'Cause we're doing this kind of amazing thing and we're all doing it together.

Of course, this community is not really *inevitable*. It has to be crafted and requires a collective commitment to reciprocity and kindness, even in the face of conflict. At one level, this is evident in the fact that Migrant Trail organizers undertake months of planning to ensure the walk reflects their most central values. This often means revisiting and tinkering with the guidelines for the walk. It also means that once the journey begins, people are, if very rarely, asked to leave if they are not amenable to living in the community that the rest of the participants create.

At the same time, the prefigurative community that arises in each of these groups often *feels inevitable;* the shared practices of fasting, protest pilgrimage, and civil disobedience are profoundly intimate and bonding. Migrant Trail participant Alex observed that the common experience of discomfort has a movement-fortifying dimension for those on the desert trek.

What unites the walkers is our common experience. You know, just the routine, the daily routine that we establish, you know, of waking up early and walking. We all know what others are feeling because we're feeling it. We know what it's like to feel hot and uncomfortable and sweaty and, you know, to smell bad and have sore feet and blisters and sunburn on the back of our necks.

Akin to the kinds of *felt* solidarity explored in the last chapter in which physically demanding tactics bring close the disavowed targets of state violence, embodied challenges create a terrain of commonality, even across various personal differences.

Joanne similarly explained of WAT's practice of gathering for a week to live together and abstain from food:

Fasting together created some bonds within the group as something that we're doing together. Many people thought of it as a way to maintain mindfulness of why we're here. 'Cause it just seems hard to everybody, and so you kind of joke about it. You're doing it together.

In using fasting to stay mindful of the injustices they contest, activists also find solidarity with each other.

Like any ascetic practice, to partake in solidarity witness means to make a choice and an ongoing commitment, despite the obvious challenges. Valantasis (2008) suggests that "what makes a performance ascetical (rather than enculturative) depends on the intention of the performer or performers to resist, to contradict, to defy, or to define the self in opposition to the dominant social context" (106). Maya suggested that prefigurative community requires just this intentionality, explaining that the choice to *trust* was central to WAT's decision to fast in community. Maya was also clear that WAT's practice of fasting was not without its drawbacks:

When we deny ourselves food, we're put into this place where we have a more visceral feeling of our bodies and hopefully trusting in the spirit, that we trust that our needs are going to be met. We're going to trust that we have enough energy to do this work.

FIGURE 5.2. *The physicality of the desert journey forges a sense of solidarity among Migrant Trail participants, here pictured at their fourth night's campsite*
Photo credit: Eric O Ledermann

We're going to trust that in not eating and being put in this emotional place that's very vulnerable, pushed to the edge, stressed out, that that space is a different space from our everyday lives. We choose that deliberately with all these other people ... And can something more creative come out of that? An action that's like more creative, more confrontational, more loving, more just? ... I believe that it can. I also believe that fasting pushes all of us to our stress levels, and so there's like even more conflict (laughs) than you would otherwise have in a group of people. So I think there are downfalls to fasting, but I think ultimately it's this choice to trust.

What Maya here identifies as the "downfalls to fasting" – high levels of stress that might lead to conflict – are located within a larger project of trust. This "choice to trust" is directed toward the spirit, and in this sense a higher power. It is a trust in bodily discipline, such as fasting, as a transformative process. It is also a trust directed toward fellow WAT activists. The element of trust is essential to the ascetic process. A mode of discipline is undertaken with the trust that it will create a different kind of consciousness and way of being. Ascetic discipline also means the willingness for something unknown or excessive to instrumental political aims to occur.

In addition to protest pilgrimage and fasting, the kind of close living that is integral to participating in these communities is itself experienced as a relinquishing of comforts in order to learn lessons and craft a self that stands in opposition to the dominant order. Bourgeois, capitalist society does not demand that people live in extended communal conditions, especially not those who are upwardly mobile, white, and in heterosexual nuclear families. The acquisition of a single-family home is often held up as iconic of the American Dream, complete with the stereotypical white picket fence. Quite literally cohabiting in close quarters, in the face of hunger, heat, and other forms of physical and emotional stress, is for many activists a key aspect of the discipline that solidarity witness requires.

Jane reflected that her experience of communal living on the Migrant Trail was multiply challenging, while also reminding her about aspects of herself that she often neglects in her daily routine. She described the walk:

It's a very intense form of community for a short amount of time, which challenges me on many levels. I learn a lot about sort of living and being with other people. I tend to be a pretty solitary person and like my space and like living by myself and doing my own thing. To live in community in a really sort of literal sense always reminds me how much I sort of need people and like to be around people to a degree. But also it always feels really good to go home at the end and sort of have my space back again.

Living in community is rarely easy, but these activists perceive it as having invaluable features. For Jane, each year's walk reminds her of a kind of social interdependence that she craves, even if she identifies as a rather solitary person.

Others remarked that the unique mode of intergenerational living that these communities instantiate was an important contrast to dominant society. Just as living in close physical proximity with extended community pushes against the bourgeois order and dominant residential geographies, white and middle-class American publics tend to be sorted by age cohort. This is especially so in terms of consumer and media markets. In the spaces of solidarity witness, social space and time contrasts with market space and time. For instance, Migrant Trail participant Raul, a community organizer in his late twenties, explained how important it was for him to connect to those with decades of movement experience:

I've been talking to a lot of my elders on this walk. There's so much knowledge that the older community on this walk has to share and is eager to share ... And I've seen traits that I would love to have. You can have a meaningful conversation, something that would take days, weeks, months, years to develop in some of our real world relationships.

The sentiment that intimacy could be created quickly in these prefigurative spaces was broadly shared. For Raul, this intimacy is so distinct from his daily life that he juxtaposes relationships forged on the Migrant Trail to those made in the "real world." The walk becomes a space apart; it also maintains its own time scale. As Raul suggests, the older generation has a mass accretion of movement knowledge because of their decades of activism. Through prefigurative community, this cross-generational knowledge can be shared quickly – in an hour, day, or week – and yet resonate deeply and enduringly. As Migrant Trail participant Dana explained, "You're doing something together that's meaningful and so those relationships feel very significant." With relationships that "feel significant" comes an emotional basis for knowledge sharing across bonds of trust. Of course, what is created and shared through prefigurative community is not just factual knowledge, but experiences, affects, and new epistemologies. These have other important impacts both on the activists themselves as well as on these groups' aims more broadly.

TRANSCENDENCE: COMMUNITY'S PSYCHIC REWARDS

WAT participants Carol and Harriet guide us in a morning reflection. They read from a book written by Jesuit priest and peace activist John Dear. In the reading, Dear references the teachings of Buddhist monk Thich Nhat Hanh. "Most of us are sleeping," suggests Hanh. "Mindfulness is a key ingredient in the spirituality of peace."

After the reading, everyone is invited to consider this aloud, if they so choose. What does it mean to be mindful? What does it mean to be awake?

When it is Donna's turn to speak, she explains her sense of being overwhelmed in the face of "global racism, climate chaos and war." Her voice cracks and she begins to cry. She cannot say much else. Someone puts a hand gently on her shoulder. We sit in a silence of shared acknowledgment.

Sam is one of the first to respond. A peace activist who has been living in a Catholic Worker community for decades, including numerous stints in prison for his civil disobedience, Sam observes that the despair Donna has expressed is one that is familiar to him. Still, he sees in the suffering an impetus. "I think the grief and despair is what drives us to find each other," he says softly. "This hole that we're in is not our origin, and it's not our destiny."

Larry sits on the floor, rocking back and forth with his knees in his hands, a motion I have learned is common for him when the group sits for extended periods. He reiterates what he has said a few times this week. "If you're gonna be a revolutionary for peace and drop out of mainstream society, you can't do it alone." He is clear that he does not mean this in the sense of acquiring a critical mass to apply political pressure. For Larry, it is a question of maintaining one's sanity; a "sense of community and collective solidarity" in the face of a culture that is "hostile, bigoted, and racist" is a lifeline.

Matt responds to Donna and the others. "The circle is a place where we can bring our full selves even as we know that as long as there are men in cages, we can't be our full selves. But taking care of each other is part of being our full selves."

The reading that Carol and Harriet have selected for the end of the reflection time concludes with the statement "peace-making begins with grief." I diligently jot down all I can to document the morning's interactions, awed by the synchronicity of this final statement. Perhaps this reflects my own ignorance or outsider status in the circle. Perhaps Carol and Harriet knew that that morning would be a conversation about sharing in grief.

It is not until the next day, however, that Donna has an opportunity to once again speak to the whole group. She reflects back on the prior day's conversation, her words straightforward and brief. "This group is really the first time I've been embraced in a community and a culture of resistance," she declares (Adapted from author's field notes).

Social movements have often been where people go to be their whole selves. Regardless of a movement's impacts on policy or the social structure writ large, a sense of camaraderie and recognition is an important recruitment mechanism for those who feel marginalized by or alienated from mainstream society. Typically, this observation has been articulated in the case of the stigmatized or structurally excluded. Gay activists, forced to choose between the closet or be ostracized, were able to love and be loved freely in LGBTQ spaces. Black communities in the US South created alternative structures of communal care and even schooling where white society threatened bigotry and bodily assault. While they might not face the same forms of stigma and oppression, solidarity activists often discover that movement communities are the most transformative aspect of their political engagement. The white, middle-class students who joined the Freedom Summer project of 1964, for instance, reported that the most significant part of their activism was finding a sense of belonging and camaraderie both among the southern black communities with whom they lived and worked as well as among each other. These white volunteers "discovered a powerful sociological truth: the most satisfying selves we will ever know are those that attach to communities and purposes outside of our selves" (McAdam 1988: 138). Akin to other forms of asceticism, prefigurative community requires intentionality and discipline, practice and patience, in order to reach an experience of transcendence. The psychic rewards afforded by prefigurative community are an important aspect of this transcendence.

Some who were newer to prefigurative community found themselves wonderstruck. During her first time on the Migrant Trail, Julie reported that the sense of generosity and kindness on the walk was a striking difference to what she had experienced in mainstream society.

I've been so overwhelmed and in awe of the community that I see here and the willingness to give something that someone else needs when you don't have much yourself, you know? I've just become so sick of a disregard for human life so I wanted to do something that values life. It just seems like there's a lack of community in the United States in a lot of places, the lacking desire to help people when there's no gain. People who are dying, people who just need help. Just help ... I think this is the most powerful thing that I've experienced here is the community. I think it's just a desire to help other people, to stand for something bigger than yourself. Just this unselfishness. It's been amazing to witness here.

For Julie, one of the most compelling acts of witness during her first desert trek was to the community forged by the activists themselves. This was a transformative experience, and it had long-term implications. Not only did Julie switch careers in order to pursue the kinds of care she saw represented on the Migrant Trail, she participated regularly in the walk after her initial encounter. Julie's experience suggests that the psychic rewards that prefigurative community can offer serve as an important recruitment and commitment mechanism, bringing new participants into the group and ensuring they stick around over the long haul.

Maya explained that while the aim of closing Guantánamo was important to her decision to join WAT, the dynamic of the community, including its spiritual elements and articulation of the sociological imagination, offered a kind of transformative engagement that has kept her involved over the long term:

The issue, I felt, was very compelling, but also the way in which we were able to talk about and process through how we were feeling and sort of the spiritual grounding of the community was really attractive to me. It felt sort of like a home. [It was] rooted in this sense that there are these large systems of violence and oppression that are working in the world, and they affect all of us, and how do they affect us, and how do we change that and all those questions. They were individuals who I really looked up to.

While the desire to close Guantánamo was important to Maya, locating the military prison within a broader analysis was critical. WAT's assessment of the security state sees those detained as the most directly impacted by state violence but acknowledges that those who enjoy relative privilege and protection are also touched by a system structured in "violence and oppression." Maya suggests that the value placed on reflection, emotions, and spirituality made this movement community feel like a kind of "home," where she can find role models from whom to learn and be inspired. Valantasis (2008) suggests that "asceticism rejects precisely in order to embrace another existence" (41). Through an ascetic political practice, these activists create an alternative existence, a form of transcendence, that Maya feels to be a home.

Many noted that standing against dominance was an isolating process, making it even more important to find solidarity among each other. SOA Watch participant Leah explained this as one of the most important features of the annual vigil at Fort Benning:

Sometimes I think working for justice and peace can feel really isolating because you're going against the mainstream and it's countercultural. So to be with people who say, "I stand with you, I agree with you, this is not right," is really powerful, especially when it's a big number of people. I think getting to be in solidarity with people from all over who are working against injustices and who are all there because they don't agree with what's going on at the hands of the school is really powerful.

Harold similarly noted of the weekend events with SOA Watch at Fort Benning:

The human contacts that you make in those situations are very valuable, and I think they're also something that we need as activists. We need that. We need to know there's other people like us out there, other people that are different than us but doing the same thing out there. And then it's this human contact that really keeps us going.

Both Leah's and Harold's sentiments harken back to WAT member Larry, sitting on the floor during most group reflections and sagely noting, "if you're gonna be a revolutionary for peace and drop out of mainstream society, you can't do it alone." What Leah terms "going against the mainstream" and being "countercultural" can lead activists to estrange family and friends and to feel alone in their places of work and even faith communities. Harold notes that "human contacts" are "something that we need as activists." Finding people that share one's values and commitments helps bolster political resolve in the face of an oppositional culture, motivating activists to continue their efforts despite confronting loneliness and ostracism.

To this end, many noted that the prefigurative community forged during this kind of activism was an "energizer." Tracy, folder of the origami peace cranes, explained that because being an activist is often "really lonely work," the annual SOA Watch vigil "energizes [people] to go back." Brother Adam similarly explained that the Migrant Trail "is an energizer for me to continue to inspire me since I live in the middle of things in Tucson." Akin to Raul learning from his elders, Brother Adam also benefited from the intergenerational aspect of the community, noting that part of this energy came from meeting "inspiring young people trying to be a part of making things better." Darlene, who only participated once on the Migrant Trail agreed that the walk helped revive her commitment to helping fairly conservative churches in her home community to take a more pro-immigrant stance. Darlene explained, "participation [in the Migrant Trail] injected me with a new enthusiasm for the work that I was already doing and [I] am eager to get down there again to be reinvigorated."

Prefigurative community is a key element of ascetic political practice. Through modes of physical and psychosocial discipline, activists create something not merely greater than the individual but expose as well the limitations and kinds of damage that a culture of bourgeois individualism creates. This community, in turn, becomes an experience of transcendence akin to other ascetic processes. It generates important psychic rewards that hedge against isolation and the incumbent burn out that radical activists often face in mainstream society. These psychic rewards also have instrumental benefits, helping to foster long-term activist engagement.

CONCLUSION

Solidarity witness is centrally about creating selves and collectives able to engage in profound and enduring resistance. This subject work is accomplished through what I am terming an ascetic political practice. The activists in this study relinquish comforts and undertake intentional modes of discipline in order to renounce the dominant order bodily, psychically, and, for some, spiritually as well. They pursue these efforts with intentionality and trust that something greater will be created, akin to the forms of transcendence that the traditional religious ascetic pursues.

Like all ascetic endeavors, solidarity witness resists individualism. As a specific social and political practice, solidarity witness intends to actively contest the myth of meritocratic individualism that is a fundamental pillar to the logic of late capitalism. Prefigurative community is key to rejecting such individualism and is a central accomplishment of the ascetic aspects of solidarity witness. By enacting the kinds of relationships and social behaviors they wish to see in the greater society, these activists craft a resistant mode of solidarity. They forge a communal existence that attractively contrasts with many activists' experience of bourgeois life.

Enacting prefigurative community is not easy, especially when activists cohabit under the physical and emotional stressors that are central to their ascetic practices, such as hunger, heat, and exhaustion. Indeed, some activists experience communal living as itself ascetic, requiring one to give up petty comforts in pursuit of a greater vision. In turn, ascetic forms of discipline help these activists forge a sense of intimacy with each other that feels transformative to many. In helping to hedge against the burnout, despair, and isolation that so many have experienced in their lives and in their activism, prefigurative community offers invaluable psychic rewards.

The solidarity that these activists pursue is enacted multiply. Through their embodied forms of discipline to better see what the state occludes and show such injustices to others, these witnesses enact the best articulation of solidarity with the targets of state violence that they can. At the same time, in order to remain steadfast in their political commitments, they must generate transformations within themselves and nurture a collective culture of opposition. Doing so requires they put into practice a different manner of existence. The ascetic political practice of solidarity witness leads them in this direction.

6

The Complications of Solidarity Witness

One of the more ubiquitous symbols at both SOA Watch's annual vigil and the Migrant Trail walk is the white cross, emblazoned with a name. Migrant Trail organizers have learned that the cross's meaning must be treated with care. The symbols of the dominant, even if repurposed to subversive ends, can cut both ways, inadvertently reinforcing histories of exclusion and oppression. Migrant Trail organizers were first asked to consider the cross when a group of Californians of South Asian descent joined the desert trek. At this point, it was still a Migrant Trail tradition that the person leading the walkers would carry a very large, wooden cross, about four feet tall and weighing over thirty pounds. There were only a few participants, generally male, who could practicably carry such an object for the miles required. The South Asian participants were uneasy with this symbolism, which evoked for them a lengthy history of Christian missionaries evangelizing non-Christians abroad. They expressed their discomfort in walking behind a large cross and their concern with the meaning this might have to various audiences. Longtime participant and organizer Jessie acknowledged that when she heard these comments, she was grateful. Having been raised Christian and still identifying as such, she had not seen the cross as others might. She explained:

I'm used to crosses … a cross to me is not a sign of oppression. It's not a sign of my religion winning over yours. But that's what the cross has symbolized for many people for many years and so it was good to hear those voices and to think about.

The organizers decided that while the small crosses emblazoned with the names of deceased migrants would stay, the big cross could go. As Jessie reflected, "No we don't have to walk behind this big, awkward white cross which might signify something very different."

The current group participation document further clarifies the meaning of the cross:

The majority of migrants who have died on the Arizona-Sonora border were most likely Christian, if not Catholic, but this does not mean that those who honor them have to be. Crosses are a simple way of representing life, death, and the faith of those who are left behind. The carrying of crosses along the Walk does not endorse or promote any particular faith or religion. The Migrant Trail is an interfaith experience that is open to all representations of peace, hope, and faith.

(Migrant Trail Participant Packet 2017)

Despite this explanation, the cross has an ineluctable association with Christianity for some. Jessie explained that despite the public discussion participants have about the cross, "[there was a participant who] couldn't take away from the cross who Jesus was to her. And so when she carried a cross she was carrying it as a symbol of her Christianity." Participants are invited to take one of the small crosses at the beginning of the week as a way of personalizing the deceased, not as a token of religiosity. Still, there is no accounting for the diversity of personal convictions.[1]

The case of the cross may seem incidental or insignificant. Certainly it never emerged as a divisive controversy at the scale that has led to movement schisms throughout history. That every tool enables certain possibilities and forecloses others is a truism to which movements are accustomed. In the moment of contest, query or reflection about everything from symbols to emotions and strategy to purpose, the activists in this study raise important questions about how best to engage in solidarity witness, considering essential issues about their political practice.

In this chapter, I examine a few of the central forms of dissonance and dissatisfaction that these activists express toward their group's approach to social change. Internal movement conflicts can be dreary to write about, even if such debates are sociologically rich (Ghaziani 2008). I focus less on the forms of petty acrimony that accompany all group interactions, examining instead

---

[1] Bruce Palmer (1980) offers a similar example in which the Southern Populists, an anticapitalist movement from the 1890s, were somewhat foiled in their efforts to wield dominant Christian signs as oppositional tools. The Populists used biblical allegories to frame their vision for a utopic social order, describing a "golden era" to come in which the evils of poverty and greed would be vanquished. The ability of the Southern Populists to portray social and economic ills as moral shortcomings through the language of religion was their key strength. Yet as the Populists introduced religious terms into their resistance, they often neglected to explicitly link these to social policies. Akin to the varied interpretations of the cross here discussed, the Populists' use of a biblical framing was reinterpreted and rearticulated by popular audiences and oppositional politicians. What the Populists intended as a widely appealing frame for social structural change was often flattened into an individualist focus on al moral failings, an interpretation in accord with a more dominant Protestant ethic. Palmer suggests that the Populists' biblical lexicon for revolution was in this way distorted, the focus turned to questions of "private morality, not those of social, economic and political change" (137).

some of the more enduring quandaries these activists suggest that their groups face. In considering how they might falter and what they might do to become stronger, we find a set of complex ideas and ideals about what these campaigns seek to achieve and how they wish to do so.

In what follows, I address the four areas of contention most commonly raised by the activists in this study. In the first section, I revisit the discipline of ritual examined in Chapter 3 to think through how this form of direct action appeals to some at the cost of potentially alienating others. The second section turns more squarely to questions of exclusion, especially as these are linked to issues of racial justice. Building on questions of privilege and intragroup relationships, the third section examines the main concerns that participants voice about the subject work of solidarity witness. With its deeply embodied and emotional features, some participants worry that witnessing may hinder rather than help newcomers in forging oppositional consciousness and creating a self-better able to resist the state. The fourth and final section builds on these debates and dilemmas while also offering something of a capstone to the study. I interrogate how witnessing as a specific form of political practice may not lead these campaigns to the tangible institutional shifts they demand but may offer an invaluable mode of political engagement nonetheless.

As these dilemmas show, the practice of solidarity witness, with its deeply psychosocial and often religious features, atypical forms of political engagement, and uncompromising utopian stance, provides a particular movement practice that may be off-putting to some. For others, the practice of solidarity witness may be attractive and compelling but allow for a "feel good" experience that impacts little on subsequent mobilization. At the same time, what might appear politically ineffectual, or even apolitical altogether, may in fact be deeply politicizing. Solidarity witness recruits some participants into forms of long-term and high-risk activism that they did not predict they would undertake. Solidarity witness offers others a means of continuing political engagement in the context of policies and institutional practices that are obviously unjust yet unresponsive to normal political channels. When the groups in this study wrestle with frustrations about process, purpose, and efficacy, they demonstrate well-considered notions of how solidarity activism should best be done in the face of the indefinite detention, militarism, and draconian restrictions on human mobility that typify the US security state.

THE DISCIPLINE OF RITUAL

As explored in Chapter 3, the ritual tactics of witnessing stand in contrast to the forms of protest that American publics usually associate with politics. For many activists, the solemn, silent, and often funereal ritual is part of the appeal of solidarity witness. Yet ritual protest, like all elements of solidarity witness, is predicated on a kind of discipline. This discipline has its own logic, and for many it achieves a desirable outcome, communicating a unified message that bystanders are unlikely to rebuke. Not all activists are equally attracted to this form of public witness, however. Some find it stifling, as well as iconic of the kind of privilege that group members do not equally share. I begin this chapter by exploring some of the conflicts that have arisen over the nature of ritual protest and the forms of discipline it demands.

Some of these activists suggested that solemn vigil was the mode of public witness most in line with their aims, recalling instances when excursions from the discipline of ritual protest have backfired. This was the case during one of the first years of the Migrant Trail, when a self-selected group decided to risk arrest at Border Patrol headquarters by staging a "die-in." This tactic was akin to the one at SOA Watch and likely informed by the fact that these participants on the Migrant Trail had also been active in the protest at Fort Benning. Those who organized this piece of "guerilla theater" believed it to be an important means of amplifying the walk's message, dramatizing the state's violence and tragedy of migrant deaths (Magaña 2008). Unfortunately, the central walk organizers, themselves members of local organizations in Tucson and the border region, were not well informed about the smaller group's plan. Organizer Ana explains how this created an odd dynamic both within the group and in terms of the message communicated to the public:

> None of us brown people were clued into it, and it was weird to be stepping over white folks pretending to be migrants ... it became about those folks and their action and not about the actual migrants and their deaths.

Certainly there was an uncomfortable racial dynamic to this in which organizers of color were not involved in planning the action and the display of white bodies seeking to dramatize the experience of obviously racialized migrants was perceived as somewhat offensive. Migrant Trail organizers were more upset, however, by the media exposure that ensued. While the action made the news, the Migrant Trail did not. The public's attention was focused on the theatrics of this controversial protest rather than about the issue for which so many had walked the seventy-five miles. The "die-in," while a familiar tactic to those who undertook it, ended up having a divisive effect within the group, monopolizing media coverage and obscuring the very issue these activists hoped to highlight.

A similar pitfall occurred in 2010 at SOA Watch, though in this instance, part of the issue was how heavily policed the vigil has become since September 11. A small group decided to create an alternative to the regular civil disobedience at the gates of Fort Benning, shutting down the major thoroughfare leading into the town of Columbus. Some explained this as an effort to reinvigorate the SOA Watch campaign at a time when the number of protesters was dwindling, and very few were willing to risk the heightened minimum jail time that came with crossing onto the base. A dozen people walked onto the highway with a banner that read "Stop: This is the End of the Road for the S.O.A" (Severson 2010). Those who planned the street action believed it was a safer alternative to actions on the Army base. Long-term SOA Watch participant

Kirk explains, "They wanted to have civil disobedience that didn't result in federal prison time." Unfortunately, among the relatively small group that intended to be arrested for shutting down the highway, some were undercover cops. Kirk continues, "It just gave the police an excuse to go berserk, and they basically arrested a whole bunch of other people who were not even involved."

Many SOA participants believed this action and the fallout distracted from the protesters' message. Burt observed that the action "caused a great hoo haa, and to what? To make a bunch of local residents angry who don't even understand what's going on?" The street arrest did little to draw attention to the SOA's violence. Rather, akin to the die-in action on the Migrant Trail, the media story focused on the dwindling number of protesters and the scuffle between activists and police (Severson 2010). While this might have been an opportunity to draw links between the SOA's military training and Georgia police forces, the message was not coherent, and little was said about SOA's record. Although various dynamics were at play in this instance, this protest effort ended up undercutting these activists' intention to highlight the stories of the most directly impacted. Instead, they became the protagonists of the narrative, in conflict with what Cameron took to be the mantra of good solidarity activism: "You're not the hero of the story. You're never the hero of a story."

Not all participants supported ritual protest and its forms of discipline, which activists across the three groups agreed included the relinquishing of certain freedoms. Maya of WAT acknowledged that when group members put on the orange jumpsuit and black hood and processed silently through public space, "individual WAT folks are silenced in a bodily way; it's difficult to see what's happening on the other side of the hood – sometimes breathing, too – and it's expected that we maintain a solemn, silent presence." Those dressed in the jumpsuits do not respond to bystanders. Instead, those activists who will engage with the public are selected ahead of time and do not dress as detainees. Maya noted that although she thought this level of discipline and silence was central to the power of WAT's repertoire, their ritual protest "also limits the freedom and autonomy of each person participating."

While Maya did not relay any anecdotes about this becoming an issue among WAT participants, relinquishing autonomy in favor of collective discipline has raised concerns among some Migrant Trail participants. Of note, not everyone has been enthused by the nonviolent stance all agree to uphold when they embark on the weeklong journey, an agreement that includes committing to treat all people encountered with respect. On the Migrant Trail, the most commonly encountered persons not part of the group are Border Patrol. Occasionally, aggressive vigilantes have also confronted the group. In 2011, one vigilante brandished a shotgun and told the walkers to "go back to the suburbs." In 2015, another vigilante, a member of the Minute Men, aggressively heckled the group for a mile. In the face of these encounters, not all who join the Migrant Trail agree that Border Patrol or anti-immigrant vigilantes deserve to be treated with respect.

During one walk, conflict arose when Julian, a longtime Chicano activist from Tucson, began flipping off Border Patrol. Organizers asked him to stop, but he resisted. While he ultimately ceased the confrontational actions, he explained that it was not because he believed he had done anything wrong. Rather, his friend, there with her young child, had asked that he not model the behavior in front of an eight years old. At the final afternoon's group reflection, Julian explained his decision to use his middle finger against the Border Patrol. He began by circulating his Nalgene water bottle where he had placed a now-faded sticker of the face of Jose Antonio Elena Rodriguez. Rodriguez was a sixteen-year-old Mexican boy who had been shot and killed by Border Patrol just eight months earlier. As participants studied the face and passed the bottle along, Julian told the story of the boy's death as a reason why he could not himself adopt a stance of nonviolence. Going further, Julian explained that such a stance had to be understood by the group of mostly white participants as an expression of their racial privilege. Julian told the group of majority white participants that they had the benefit of greeting security forces with a stance of welcome rather than the self-defense required of a person of color.

As one example, Julian described the Border Patrol checkpoint the group had walked through a few days prior, a checkpoint well into the interior of Arizona, as a "sugarcoated checkpoint." The way Border Patrol officers had treated the group was nothing like the harassment and threats he and his Latino friends received when they were regularly stopped. Wanting to flip off the Border Patrol, Julian concluded, was a completely appropriate response to a viciously racist system.

The group was generally receptive to Julian's comments, sitting quietly as he spoke and thanking him for raising important issues of racial privilege. A few core organizers did walk away. Some had to attend to other obligations. Others did not believe that this circle was a productive site for such a conversation as the group of fifty people would not see each other again for a year, and this was the final night of an exhausting journey. Some of these organizers were people of color who also disagreed with Julian's analysis, at least that the Migrant Trail should be understood as an expression of white privilege.

Long-term organizer Ted, a white activist now in his late sixties, remained in the conversation and stood to speak, respectfully disagreeing with Julian. Ted, at over six feet in height, seemed a towering presence while speaking to the walkers who all sat or lay under the makeshift tarp structure. Ted began by repeating a phrase he had used for years: "no institution is a monolith." By saying this, he meant that the employees of any government institution, including branches of the military and of law enforcement, should not be individually blamed for the operations of the larger system. Such a logic extended to the Border Patrol. Ted then exhibited his conception of what nonviolent witness looks like in encounters with Border Patrol agents. He did so by tipping his sun hat. "I do that," Ted told Julian and the group, "and I say to him or her, 'I see you. And I want you to see me.'" The tipping of a hat could be dismissed as a gesture of antiquated masculinity, but Ted explained a different logic for his gesture. The hat tip was an act of respect and recognition of the Border Patrol officer as a fellow person, with a complex humanity and a set of profound responsibilities.

Migrant Trail organizers did not make any structural changes in response to Julian's concerns, but this instance revealed important debates about the mood and message these activists communicate. Throughout their years doing the walk, Migrant Trail participants have found that some Border Patrol officers are quite sympathetic to their cause. Even if and when this is not the case, many Migrant Trail participants hope to bring their message to the officers as well. This is a central ethic to the practice of solidarity witness. As they seek to challenge systems of oppression, most of these activists adamantly refuse to villainize any individual, even those employed as executors of the "legitimate violence" of the state. Doing so goes against their sensibilities regarding the innate humanity and potential for good in every person.

There is also some instrumental logic here. Through years of involvement, many find that officials in law enforcement and the military, as well as certain politicians, are quite receptive to activists' message, at least in their capacities as individuals. What the practice of solidarity witness reveals is that most individual employees of the state and even many elected officials are relatively powerless to effect systemic change. At the same time, sometimes dissent that arises from within the state's ranks can be as or more effective at exposing state secrets and convincing the public of official wrongdoing than the work of external activists (e.g., Edward Snowden, Daniel Ellsberg).

A third consideration that activists and scholars have long observed is that maintaining permanent hostility toward activists' opponents, no matter how deserved, can prove quite exhausting, leading movement groups to despair and burn out. Even when activists disagree with those who are actively complicit in oppressive systems, attempting to cultivate a sense of compassion rooted in structural analysis can actually help movements to endure. This compassion is something akin to Dr. King's suggestion of agapeic love. Ioanide (2015) suggests that such compassion, or acceptance, might be central in helping activists maintain a sense of "psychic integrity and spiritual strength" (217).

For these reasons, demonizing individuals charged with upholding the system is not only against the moral cosmology of many witnesses but could be politically and emotionally counterproductive. This is not to dismiss Julian's concern with nonviolence as an expression of racial privilege. As one might expect given the nature of solidarity activism and the kinds of state violence these groups contest, issues around internal racial dynamics were of central importance to these activists, a point that I now explore further.

"WE STILL HAVE A LOT OF WORK TO DO"

On January 12, 2015, Witness Against Torture members stood with symbolic coffins in the freezing drizzle in front of the Justice Department. The Black Lives Matter campaign was continuing to gain attention, and its DC-based Hands

Up Coalition had invited Witness Against Torture to join this evening's vigil memorializing the black victims of police violence. The guest of honor was the mother of Emmanuel Okutuga, who been shot and killed by police in Silver Spring, Maryland, in 2011. WAT members flanked her on both sides. Some wore the quintessential orange jumpsuits, protected by transparent ponchos. Those not holding the symbolic coffins propped up banners reading "From Ferguson to Guantánamo," "White Silence = State Violence," "We Demand Accountability for Torture and Police Murder." After Okutuga's mother spoke about losing her son to state violence, WAT member Sumaira, a Pakistani American woman and central organizer of the evening's actions, explained,

Just as the military occupies Afghanistan, so the police occupy our streets here, picking off brown and black bodies ... We challenge the white supremacy that underlies anti-black racism and Islamophobia both. We are here to break the silence.

The coalition of Hands Up and WAT had decided to march to the DC Central Cell Block, a nearby jail, in which many WAT members had spent ample time imprisoned for various Guantánamo-related direct actions over the past decade. As is the case with most US detention facilities, time spent in the jail offered a stark depiction of the disproportionate incarceration of black men. It was decided that the jail would be an appropriate place to link Guantánamo to domestic policing.

Led by Mrs. Okutuga, the group marched through downtown Washington, DC, at rush hour, singing "We remember all the people the police killed, we feel their spirits, they're with us still." Upon arrival at the jail, twenty WAT members wanting to risk arrest entered the building. Everyone else remained at the top of the steps outside, where each person who identified as white was invited to take the microphone and finish the sentence, "I am breaking white silence because ..." Tens of WAT members finished the statement as a personal reflection and then made a systematic call to "all white people around the country," asking that they "also break their silence and stand against racism."

While a few white members of WAT judged this part of the day's events as hokey, participants of color later reflected on how moving this public call to "break white silence" had been. Ángel, an Afro-Latino man, recalled looking around at the other people of color during the action. "We were all in a bit of shock," he remarked. "As a person of color, you grow up with this sense that you're a bit crazy, and even when you get all this education and consciousness, this still haunts you." Having a group of white people affirm in a public way their acknowledgment of unearned privilege and how it dehumanizes and materially disadvantages the lives of others was a kind of affirmation. As Ángel put it, "I guess the wound needs a witness."

Inside the jail, the twenty seeking arrest explained their intention to get past the metal detectors. A black police officer spoke quietly with WAT's designated leader for the action, Leo. After a short exchange, the officer asked, "So you're doing this for people that look like me?" Leo explained the officer's reaction during that evening's debrief. The officer explained that he agreed with the group's message but asked that they not push past the security scanners. They were welcome to stay in the lobby, where they would still be highly visible without forcing the officers to arrest them. The group had to make a hard decision quickly. Leo consulted with the others as best as he could, and it was decided that WAT would not push for confrontation in this instance. A majority white group seeking to challenge a majority black police force was not in line with WAT's message, intention, and stance of nonviolence. This decision was not necessarily unanimous. As one WAT member later asked me with some frustration, "when did we decide that a person's race trumped their office?" The group ultimately stayed in the lobby for twenty-eight minutes to symbolize the fact that a black person is killed by US law enforcement or vigilantes every twenty-eight hours. With a list of names they had prepared ahead of time, the activists proceeded to name black men killed by the police and to sing quietly in their memory.

This action represents one step in an ongoing transition by WAT toward a greater focus on racial justice. While this transformation is one that group members had long been seeking, they have often been uncertain of how to get there. Just months earlier, core organizers spoke to me about the implicit forms of racial exclusion in their group, an issue they had been grappling with for almost a decade. As one of many instances, Carol explained to me her sense that some US-based racial justice activists were frustrated or at least confused by WAT. "Why does a group of white Americans concentrate so much on one US prison overseas, when such egregious abuses are being perpetrated in prisons all over the country?" she recalled being asked. She understood the logic and sentiment behind the question.

The coalition action with Black Lives Matter in January 2015 offered a clear means for WAT to extend their almost exclusive focus on closing Guantánamo to include pressing domestic racial justice issues, such as abusive policing and the disproportionate incarceration of people from communities of color. WAT's leaders and activists on this day, and in the months since, have included more people of color and US Muslims than ever before. The group's hours of conceptualizing this action included challenging conversations around racial power and privilege.

Yet WAT's shift to more explicitly include a domestic racial justice agenda was about organizational learning and political context, not merely activists' shame or guilt about white privilege. Throughout history, social movement leaders have observed that when you work on one issue, you come to care about innumerable interlocked struggles (Payne 1995; Lipsitz 2008). No form of oppression or mechanism of violence can so easily be isolated, as the activists in this study understand.

Participants across all three groups spoke often about pursuing greater racial awareness and inclusion. There was good deal of frustration as well as variability as to how racially inclusive participants understood their groups to be. Akin to the ways that WAT has grown as an organization, SOA Watch participants tended to view their group as making hopeful strides toward greater inclusivity, broadly considered, with race an important part of this. Damien, himself a black man, explained this evolution to me:

If I had come across SOA Watch in the early 1990s, it could've easily been something that I did overlook. I think that we are all impacted by imperialism, militarization, state-sponsored violence, racialized repression [but] it was a certain demographic initially represented by SOA Watch – older, white, middle class and from faith communities. These like "elder statesmen" in a way have a role ... They were there doing the work. A lot of them lived abroad throughout like the thirty [years dirty] wars period in Latin America, and have a lot to give to the movement.

Damien noted that since the early 2000s, SOA Watch has also been committed to becoming more diverse and taking guidance from aggrieved communities. This has included opening offices in Santiago, Chile, and Barquisimeto, Venezuela, "each of which are staffed by people who have been members of Latin American social movements for several years or even multiple generations." Damien suggested that SOA Watch has grown in many ways over its second and now third decade of organizing. As part of this, many of the original activists had made space for new voices: "I think that it's been important that [the original activists] have been able to step back and realize that there were forces missing from the conversation: youth, people of color, indigenous people."

Siobhan, herself an older, white, middle-class Catholic agreed with this. She emphasized that since 2004, SOA Watch has implemented a new organizational structure committed to increasing diversity as well as hemispheric representation. She further pointed to what she saw as the invaluable role of anti-oppression workshops that SOA Watch organizers and staff participate in regularly. Siobhan believed that the recruitment and retention of a younger generation of activists over the past ten years was likely the most important means for growing the campaign's awareness and productive engagement with internal power dynamics:

As younger people come in ... they kind of teach the older people, who think [increasing our diversity] isn't an issue, because obviously we're a group that's trying to do good. But you can't mimic the structures that you're basically opposed to. So it has been an evolution, a learning experience for all of us. And I think it's a way that we need to go forward. We'd like to have diversity. We'd like to truly reflect people who believe in the issue, and would consider themselves SOA watch supporters.

SOA Watch participants seemed to feel that they were already a decade into important and ongoing anti-racism and anti-oppression work. While SOA

Watch activists made no claims about having somehow "arrived" in this regard, WAT and Migrant Trail participants spoke much more about how white dominance may be perpetuated in their groups.

Of the three groups, participants on the Migrant Trail seemed to have implemented the fewest intentional means of addressing issues of racial privilege. Further, Migrant Trail organizers were not generally optimistic about having achieved greater diversity over time, especially in terms of race. While the racial composition of the group changes some from year to year, the walk is always majority white. This is an interesting juxtaposition to SOA Watch and WAT, which were both originally majority white, as people of color have been central to the Migrant Trail since the walk's founding. Core Migrant Trail organizers agreed that there is a need to consider dynamics of racial inclusion and exclusion on the walk without rendering invisible the important contributions of leaders of color.

Both Migrant Trail and WAT participants believed that racialized socioeconomics were a key reason certain people could not join a weeklong action. Jane explained that on the Migrant Trail, "One reason why it pulls mostly white people [is the] class and racial politics that play into who can take a week to choose to walk across the desert." Maya of WAT similarly noted:

There's a reason why those of us who come from upper middle class backgrounds have time to go to DC for a week in January and protest the entire week. Like we have the flexibility in our schedules to do that.

The idea that one's race and class might make it easier to participate in certain kinds of activities is captured by what social movement scholars have termed "biographical availability," defined as "the absence of personal constraints that may increase the costs and risks of movement participation" (McAdam 1986: 70). If biographical availability has traditionally been understood to be greatest in the life phase between emancipation from one's parents and starting a family and career, with little consideration of race and class, these activists expanded such a notion. Cameron, for example, considered how biographical availability was an obviously racialized category, noting that the tactics central to WAT's repertoire are made possible in part because of the protections of whiteness:

One of the main components to our resistance – the focus on nonviolence and civil disobedience – relies probably a lot on privilege. A lot of people of color aren't just like "let's get together for a week and get arrested." When I think about my experience in communities of color, they don't have to try really hard to get arrested.

Whereas white activists committing civil disobedience exercise a good deal of control over when to push for arrest, the freedom to choose when and where to risk arrest is withheld from US communities of color. Many of these solidarity activists select high-risk tactics precisely because they wish to utilize and confront their unearned privileges, as explored in the discussion of embodied resistance in Chapter 4. Moreover, no one is compelled to get arrested to participate with WAT or SOA Watch. Nevertheless, Cameron points to a cultural emphasis on nonviolent direct action that might not be equally appealing to all, and may in fact be alienating to some.

Other participants observed that their object of struggle might lack broad appeal, even if much of the political work of solidarity witness is in drawing connections across seemingly disparate nodes of the US security state. Maya observed that the focus on Guantánamo, as one example, might not respond to the urgent issues facing certain communities. Nearly a year before WAT's coalition work with Black Lives Matter began, Maya reflected on the lack of racial diversity in the group, explaining:

My experience with working with the black community in Chicago is that communities here are concerned about mass incarceration and the prison industrial complex, like right here in Illinois where super max prisons are being built and all of these people are being picked up, drugs are being planted on them, and then they're going to prison for many, many years on nonviolent charges. Those communities are wanting to work on issues that are very close to home.

Maya suggested that communities of color are compelled to address the violence targeted at them on a daily basis in ways that these solidarity activists are not.

Jane similarly explained the overwhelming whiteness on the Migrant Trail as reflecting different approaches to immigrant rights work: "Most of the organizations that I've been involved with that do humanitarian work are mostly white. And advocacy organizations are definitely more diverse." Groups in and around Tucson that focus on getting water and medical aid to distressed migrants in the desert are often majority white, whereas advocacy organizations that push for concrete policy shifts tend to involve more people of color, including undocumented participants. This distinction in orientation may be linked to Maya's account of aggrieved communities needing to struggle against the daily violence dealt them, seeking the most tangible and immediate remedies possible. Moreover, linked to Cameron's observation regarding the differential risk of tactics for different groups, the act of delivering humanitarian aid to stranded migrants in the highly patrolled borderlands constitutes a substantial risk for undocumented migrants and people of color in ways that it does not for white people. For communities of color, then, taking a week to witness in the borderlands may be a luxury they cannot afford. Julian seemed to corroborate this, when he recalled being asked to defend the walk to activists of color working on migrant justice issues in Tucson, who perceived the Migrant Trail as "a bunch of white people walking in the desert." Julian concluded, "Spending a week out in the desert does not really have an impact on the issue. It impacts us who walk much more."

Most agreed that while all of these features might explain why their groups were overwhelmingly white, it was incumbent on each group to make the necessary transformations for greater racial inclusion to occur. Before WAT began their coalition work with Black Lives Matter, Maya observed,

The responsibility falls on our shoulders as far as recruiting people of color to be a part of our group and just not being successful in that or not holding that as a priority ... Witness Against Torture is a white space, and so my sense is that people of color who come in may not feel welcomed into it or feel welcomed to have power or decision-making capabilities in it.

This is a responsibility that WAT has taken seriously and continues to pursue. Yet Cameron acknowledged specific moments in which racial ignorance might prevent people of color from wanting to stay involved in the group. He recalled being in a conversation with two other white Christians and one Arab Muslim, in which an "older white gentleman" explained, "'I don't see color. I just think we're all equal.'" Cameron reflected,

Like the whole color blind statement, right? And I'm like, "I think we should see Saad as a Bangladeshi man that's a person of color." And [Saad]'s like, "yeah, damn right. I'm proud of it." When you hear something like that, [it's] like, oh, wow, we still have a lot of work to do to think about how we embody racism in our comments and stuff. But I think we just need to do that work, like I think all of us.

Jane also suggested that the Migrant Trail could benefit from considering racial justice issues within the group with greater attention:

It's mostly white people that do this walk [and] we talk about white privilege a certain amount, in relation to migrants, ways in which we have privilege that migrants wouldn't have. But we don't talk about [privilege] in terms of the differences within our group and how my whiteness just, for example, positions me differently than the people of color who are in this group.

Certainly every group has those who believe these kinds of internal movement conversations are a waste of time. Some understand them to be a further expression of racial privilege, white people congratulating themselves for having conversations with little action. Others assert that they detract important energy and resources from the campaign's central aims. A rare few perceive white privilege to be a nonissue. However, participants continue to report instances that might push people of color out of the group, from moments of the kind of ignorance reported by Cameron to attempts at humor that are experienced as racial microaggressions.

Susan explained that on the Migrant Trail,

I overhear stuff, and I'm surprised what I hear sometimes in terms of the ignorance ... like comments that are not inclusive or almost racist or nativist. Just like, we're not all in the same place. So I guess the question is how do you create a space for all of these people to come together and participate?

During her first and only time participating on the walk, Miriella, who was born in Mexico and brought across the border as a child, shared with the group two experiences that had upset her during the week. One instance was when the group was getting ready to go through the Border Patrol checkpoint, twenty-five miles north of the border. The group had agreed they would obey the regulations of this checkpoint even though many believe it to exemplify the legally questionable advances of militarized border enforcement into the nation's interior. Under US law, those who are not US citizens, such as legal permanent residents or those in the country on a temporary visa, are required to carry and show documentation when state authorities request it. US citizens, on the other hand, are not required to show proof of their citizenship except when at a port of entry. In a likely attempt to expose the absurdity of the checkpoint and bolster group morale, one walk organizer announced, "foreigners should get their papers out." Miriella believed this trivialized the experience that so many face because they do not have documents.

A second instance that Miriella recounted, arguably more egregious than the first, was when she was in line for a meal with other family members and friends, all people of color. They happened to be at the front of the queue when someone said to them, "look, the natives can't wait!" As Miriella recounted this instance to the group during the final afternoon's reflection, it was likely evident to most why such a comment would be offensive. Nevertheless, she explained to those who might not understand the racism embedded in this statement, "this reiterates ideas about indigenous savagery." Before she concluded, Miriella asked that the other walk participants not comment immediately: "If this makes you uncomfortable, I encourage you not to respond right away and to sit with the discomfort."

The group was fairly receptive to this. After a long pause, the person who had made the comment at the Border Patrol checkpoint apologized simply and clearly without qualification. No one took responsibility for the food line comment. Others expressed their gratitude that Miriella had brought these issues to the group, agreeing that these kinds of conversations were important and necessary.

Solidarity activists are in part distinguished from the state's targets because of their stance of privilege. While most of these activists consciously engage with their role in dominant social arrangements as a key element of their political practice, part of this engagement is also reflecting critically on how their groups might perpetuate forms of oppression or false consciousness. I now turn to concerns participants expressed about the potential of solidarity witness, with its embodied and emotional dimensions, to lead some activists to collapse the distance between themselves and the state's targets.

THE TRICKINESS OF FELT JOURNEYS

There is a little bit of a danger that you can blur the line between you and the detainee. This is the problem of secondary witness. We are not the victim. This whole "We are all German Jews" that the French *Enragés* said in 1968 – at some level, no, you are not. That is the whole point. We never want to blur that line. We will un-costume when we want to affirm our role as sympathetic citizen. We wear the regalia when we want to be these haunting avatars of this abused population.

(Grele 2011: 88–9)

Using the example of the 1960s student movement in France, the French Enragés, Jeremy of WAT identified the potential to collapse distinctions between solidarity activists and the direct targets of state violence as a challenge endemic to witnessing. The Enragés sought to craft a collective subjectivity by identifying with Nazi Germany's most persecuted; they adopted the common mantel of German Jew to express the fact that all are under the state's thumb and potentially exploitable. Most of the activists in this study understand the US security state as a complex system that impacts everyone, including themselves. Yet in their stance of solidarity, these activists are regularly attentive to the privilege and protections that distinguish them from those who are incarcerated, disappeared, and terrorized. As Jeremy suggests, being an ethical witness requires maintaining the distinction between oneself and the directly violated. If the subject work of solidarity witness seeks to make the state's targets more morally proximate, the activists in this study reiterate time and again that they do not pursue similitude with the state's targets. Making such a distinction is a dynamic that many believed needed to be continually revisited. Moreover, participants suggested that one of the ways the subject work of witnessing goes awry is when the distinction between Enragé and Jew, solidarity activist and state target, is not maintained.

As explored in Chapter 4, embodied tactics serve as an important mode of witnessing, allowing activists to see and feel the sites and machinations of state violence that are otherwise obscured. Nevertheless, some worried that the physicality of these experiences might be misleading to some participants. This concern was specific to cases of entry-level activism, the Migrant Trail and SOA Watch vigil, to which participants come with more varied levels of commitment, experience, and consciousness. While all are sympathetic to the cause that they protest, some are on early journeys of learning as opposed to veterans who have spent large portions of their lives involved in social movements. Ana explained that while the Migrant Trail began among people who were all involved in border justice activism throughout the year, this has changed as the effort has grown: "We were all like people who had an understanding. We all had had friends who'd crossed ... that's different than now because some of the people are new and they don't have that other piece." It is worth noting that veterans of the Migrant Trail and SOA Watch are more likely to be critical of first-time participants whom they may not know and so their criticisms and concerns may be influenced by in-group, out-group dynamics.

Given this shift, some Migrant Trail veterans believed that the experiential learning aspect of the walk – contingent upon deep emotions and intense physical experiences – might be misleading to certain participants. Jane noted:

For the people who haven't been out here and been involved with these issues, it's really easy to forget that migrants are walking on really different terrain. We're walking on roads. They're dirt roads but they're roads. We're not walking through the mountains. This is very much not the intention of the organizers or of the walk, but people can fall into the idea that we're experiencing what migrants experience, and it's just blatantly not like that.

Susan, too, was concerned by how "folks who are not on the border" and new to the Migrant Trail might interpret the embodied experience of the walk:

I definitely can't imagine that someone participates on the walk and their hearts and their minds aren't shifted. But they have a solid understanding of the experience they had. And it's not a full picture of the reality. It is a snap shot.

Susan's concern was clearly not that participants would lack empathy but that perhaps empathy was insufficient. "If this is a starting point for people," she acknowledged, "that's great."

Embodied experience and the incumbent emotions are ways of knowing and certainly a powerful source in the social change arsenal. Still, as Carolyn Pedwell (2012) suggests, "emotions are interpreted most productively not as affective lenses on 'truth' or 'reality', but rather as one important (embodied) circuit through which power is felt, imagined, mediated, negotiated and/or contested" (176). Embodied experience on the Migrant Trail and the accompanying emotions are not necessarily complete or "truthful" in the sense of representing the reality of another. Rather, embodied experience is a powerful way of gleaning new ways of seeing and understanding state violence.

If many shared concerns that the Migrant Trail could be misleading, no one had a clear sense of how to address this beyond the current disclaimers of the organizers, in shared documents and at orientation, that "the Migrant Trail Walk is not intended to simulate the experience migrants face." A few suggested that the walk itself should be made more physically challenging but quickly realized that this might further the ontological collapse between acting in solidarity and being a migrant. Alex proposed leaving tents and sleeping bags behind, taking a few cans of tuna fish and a gallon of water each: "I think that all the softer sides of the Migrant walk, which I've become accustomed to and love, don't give people a realistic experience, or maybe enough of an idea of the suffering that migrants experience." Alex understood that the controversy with this suggestion was twofold. On the one hand, making the Migrant Trail even more intense could just as easily increase the propensity of both participants and bystanders to presume this was an effort to replicate migrants' experience. Alex acknowledged this: "We're not trying to replicate the exact experience of migrants." Alex's second concern was that in making the Migrant Trail more physically demanding, it would be "inaccessible for people." This would be counterproductive, Alex surmised, as the walk's point was to reach as many people as possible to "have the experience and then take back what they've learned to their community."

Others suggested that more informational programming during the walk, which newcomers have at times requested, would be beneficial. However, after considering this suggestion, organizers have decided that the Migrant Trail should not be what one leader termed "a traveling conference" with "speakers every night." There are many ways that people can learn more about the border, whether through their own research – Migrant Trail organizers provide a list of resources – or by joining one of the many educational delegations on the border coordinated by groups that also help organize the Migrant Trail. As importantly, Migrant Trail veterans are themselves seeking a space away from their daily activism and organizing. Ana explained, "We don't want to feel like camp counselors; we don't want to feel like delegation leaders. We wanna be able to just walk and that's really what it's about." Ana's assessment went further than this. She argued that the structured provision of more information on the walk would likely complicate rather than clarify the process of this witness. As Ana put it:

[The Migrant Trail] is about walking more than anything. Just being in that space ... I mean my feeling is come and walk and you're gonna be changed. I don't know how. But you will. And what are you gonna do with that when you leave is sort of the question. But I don't think that you should set a formula that people should go away and do X, Y and Z. I think it should just be about that willingness to be changed. That, to me, is more important.

The lack of this "formula," of a clear action plan or effort at mobilization, was believed by some to be part of the value of witnessing, a point I probe further in the next section. Yet others were frustrated by the lack of a political agenda. As Susan reflected, "I'm wanting to really move people toward more action, not just participation but action after they leave here. This is an experience, and I'm not convinced that they're actually going to take action past this." Jane concurred: "I just wish that there was more of an end result from [the Migrant Trail] on like a bigger level than the personal level that many of us experience it."

Both of these Migrant Trail veterans suggested that the personal journey and focus on remembrance might inadvertently be depoliticizing. This is likely true for some participants. Yet the contrary is also the case. Migrant Trail participant Julie explained that her initial motivation to walk was distinctly apolitical: "Honestly a big part of it for me was the personal journey. You know, you come to the desert and just personal things are going to happen. You're gonna learn stuff about yourself." While Julie sought and found something internal, she also found that she was politicized in an unexpected way. She continued:

Before I would always say [of the choice to walk the Migrant Trail], "It's not a political thing for me" because I'm afraid of offending people. But after hearing stories and seeing things that we've seen, I'm not afraid to say what I've experienced and what I believe about it. I'm not afraid to offend anyone. I think my heart's growing for it a lot. It can't help but not.

Julie's experience was not unique, and experiences such as hers reveal something important about solidarity witness. Concerns that the Migrant Trail's lack of a political program squanders its potential to mobilize participants, while understandable, do not account for the fact that it is precisely this "apolitical" stance that might attract unlikely individuals to a cause they did not know they would join. What begins for many as a personal or spiritual journey ultimately becomes a political one.

SOA Watch activists also shared concerns that the emotional aspects of witnessing might be depoliticizing. For instance, Damien acknowledged that by evoking powerful emotions, public mourning could offer activists an important resource in pushing against the dominant political frame: "The vigil itself, which includes the funeral procession, it jars you. That's the purpose it serves." At the same time, Damien worried that activists' emotions might short-circuit meaningful action. As he explained:

I also think that there's a downside to the vigil in that I've seen a lot of people go to [it] almost as if to manage their emotional state ... People take too much of that with them and not enough of the momentum that we need. This isn't something to assuage people's guilt, to make someone absolve themselves in their tears ... that's not the end of the work.

Damien's observation speaks to an enduring debate among both activists and scholars regarding the role of empathy in contesting systems of dominance. Pedwell suggests we consider empathy as an important first step for undoing systemic oppression if it moves "the 'privileged' subject from self-transformation, to acknowledgement of complicity and responsibility, to wider social action and change" (2012: 165). By this developmental arc, moving beyond the stage of self-transformation is a crucial part of the process. This is also an interesting consideration in regard to the ascetic dimension of solidarity witness. Due to the deeply interior work of solidarity witness, tactics that for some might help to shrug off the yoke of individualism might become overly individualistic undertakings for others. As Damien suggests, political change is not secured when solidarity activists absolve themselves in tears.

Samantha, a college student who was attending the Fort Benning vigil for the first time reflected on her experience in a way that seemed to affirm some of Damien's concerns. At the end of a long interview in which she expressed great excitement about the SOA Watch weekend, a final question regarding whether or not she would change anything caused her to pause. After a few seconds, Samantha concluded: "The way that I felt changed afterwards, it was more in myself than that I really feel like I made a huge impact on the actual SOA or anything." Samantha was clear that the personal journey had been impactful, that she felt like the "veil was coming off her eyes." But she reflected on her concern that she had not really made any difference:

I think there are people who are making a huge impact. But personally I don't feel like going to that protest that I really had a huge impact on anything. I know that just by being around hundreds and hundreds of people and talking to so many interesting people that I really benefited from it, which I think is an interesting aspect of protesting. I'm not really sure how I would change it. I just know that I want to be involved in something where I feel more tangibly that I'm creating a change.

The fact that Samantha felt herself changed by the Fort Benning experience speaks to the powerful transformations of solidarity witness. Such transformative experiences have the potential to endure, to change people's lives, and to mobilize them to undertake further action. They also have the potential to be understood as an end in themselves and in this way to be depoliticizing. This is a central promise and pitfall of solidarity witness as a political practice upon which I now elaborate.

"WE STILL NEED TO BE ABLE TO ACT"

In 2008, WAT members Jeremy Varon and Frida Berrigan were having a conversation in a Greek diner after the group had screened a movie. Though Jeremy had only recently become involved with Witness Against Torture, he had been an activist for years, though always a secular one. Frida was a lifelong activist too, but from a different tradition. Raised by some of the most dedicated radical pacifists of the nuclear disarmament movement, she had grown up in a Catholic Worker-type community in Baltimore, Maryland, called Jonah House.

As they chatted in the diner, Jeremy asked Frida about Witness Against Torture's long-term vision. "What is the end game? What are we trying to change? Are we trying to change policy? What about Congress?"

Frida's response was clear and concise. "Power never listens. It is not really about changing the people in power. We are not going to change them. I do not care what the institutions [do]."

Jeremy was flabbergasted. "Really? Don't you want to free prisoners and win court cases and defeat the Military Commissions Act?"

Reflecting on this conversation years later, Jeremy observed:

I am not in it just to witness and not have that witness make a difference ... [Frida] had, it seemed to me, this cosmic cynicism about the fallibility of earthly justice and this commitment to some sort of divine conception of righteousness without much mediation between the two.

Frida and Jeremy made a bargain while in that Greek diner. He would write a piece of guerilla theater for WAT, and Frida would entertain Jeremy's way of thinking. Years later, the two are still close friends. (This story is based on the account in Grele 2011: 72)

Frida and Jeremy's exchange represents an important distinction in orientation among the activists in this study. Many, like Frida, are indeed witnessing as an alternative to what they understand to be "politics." For these activists, witnessing is a means of staying engaged when the official political system offers no other meaningful avenues for dissent. Others, like Jeremy, are unwilling to forego more direct engagement with state institutions and representatives. They believe that the act of witnessing must be instrumental, part of a larger plan to apply pressure to change policies. While not always the case, those who espouse the former perspective tend to come to their activism with a faith-based cosmology. Frida, raised by an ex-priest and an ex-nun in a Christian community, was not so concerned about how institutions would respond to WAT's efforts. Jeremy, ardently secular in his approach to politics, felt otherwise.

This study contends that solidarity witness is a political practice even if and when instrumental aims are deprioritized or traditional engagement with the state does not occur. Solidarity witness also makes important impacts, even if measurable institutional changes are not often achieved. However, the activists in these groups have differing ideas about what it means to engage politically and to what extent witnessing can be considered a political strategy. These differences of opinion do not tend to manifest as conflicts *between* activists, but they do drive differences in how participants think about their involvement with these groups.

Burt of SOA Watch explained the relationship between witnessing, politics and religion in a way that was fairly representative of how the activists in this study understand these concepts:

Bearing witness – I don't want to say it's an end in itself, but it stands alone. It may not accomplish anything, and that's where it's part of but not the same as activism, which may have an objective of accomplishing something. Bearing witness is certainly a part of activism, but from a religious standpoint it can stand alone.

This idea that witnessing can stand alone when taken as a religious concept is significant. Many activists across these groups articulated witnessing as a practice that not only can be, but indeed must be, disentangled from outcomes. This is linked to a core principle for many of the faith-driven activists in this study, that in order to do God's work, one must relinquish an attachment to this-worldly results. While many theologians and Christian leaders have espoused such a stance, such a teaching is perhaps most famously articulated in the work of Catholic author Thomas Merton, whom many referenced when explaining to me the ethos of witnessing. In a famous letter to his younger friend and peace activist, Jim Forest, Merton advised:

[D]o not depend on the hope of results ... you may have to face the fact that your work will be apparently worthless and even achieve no result at all, if not perhaps results opposite to what you expect. As you get used to this idea, you start more and more to concentrate not on the results, but on the value, the rightness, the truth of the work itself.

(Merton 1985: 294)

In this sense, a religious approach to witnessing defies any traditional understanding of social movement strategy. Joanne of WAT explained:

[Witnessing] is not about being successful. It's about speaking the truth, and that's what witnessing in this context is about. We don't know what effect our words will have.

It can seem hopeless, but the important thing is to speak, to speak the truth ... we use that word on a witness stand in the court process. You take an oath to speak the truth.

Joanne's comparison of solidarity witness to being in the court system, a central institution of the state, might seem odd considering how pessimistic most of these activists are about the state's propensity for good. Yet Joanne's explanation has many implications. At one level, she is explaining that the tradition of witnessing is actually quite central to the American political process. Even if the way in which these groups witness and testify in the streets looks very different than an individual being on a witness stand in a courtroom, the logic behind the act is similar. The second aspect of this comparison, meaningful to faith-driven activists, is the idea of putting the state on trial under divine law. These activists do not know what impact their testimony will have. Instead, they trust in a higher power – and the human potential for goodness as an extension of this – that the act of truthful testimony can transform the conditions of dominance. This is linked to the ascetic dimension of solidarity witnessing – by engaging in a set of practices, these activists trust that something more moral and transformative can occur.

Such an approach might appear to be highly abstract or a complete replacement of political thinking with religious ideals. I would argue that this is not the case. Witnesses are quite politically savvy even when they refuse to participate in politics as traditionally defined. This became evident in an extended discussion with WAT member Harriet on the topic of witnessing and conceptions of the political. In our conversation, Harriet began:

The people that I'm an activist with, for the most part, are very religious. [Though] my faith is more diffuse than theirs, those are the people that I want to be witnessing with because their impulse feels right to me. Their need to witness comes from a place deep within as opposed to being some sort of a political thing. It's very deeply personal. My motivation to be an activist comes from within myself, and my faith is part of that.

Surprised that Harriet would not understand WAT's work as a political practice, I asked her to elaborate on what she meant by the term "political," to which she responded:

Doing things for political purposes to me means doing things to make change, to address grievances to the government or elect officials, or do the sorts of things that typical political organizations do. My feeling is that this government is so heavily powerful in its military industrial arm that it probably isn't going to respond to that. I don't believe we're going to make change.

Harriet's sense that traditional political work is not going to change the way that the state perpetuates war-making, imprisonment, and border enforcement is perhaps the "cosmic cynicism" that Jeremy describes in his conversation with Frida. At the same time, it may well be an accurate assessment of the current configuration of state power. Harriet and I were speaking in the spring of 2014. While the Obama Administration had reaffirmed its efforts to close

Guantánamo, the president had already broken this promise in 2009 and current progress was slow. Given these realities, it was clear why traditional political engagement would not be very appealing. Harriet continued:

If I were just doing things politically I would simply give up and say it's useless. But I feel as if I have to respond personally to maintain my own integrity, and to be part of history and be in the place in history where it's important for there to be a response even if it fails ... So that's where my faith tells me, my inner integrity tells me, that I need to be active in expressing and trying to change on some level what's happening.

Such a response might seem to have traded on tangible, political gains to achieve only personal, spiritual aims. Yet there are important implications to such a stance, both in what it tells us about the nature of the US security state as well as the approach that some of these activists need to adopt in order to maintain commitment in the face of despair. As a political practice, solidarity witness offers another way in, a form of engagement and a commitment mechanism to confront a state security apparatus that seems impenetrable to acts of popular dissent.

WAT member Maya also considered the interplay between witnessing and politics carefully, suggesting that it was this continued engagement despite limited tangible victories that gave witness its political purpose:

I think we have to ask the question about effectiveness. The word "witness" offers a different perspective on that question. I think that we're much more powerful than we think that we are, our little group of however many. But when you put that amount of power up against the amount of power of the US military, it just doesn't quite equate. So recognizing that and seeing it clearly, how can we still act in the world because that's the right thing to do, even though it might not be "effective," [scare quotes] or might not create the exact change that we want to see? We still need to be able to act.

Here Maya identifies that witnessing is not merely seeing and acting on the realities of state violence but also having a clear appraisal of the political context. Witnessing allows these activists to push for the social and moral vision they know to be just while still being cognizant of the gloomy political calculus.

Betsy offered a similar sense of how witnessing works on the Migrant Trail, framing the walk as a form of healing and spirituality for those engaged in the day-to-day struggle of border justice politics:

I think the vision of the walk is to give people who do long-term work or who identify with the reality that migrants go through [in order] to come to the US, some kind of response that's individual and collective, that can be meditative and memorial for people who die in the desert, who have to make that walk. It's part memorial and part like an active thing people do to have some kind of response to people dying in the desert.

The notion that witnessing is an "active thing" and "some kind of response," regardless of clear instrumental and political gains, was centrally important for those who found value in being a witness.

This is not to say that those who believed one should witness regardless of political efficacy were at ease with this arrangement. Long-term Migrant Trail participant Dave explained how he had transitioned from what he termed a more "political" orientation to understanding the Migrant Trail as a witness, even if he still hopes the group will make an impact and be seen.

[The Migrant Trail] is a way for us to see and experience the environment that people walk through and to explore our emotions about the deaths in the desert. Now if in the process it gains some political clout or impact, that's all the better. At first I saw that as probably the primary part, but I'm not so sure it's the primary part anymore. I concur with [Ana] when she says "it's not as much a political march as it is a way to be aware of the tragedy of people dying." Although sometimes I'm disappointed that we don't have more press, I understand how fickle the press is.

Dave's explanation of what the Migrant Trail intends to accomplish, his own shifts in orientation and continued disappointment when media coverage is limited, reveal core ambivalences that many activists navigate as they seek to be witnesses to what they also understand as vexing political issues.

For WAT member Faith, being a witness to horror and violence came with an even heavier combination of conviction, distress, and doubt. Aware of the devastating stakes of not having successfully impacted on the issue of Guantánamo, Faith lamented:

Sometimes I feel like all I can do is keep my eyes open and not avert my gaze. I don't know what else to do. And is that enough? (big sigh) I don't know ... I'm not so inclined to say, "yeah, I'm making this huge difference." I do feel that I'll keep doing what I'm doing ... The reason I stay with WAT is this bearing witness. It is vital to me. That's why I stay. And I feel that for the men at Guantánamo I will keep hanging on. For their sake. For their families' sake. For their children's' sake.

Other activists were more critical of witnessing altogether, believing that the very tactics that allowed activists a personal witness might actually hinder movement success, or at least not promote it. This sentiment was usually expressed by SOA Watch protesters who, unlike the other two groups, can reflect on decades of witnessing experience at Fort Benning. For instance, Theresa Cusimano, who had committed civil disobedience twice at Fort Benning and suffered immensely during her time in jail, expressed general cynicism about this tactic:

The non-violent civil disobedience, its only function is for personal witness. So if you need to come out to yourself with your values, it is a venue. But it's not changing minds; it's not changing votes. People who might be for us are actually against us when they see the civil disobedience because most people don't want any disobedience. So there's not the solidarity of Martin Luther King, there's not the solidarity of Gandhi. I just think it's the wrong tool, wrong time, wrong purpose.

Theresa was somewhat of an outlier among the activists in this study in how critical she was, likely linked to how uniquely brutal and destructive her time in prison had been. At the same time, Theresa assessed that she could not propose an easy alternative. "Part of my frustration is that I don't know what we should be doing to impact on this issue. I don't know how to change the course of how we spend on violence and how we invest in torture."

Also frustrated with the event at Fort Benning, Burt discussed SOA Watch's work not as damaging so much as ineffectual:

There's a difference between individual martyrdom and bearing witness in that way versus when a mass of people do it, they kind of upset the system. I think the event at Fort Benning – I don't think there is much scope for a mass [disobedience]. I've been frustrated with this for ten years, but I've just never come up with anything that seemed plausible or feasible ... It's difficult to confront the power brokers. You can hold a vigil outside Fort Benning. And they say, "okay, well, that was cool," and nothing changes.

Burt concluded that the vigil at Ft. Benning had become an act of witness with little political impact. In recent years, Burt suggested, the effort to close the SOA has had much more success by going to Latin America and pressuring governments there to stop sending militia and police to be trained at the school. While successful, Burt perceived that this work had been largely undertaken by Father Bourgeois alone, and so as a strategy, it "doesn't help the mass of people that want to do something themselves."

Yet further research suggests that Burt may be wrong on this account; the effort to pressure Latin American governments has actually been a mass movement, not the work of an individual. Those involved in this movement have been predominately Latin Americans, not the solidarity activists that converge on Fort Benning every year. As distinct from Burt, Damien understood the vigil at the SOA as an important expression of solidarity with the most directly impacted. Through their relentless, yearly presence, Damien suggested, this witness was targeting "the culture":

I think that one of the broadest tactics that SOA Watch adopts is this changing of the culture. A culture change doesn't necessarily disrupt the power structure, but it can facilitate the place in which directly impacted communities can continue to challenge that power structure. If we can be in solidarity with those who are defending their self-determination, then we can be the arm of resistance to the School of Americas while people continue to fight the battles that are delivered to their doorstep day by day as a result of these policies ... Changing the culture is necessary work, but I do believe that it's only half the work. I don't think that we should trespass on the work that other communities need to do for themselves.

Damien's distinction between culture and structure, in which witnessing targets the former, political action the latter, may be an overly simplistic rendering of how social and political dynamics work. Nevertheless, his delineation serves as a useful heuristic. This understanding of how to best be in solidarity is also quite specific to SOA Watch, which among these groups is most able to support directly impacted communities as they contest state violence from a different geopolitical location and perspective.

The possibilities for solidarity activism are of course very different in the case of Guantánamo in which the directly impacted have been stripped of rights, held indefinitely and in an offshore location that is hard to reach. In this context, many WAT members were committed to witnessing against the odds of success. However, some saw this to be an approach that actually contradicts what it means to be in solidarity. As Jeremy explained:

If we go spiritual and say this is all about soul connection and this abstract concept of witness and raising consciousness and educating the public, and do not actually try to get them out of prison, we have allowed the central evil to persist ... We owe it to them [Guantánamo detainees] to use every available channel within the limits of our concept and our community for the circumstances of their lives to meaningfully change.

(Grele 2011: 98–9)

These distinctions in orientation among WAT members do not ultimately lead to infighting so much as a division of labor. Indeed, WAT's regular planning retreats are centrally concerned with political calculus. A few organizers will collect information from various allied organizations and present detailed intelligence to the rest of the group. It is then up to the collective to develop the most creative and impactful forms of protest they can, given this political information.

Jeremy explained that his role was a specific one within the way that WAT organizes itself:

Being an academic and text junkie, I – probably more than anybody else in the group – have made a point of trying to master some of the detail ... We are very careful to build our actions on a command of the facts and our understanding of the political meaning of the facts.

(Grele 2011: 73)

Faith explained her role in contrast to this:

We are absolutely doing what we know to be the right thing to do and the most effective thing to do ... but I'm not necessarily the person who has the pulse. I do trust that there are other people in the group who do.

Jeremy concluded that the division of labor allowed WAT to include these very different orientations into a consistent whole: "There is the cosmic and then there is the grind of all of this. My role has been to remind the group of the micro moves of the grind" (Grele 2011: 100).

The activists in these groups vary some in how they think about political engagement and questions of efficacy. These different ideas manifest less as conflicts within groups or between activists as they do as frustrations about a sense of powerlessness in a system that is overwhelming in its scope, reach, and violence.

Even if witnessing has its own political logic that situates it outside of conventional understandings of politics, continuing to witness against the odds of institutional change can also be understood as a political act in itself. Insofar as solidarity witness is a way of being and acting against global dynamics of injustice and impossible divides of power, this political practice must rely on alternative logics, psychic rewards, and commitment mechanisms to those which dominant society proffers. A pursuit of rightness in process and ethical existence in lieu of what many would measure as political results provides this alternative for some, even if the very activists who espouse this stance understand theirs as a necessary if insufficient enactment of solidarity. For others, the cosmic is not nearly enough. The grind must also be articulated and pursued as so many lives are held in the balance.

CONCLUSION

Solidarity witness is a political practice that challenges conventional understandings of what counts as political activity and holds out against a common sense that posits policy reform as more meaningful than other shifts of epistemology and imagination. At the same time, because witnessing provides deeply interior and often religiously meaningful forms of transformation, some worry that its political edge can be subsumed by other impulses. There is concern that mass forms of mobilization have not been prioritized and that these groups' annual gatherings might lead newcomers to false conceptions. Just as importantly, solidarity witness is not for everyone. Its forms of discipline and its unwavering commitment to a certain understanding of "nonviolence" are alienating for some.

In exploring the frustrations that all activists are bound to express toward their chosen approach to social change, we gain some purchase on what a given political practice accomplishes and where it falls short. We also deepen our understanding about the political and ethical commitments these activists hold regardless of what they have the power to achieve. Social life is riddled with ambivalences, contradictions, and unexpected outcomes. When these groups articulate what they perceive to be their limitations, constraints, or areas for growth, they tell us that no political project is complete, that solidarity activism will always be an imperfect approximation, and that solidarity witness is both capacious and flawed.

7

"Knowing Things Impossible to Un-know"

The act of bearing witness truly is a life-changing one. You know things that are wonderfully and terribly impossible to un-know. You are standing somewhere sacred, and now, you have to do something about it, because bearing witness carries with it the responsibility of doing something with this new knowledge.

Kat Rodriguez, Migrant Trail organizer, 2015 TEDx talk given at the City University of New York

Many of them indeed know better, but as you will discover, people find it very difficult to act on what they know. To act is to be committed and to be committed is to be in danger.

James Baldwin, *A Letter to My Nephew* 1962

In November 2015, during her TED talk, Kat Rodriguez discussed the Migrant Trail as part of her years of work on the US–Mexico border. Kat reiterated what many of the activists in this study observe. The practice of solidarity witness is "a life-changing one." Solidarity witness is a way of coming to know, see, and act beyond the deeply limited forms of knowledge and politics that underwrite the US security state. This is not merely a cognitive process. Solidarity witness forges an embodied, affective, sometimes spiritual, and always committed mode of knowing. As Kat suggests, knowing "things that are wonderfully and terribly impossible to un-know" is a profound responsibility.

The responsibility that comes with this kind of knowing about injustice, violence, and one's own complicity in the system is dangerous, even for those who are not most acutely violated. James Baldwin made this observation in 1962 when he penned a now famous letter to his teenage nephew. Baldwin explained that even for white people, the obvious "winners" in a system of white supremacy, the stakes of knowing and acting against racism were not small. Baldwin explained that while many white people do "indeed know better," they do not act on what they know. Acting on what they know, Baldwin suggested, requires commitment. With such commitment, there is vulnerability, exposure, and risk – what Baldwin calls "danger." The solidarity activists in this study might agree. To bear witness and to "do something with this new sacred knowledge and understanding," as Kat puts it, is the commitment of solidarity witness. This is a commitment borne of having seen things that one cannot un-see. It requires a willingness to take risks. It also offers the hope of an alternative to the alienation of everyday bourgeois life and the fear-based politics of the US security state. Such a commitment portends a better form of life.

This study set out to understand how three movement groups, all broadly from the Christian left, predominately white and middle class, imagine and enact solidarity across the divisions of power and reverberations of violence that organize today's global society. Such an inquiry also directs us to understand how those who are not the state's targets experience the US security state politically and subjectively. The study identifies and elaborates a political practice I term "solidarity witness." Solidarity witness is an embodied, affective, and often religious means of pursuing solidarity with those who lack the practical freedoms to advocate for themselves. Just as importantly, solidarity witness allows those who are otherwise expected to buy into the fundamental logics and behaviors of the security state to refuse to do so.

As a political practice, solidarity witness is both performative and prefigurative. Ritual protest, a testimony to this witness, is political theater *and* solemn meditation. These activists stage evocative public dramas to share compelling messages with various publics. Yet the activists in this study design their ritual protest with a particular mood and aesthetic, making such performances feel more authentic to those involved and enhancing intra-group solidarity. The embodiment of solidarity witness also serves both expressive and instrumental aims. By putting their bodies on the line, solidarity activists learn lessons that they would not otherwise experience while amplifying the resistance of the state's targets for diverse audiences. The embodiment of witness makes more visible and morally proximate the state's targets, whom the dominant culture fears and abjects. The ritual protest and embodied discipline of solidarity witness can be understood as components of what is ultimately an ascetic political practice. The activists in this study engage in a form of sociopolitical withdrawal, intending to craft selves and collectives that can resist the US security state with enhanced conviction and commitment. Their fasting, pilgrimage, and jail time are ultimately a mode of training for long-term, nonviolent resistance. The power of solidarity witness as an ascetic practice derives in part from the fact that it is undertaken collectively, as a form of prefigurative politics. These activists model the interactions, relationships, and ways of being that they wish to see in the world writ large. In turn, they experience psychic rewards that help prevent despair and burnout and find a mode of existence that offers a much-desired alternative to more conventional social arrangements.

Like all political practices, solidarity witness is not without its complications and conflicts. Participants in these groups worry that the core features of solidarity witness – the intensive subject work and the relatively unstructured nature of witnessing as a political act – might fail to be mobilizing for certain participants, especially newcomers to these efforts. Participants in these groups are also aware and often frustrated that forms of racial exclusion, ignorance, and microaggressions continue to make their way into the communities they have carefully built. By exploring such dilemmas, we gain a sense of these activists' richly considered notions of solidarity activism in contesting the US security state. Movement work is always incomplete, and the tools used for political struggle are often double edged. Part of the artistry of social movement efforts is to effectively navigate such contradictions without allowing them to derail progress toward a more just and equitable horizon.

Through solidarity witness, the activists in this study work to expand the sphere of politics. They contest dominant ways of seeing and understanding the impacts of the US security state. They create avenues for dissent and political analyses that would not be tolerated, and would likely be wholly unrecognizable, in official halls of state power. These activists expose the US security state's contradictions in visceral, emotional, and culturally provocative ways. They invite bystanders to interrogate today's dominant solidarities as fear-based and chauvinist. At the same time, they cultivate alternatives – cultures of opposition by which they prepare themselves for enduring resistance.

LEARNING FROM SOLIDARITY WITNESS

This book does not intend to argue that solidarity witness is the only or the best way to respond to the US security state. Yet by examining movements' choices and strategies, we better understand how society is governed and how such governance functions in practice. As a political practice solidarity witness can tell us something not just about a kind of activism but also about the US security state as a target of struggle.

Much of the formative research on social movements, responding to the movements of the New Left and the 1960s, emerged under a different political context than we find today. As Chapter 1 outlines, the 1970s' rise of transnational neoliberalism has generated a host of concomitant shifts in global governance. One of these is that the nation-state, as a handmaiden of the market, has shifted its investments to so-called security purposes – policing and incarceration, waging wars, and organizing regimes of human immobility. For movements seeking greater democracy and social justice, this creates a new terrain of struggle with its own set of political possibilities and prohibitions. Globalization provides new potentials for connecting across time, space, nationality, and language – the forging of new solidarities, mobilities, and imaginaries. At the same time, the kind of democratic pressure on the state that won concessions in the Civil Rights era will not work today as it did a half a century ago.

The contemporary US security state is predicated on the most minimal pretense to democracy, organized around closed institutions and false transparency. The traditional means for mounting political alternatives are profoundly narrowed. The biggest protests in history offer no protection from war. The legal system has amassed exceptions to its own rules, and those most in need of legal protections are often simply denied access to the courts. Yet beyond its most evident structural manifestations, the US security state depends upon a deeply sociocultural motor. National security is not something that the American public is allowed to debate. Those who openly critique detention, torture, and disappearance, who point out that the security state only makes us more insecure, are labeled unpatriotic and treasonous (Butler 2004). Their forms of analysis certainly do not make it into top-level decision-making.

While the political opportunities for the campaigns in this book have long seemed fairly bleak, the US security state has seen real shifts in the extremity of its implementation. It is worth noting that data collection and most of the writing for this book was undertaken during the Obama Administration, a presidency that many in these groups argued at the time was as bad as any on issues of immigration, military intervention, and indefinite detention. Nevertheless, Trump's 2016 election and early tenure introduce a qualitative shift in rhetoric and policy. Racist discourse, centrally targeting Muslims, Mexicans and other migrants, was popular enough to win a presidential election.[1] Trump has supported keeping Guantánamo open, bringing new prisoners there, and pursuing torture as an effective means of intelligence gathering. He has issued draft memos that reverse Obama's 2009 order, which sought to close the prison and limit military interrogation techniques to those that meet basic standards of humane treatment (Finnegan 2017). Trump has also been a bombastic proponent of the Islamophobia that WAT has long claimed animated Guantánamo's existence. Whereas most politicians have been much more cautious in expressing outright racism and religious intolerance, Trump has proposed Muslim registration lists reminiscent of US policies toward the Japanese during World War II. In June 2018, the Supreme Court ruled along partisan lines to uphold Trump's third iteration of a "travel ban," preventing those from five Muslim-majority countries, as well as Venezuela and North Korea, from entering the US. Trump also continues to highlight his commitment to constructing a wall at the US–Mexico border, one of his more controversial pillars during the campaign. His administration has taken the unprecedented measure of separating migrant children from their guardians, without records or identification, and placing them in detention, a practice that has generated horror and worldwide condemnation. Without overemphasizing the power of a given individual or

---

[1] It is of course beyond the purview of this project to determine the various factors that led to the outcome in the 2016 presidential race. I am not arguing that organized racism and support for state violence against vulnerable populations was *the* winning strategy but rather an undeniable part of a successful effort to win support from large contingents of the American public.

political office to usher in new policies on torture and immigration, this nevertheless appears to be a particularly dark time for the state's targets and the activists in this study. At this conjuncture, we urgently require new understandings of what political activity to contest the state might look like. Solidarity witness offers some ideas.

First, contesting the US security state requires endurance. In seeking to find a mode of struggle that aligns with their own moral visions, those involved in the practice of solidarity witness demonstrate a level of commitment that is quite unusual, even among political activists. These groups are important to pay attention to not because of their short-term successes but because of their longer-term preparation. By crafting resistant and collective subjectivities that renounce the dominant order and forego many of its core logics and seductions, these groups are involved in a form of productive refusal. No matter how active (or not) they appear, these activists are engaged in a committed, intentional, well-considered process of movement preparation. Mass mobilizations are never as spontaneous as they appear. Activists are always preparing, strategizing, forging ahead in the face of unlikely odds. Yet it is also this preparation that can turn the political tides when the moment is right and a struggle is taken to scale. Mass mobilization in opposition to the Trump Administration's most draconian proposals might be one of these moments.

Second, claims making on the nation-state – what social movement scholars have long assumed was the animating feature of collective action for political change – might make less sense in today's transnational order than it once did. By seeking to enact solidarity with the targets of the US security state's most draconian policies, the groups in this study are tackling structures of injustice beyond the scope of any feasible effort at policy change. Insofar as these groups do seek tangible institutional reforms, they do so as a way to both impact the behemoth of the neoliberal order as well as expose its contradictions. These groups demonstrate that a supposed national security assured through the torture and indefinite detention of some, the enforcement of impossible borders against others, and mass military interventions the world over is no security at all. These campaigns make the human stakes of state violence evident. In so doing, they give themselves and their audiences a feasible target of struggle in the context of transnational dynamics that exceed what any movement can realistically confront. The practice of solidarity witness in this sense highlights the limitations of piecemeal policy change at the level of the nation-state under a global, neoliberal security complex.

Third, the policies of the US security state depend on narrow ways of seeing, knowing, and living. When the activists in this study undertake many of the core practices of solidarity witness, they push past the perspectives of rational choice, frame alignment, and liberal individualism that continue to dominate how we think about social movements. These groups do things that are frankly illogical if measured by such perspectives – fasting for days, walking in the desert in great discomfort, getting arrested and spending months and even years in jails and prisons. When these groups envision and enact solidarity with the most degraded, they speak back to the narrow notion of self-interest that dominates not just American political culture but our understanding of what motivates and sustains activists, even when traditionally defined victories are few and far between.

Part of the conception of solidarity at play for these activists is that the abuse of state power impacts everyone but in ways that must not be made equivalent. These activists experience moral outrage and profound grief in the face of the state's acute violence. They fight mightily so that militarism, over-zealous policing and incarceration, rampant legal exceptionalism, torture, and the undergirding racism are made visible for all to behold. The neglect, disappearance, and abuse of society's most vulnerable pose indisputable evidence that something in the social body is damaged. They expose the contradictions of dominance and point to the ways in which the system impoverishes all.

At the same time, many of these activists are driven by the despair and disillusionment that accompany the ways that the US security state shows up in their daily lives, often as a sense of isolation and meaninglessness. As a form of struggle, solidarity witness allows these activists to satisfy a desire for self-respect, to craft a current existence that seems more dignified, moral, just, and imaginative than their lives previously permitted, and to attach themselves to a collective struggle for a better future. They articulate an ethical alternative, speaking back to power in a manner that is legible, subversive, and, for many, transformational.

Methodological Appendix

When I initially conceptualized this project, I presumed that I would focus on an *event* rather than a *group*. This is in part because I had already begun research with the Migrant Trail, which incidentally is both. Thus, I planned to examine the Fort Benning vigil as opposed to SOA Watch in its entirety, the Migrant Trail as a weeklong journey, and Witness Against Torture's week of fasting and civil disobedience in Washington DC every January. Part of this was a question of scope. The fact that SOA Watch now encompasses many campaigns and projects, for example, made a focus on the vigil seem a more reasonable undertaking. The other reason to look at events was my interest in what these groups *do* when they witness as an act of solidarity. I intended to focus on embodied, emotional, and quasi-religious forms of nonviolent protest as a kind of patterned culture of resistance. In so doing, I believed I might also be able to offer some insight into the nature and reach of the state violence that these groups contest. This kind of inquiry remained my preeminent concern.

As I began to get more involved in observant participation (Costa Vargas 2006) and interviewing, however, I realized that focusing solely on annual gatherings as opposed to a more expansive conception of each group's work created false limitations regarding what I could ask and examine. These were limitations that the activists did not share. Much of what WAT has done, such as the two journeys to Cuba, did not occur during the group's January weeks of action. To tell WAT's story in any complete measure requires considering actions, activities, and processes beyond their yearly convening in Washington DC. SOA Watch has also done a great deal of work outside of the Fort Benning vigil, with yearly advocacy days in Washington DC as well as delegations and projects throughout the hemisphere. I did not personally participate in these latter activities, and I still focus on the group's effort to close the school. Yet SOA participants made common reference to the movement's other efforts. Thus if the majority of my observant participation has indeed occurred during the weeks of action I initially intended to study, what I might term "my unit of analysis" in traditional social science terminology has become *communities* in resistance as opposed to annual events.

The data for this project include weeks of observant participation (Costa Vargas 2006), semi-structured interviews, follow-up surveys, and an archive of hundreds of courtroom statements. All interviews began by inquiring into the participant's basic demographic information – age, occupation, racial identity, religion, and class background, for instance. I then asked about personal history with activism and what drew people to their group. The next set of questions focused on group vision and tactics, the kind of people involved, and if activists would change anything about their group. For SOA Watch and WAT, I inquired into participant experiences with civil disobedience. Data collection was not identical across the cases, which I now treat in turn.

My research with Migrant Trail participants was unique in that my experience with the walk far exceeds my level of immersion with either of the other two groups. Ahead of the 2011 Migrant Trail, which was my first time doing the walk in the capacity of a researcher, I contacted four walk organizers and two prior participants. They were all excited to be interviewed. Doing so in the comfort of homes and offices, as opposed to in the searing hot desert, led to longer and more nuanced discussions. During the walk itself, I conducted twelve more interviews in the desert, for a total of eighteen digitally recorded conversations. I also administered demographic information surveys to fifty-four of that year's fifty-eight participants and conducted sixteen follow-up surveys in 2012 with those who were newcomers on the Migrant Trail in 2011. These surveys allowed me to measure what, if any, enduring impact the walk has had on activists themselves (Russo 2014). While I have conducted no official interviews since 2011, I have walked the Migrant Trail in an official research capacity three times, in 2011, 2013, and 2014, with twenty-one total days of note-taking, digital recording, and photo documentation. My five other Migrant Trail experiences, of course, cannot be cleanly partitioned from the archive of experience from which I draw.

I did not commence research with SOA Watch or WAT until 2013. In both cases, I began by doing exploratory interviews with key organizers followed by multiday trips to each group's annual gatherings. My first contact with members of these groups was made through people I had met during my years in immigrant rights organizing. While the central organizers in both groups were incredibly busy – often balancing jobs, schooling and care-taking responsibilities with their activism – most were eager and willing to talk to me. Many of the activists across all three groups have pursued extended college and graduate educations and are themselves teachers, educators, and independent journalists. In addition to our shared social networks, these activists have tended to be familiar with and excited by the idea of having someone document their communities. I undertook two research trips to the WAT weeks of action in January 2014 and 2015, with an additional research trip to the group's 2014 planning retreat. This totaled fourteen days of observant participation. In total, I conducted sixteen semi-structured interviews with WAT participants over videoconference or telephone. Akin to the demographic information survey administered with Migrant Trail participants, I conducted a similar assessment with WAT in 2015 in which thirty-eight of an estimated forty-five weeklong participants took part.

I also conducted two research trips to SOA Watch's Fort Benning vigil in 2013 and 2014 with six days total of observant participation and fifteen semi-structured interviews, ten of these by phone and five in person. Collecting representative survey data at SOA Watch as I had done with the other cases was not possible for a single researcher confronted with no less than 2,000 people at both the 2013 and 2014 Fort Benning gatherings. Though I lack the kind of overarching demographic portrait of SOA Watch that survey data provide, there are other sources of information available for this case that do not exist for the Migrant Trail or WAT. There has been a fair amount of published research on SOA Watch, making it possible for me to supplement my own information with data collected by others (Nepstad 2000; Gill 2004; Sundberg 2007; Koopman 2008). Moreover, SOA Watch itself has maintained hundreds of courtroom statements made by those who have stood trial for their civil disobedience. This archive allows me to tell a story about a twenty-five-year-old movement with a level of historical depth and nuance that observant participation, interviews, and survey methods alone would not provide.

Bibliography

"2015 CWU Human Rights Award Recipient: Margo Cowan." 2015. *Church Women United in Tucson*. http://cwutucson.org/margo-cowan.html

Aamer, Shaker. 2014. "In Guantánamo, National Security Rides Roughshod over Human Rights." *The Guardian*. www.theguardian.com/commentisfree/2014/jan/05/guantanamo-national-security-human-rights-us-military-constitution

Adorno, Theodor W. 1973. *Negative Dialectics*. Translated by E. B. Ashton. New York: Routledge.

Ahmed, Sara. 2004. *The Cultural Politics of Emotion*. New York: Routledge.

Alexander, Michelle. 2010. *The New Jim Crow: Mass Incarceration in the Age of Colorblindness*. New York: The New Press.

Anderson, Benedict. 1983. *Imagined Communities: Reflections on the Origin and Spread of Nationalism*. New York: Verso.

Andreas, Peter. 2009. *Border Games: Policing the U.S.-Mexico Divide*. 2nd edn. Ithaca, NY: Cornell University Press.

Anzaldúa, Gloria. 1987. *Borderlands/La Frontera: The New Mestiza*. San Francisco, CA: Aunt Lute Books.

Appelbaum, Patricia. 2014. *Kingdom to Commune: Protestant Pacifist Culture between World War I and the Vietnam Era*. Chapel Hill: The University of North Carolina Press.

Arendt, Hannah. 1963. *On Revolution*. Harmondsworth, UK: Penguin Books.

Armstrong, Elizabeth A., and Mary Bernstein. 2008. "Culture, Power, and Institutions: A Multi-Institutional Politics Approach to Social Movements." *Sociological Theory* 26 (1): 74–99.

Bacevich, Andrew J., ed. 2009. *The Long War: A New History of U.S. National Security Policy since World War II*. New York: Columbia University Press.

Baldwin, James. 1962. *The Fire Next Time*. New York: Vintage International.

Bandow, Doug. 2009. "The Problem of Guantanamo." Cato Institute. http://social.cato.org/blog/problem-guantanamo

Bayoumi, Moustafa. 2009. *How Does It Feel to Be a Problem? Being Young and Arab in America*. New York: Penguin Books.

Bellah, Robert N. 1967. "Civil Religion in America." *Daedalus*, 96 (1): 1–21.

Bellah, Robert N., Richard Madsen, William M. Sullivan, Ann Swidler, and Steven M. Tipton. 1985. *Habits of the Heart: Individualism and Commitment in American Life*. Berkeley: University of California Press.

Blackwell, Maylei. 2011. *Chicana Power!: Contested Histories of Feminism in the Chicano Movement*. Austin: University of Texas Press.

Boggs, Carl. 1977. "Marxism, Prefigurative Communism, and the Problem of Workers Control." *Radical America: Special Double Issue* 11–12 (6/1): 99–122.

Boltanski, Luc. 2004. *Distant Suffering: Morality, Media and Politics*. Translated by Graham Burchell. Cambridge, UK: Cambridge University Press.

Boyd, Andrew, and Dave Oswald Mitchell, eds. 2012. *Beautiful Trouble: A Toolbox for Revolution*. New York: OR Books.

Branch, Taylor. 1989. *Parting the Waters: America in the King Years 1954–63*. New York: Simon & Schuster.

Bravin, Jess. 2014. *The Terror Courts: Rough Justice at Guantanamo Bay*. New Haven, CT: Yale University Press.

Breines, Winifred. 1980. "Community and Organization: The New Left and Michels' 'Iron Law.'" *Social Problems* 27 (4): 419–29.

Brown, Anna J., Michael Stewart Foley, Patrick Stanley, and Matthew Vogel, eds. 2008. *Witness against Torture: The Campaign to Shut Down Guantanamo*. New York: Yellow Bike Press.

Brown, Wendy. 2005. *Edgework: Critical Essays on Knowledge and Politics*. Princeton, NJ: Princeton University Press.

    2015. *Undoing the Demos: Neoliberalism's Stealth Revolution*. New York: Zone Books.

Butigan, Ken. 2003. *Pilgrimage through a Burning World: Spiritual Practice and Nonviolent Protest at the Nevada Test Site*. Albany: State University of New York Press.

Butler, Judith. 1993. "Gender as Performance: An Interview with Judith Butler." *Radical Philosophy* 67: 32–9.

    2004. *Precarious Life: The Powers of Mourning and Violence*. New York: Verso.

    2009. *Frames of War: When Is Life Grievable?* New York: Verso.

Byrne, Malcolm. 2014. *Iran-Contra: Reagan's Scandal and the Unchecked Abuse of Presidential Power*. Lawrence: University Press of Kansas.

Calavita, Kitty. 1984. *U.S. Immigration Law and the Control of Labor: 1820–1924*. London, UK: Academic Press.

Calhoun, Craig. 2013. "Occupy Wall Street in Perspective." *The British Journal of Sociology* 64 (1): 26–38.

Chakrabarty, Dipesh. 2000. *Provincializing Europe: Postcolonial Thought and Historical Difference*. Princeton, NJ: Princeton University Press.

Chavez, Leo R. 2008. *The Latino Threat: Constructing Immigrants, Citizens, and the Nation*. Stanford, CA: Stanford University Press.

Christensen, Carol, and Fazal Rizvi, eds. 1996. *Disability and the Dilemmas of Education and Justice*. Berkshire, UK: Open University Press.

Chun, Jennifer Jihye, George Lipsitz, and Young Shin. 2010. "Immigrant Women Workers at the Center of Social Change: AIWA Takes Stock of Itself." *Kalfou* 1 (1): 127–32.

"Close to Slavery: Guestworker Programs in the United States." 2013. *Southern Poverty Law Center*. https://splcenter.org/20130218/close-slavery-guestworker-programs-united-states.

Cobb, Stephen. 1976. "Defense Spending and Defense Voting in the House: An Empirical Study of an Aspect of the Military-Industrial Complex Thesis." *American Journal of Sociology* 82 (1): 163–82.

Cocks, Joan. 1989. *The Oppositional Imagination: Feminism, Critique, and Political Theory*. New York: Routledge.

Cohen, Stanley. 2001. *States of Denial: Knowing about Atrocities and Suffering*. Cambridge, UK: Polity.

Coleman, Mathew. 2012. "The 'Local' Migration State: The Site-Specific Devolution of Immigration Enforcement in the US South." *Law & Policy* 34 (2): 159–90.

Collins, Patricia Hill. 1991. *Black Feminist Thought: Knowledge, Consciousness, and the Politics of Empowerment*. New York: Routledge.

Comaroff, Jean, and John L. Comaroff. 2012. *Theory from the South, or How Euro-America Is Evolving Toward Africa*. Boulder, CO: Paradigm Publishers.

Costa Vargas, João H. 2006. *Catching Hell in the City of Angels: Life and Meanings of Blackness in South Central Los Angeles*. Minneapolis: University of Minnesota Press.

Coutin, Susan Bibler. 1991. *The Culture of Protest: Religious Activism and the U.S. Sanctuary Movement*. Boulder, CO: Westview Press.

Crenshaw, Kimberlé. 1991. "Mapping the Margins: Intersectionality, Identity Politics, and the Violence against Women of Color." *Stanford Law Review* 43 (6): 1241–99.

Crittenden, Ann. 1988. *Sanctuary: A Story of American Conscience and the Law in Collision*. New York: Grove Press.

Cunningham, Hilary. 1995. *God and Caesar at the Rio Grande: Sanctuary and the Politics of Religion*. Minneapolis: University of Minnesota Press.

Cusimano, Theresa. 2011. "Theresa Cusimano Crossed The Line To Close The SOA." *SOA.org*. November 20, 2011. www.soaw.org/about-us/pocs/246-2011/3834-theresa-cusimano.

Danielson, Leilah. 2014. *American Gandhi: A. J. Muste and the History of Radicalism in the Twentieth Century*. Philadelphia: University of Pennsylvania Press.

Deligio, Liz. 2004. "Taking a Stand at School of the Americas." http://soaw.org/index.php?option=com_content&view=article&id=992

Demerath, Nicholas Jay, Gerald Marwell, and Michael T. Aiken. 1971. *Dynamics of Idealism: White Activists in a Black Movement*. San Francisco, CA: Jossey-Bass Inc. Publishers.

Denbeaux, Mark, Josh Denbeaux, and David Gratz; John Gregorek, Matthew Darby, Shana Edwards, Shane Hartman, Daniel Mann, and Helen Skinner, students. 2006. "Report on Guantánamo: A Profile of 517 Detainees through Analysis of Department of Defense Data." Newark, NJ: Seton Hall University School of Law.

Department of State. The Office of Electronic Information, Bureau of Public Affairs. 2005. "President Hosts United States – European Union Summit." June 20. http://2001-2009.state.gov/p/eur/rls/rm/48389.htm

Derwin, Susan. 2012. *Rage Is the Subtext: Readings in Holocaust Literature and Film*. Columbus: Ohio State University Press.

Diani, Mario. 1995. *Green Networks: A Structural Analysis of the Italian Environmental Movement*. Edinburgh, UK: Edinburgh University Press.

Diani, Mario, and Doug McAdam, eds. 2003. *Social Movements and Networks*. New York: Oxford University Press.

Dominguez Villegas, Rodrigo. 2014. "Central American Migrants and 'La Bestia': The Route, Dangers, and Government Responses." *Migrationpolicy.org*. September 10. www.migrationpolicy.org/article/central-american-migrants-and-la-bestia-route-dangers-and-government-responses

Doty, Megan. 2005. "Prisoner of Conscience Court Statements." www.soaw.org/about-us/pocs/153-court-statements/995

Duggan, Lisa. 2004. *The Twilight of Equality? Neoliberalism, Cultural Politics, and the Attack on Democracy*. Boston, MA: Beacon Press.

Dunn, Timothy J. 2009. *Blockading the Border and Human Rights: The El Paso Operation That Remade Immigration Enforcement*. Austin: University of Texas Press.

Durkheim, Emile. 1893. *The Division of Labor in Society*. New York: Free Press.

——— 1912. *Elementary Forms of the Religious Life*. Translated by Karen Elise Fields. New York: Free Press.

Eberhardt, Jennifer L., Phillip Atiba Goff, Valerie J. Purdie, and Paul G. Davies. 2004. "Seeing Black: Race, Crime, and Visual Processing." *Journal of Personality and Social Psychology* 87 (6): 876–93.

Emerson, Robert M., Rachel I. Fretz, and Linda L. Shaw. 1995. *Writing Ethnographic Fieldnotes*. Chicago, IL: University of Chicago Press.

Erdozaín, Plácido. 1981. *Archbishop Romero, Martyr of Salvador*. Maryknoll, NY: Orbis Books.

Ewing, Walter. 2014. "'Enemy Territory:' Immigration Enforcement in the US-Mexico Borderlands." *Journal on Migration and Human Security* 2 (3): 198–222.

Ewing, Philip. 2016. "Fact Check: Is Obama Handing Guantanamo Bay Back to Cuba?" *NPR*, February 25. www.npr.org/2016/02/25/468044107/fact-check-is-obama-handing-guantanamo-bay-back-to-cuba

Eyerman, Ron. 2005. "How Social Movements Move: Emotions and Social Movements." In *Emotions and Social Movements*, edited by Helena Flam and Debra King, 41–56. New York: Routledge.

Eyerman, Ron, and Andrew Jamison. 1991. *Social Movements: A Cognitive Approach*. University Park: Pennsylvania State University Press.

Falkoff, Marc, ed. 2007. *Poems from Guantánamo: The Detainees Speak*. Iowa City: University of Iowa Press.

Farmer, Paul. 2013. *To Repair the World: Paul Farmer Speaks to the Next Generation*. Berkeley: University of California Press.

Feldman, Allen. 1994. "On Cultural Anesthesia: From Desert Storm to Rodney King." *American Ethnologist* 21 (2): 404–18.

Felman, Shoshana, and Dori Laub. 1991. *Testimony: Crises of Witnessing in Literature, Psychoanalysis and History*. New York: Routledge.

Ferguson, Kathryn, Norma A. Price, and Ted Parks. 2010. *Crossing with the Virgin: Stories from the Migrant Trail*. Tucson: University of Arizona Press.

Finnegan, William. 2017. "President Trump's Guantánamo Delusion." *The New Yorker*, March 9. www.newyorker.com/news/daily-comment/president-trumps-guantanamo-delusion

Fitzpatrick-Behrens, Susan. 2011. *The Maryknoll Catholic Mission in Peru, 1943–1989: Transnational Faith and Transformations*. Notre Dame, IN: University of Notre Dame Press.

Flood, Gavin. 2004. *The Ascetic Self: Subjectivity, Memory and Tradition*. Cambridge, UK: Cambridge University Press.

Foley, Michael Stewart. 2003. *Confronting the War Machine: Draft Resistance during the Vietnam War*. Chapel Hill, NC: The University of North Carolina Press.

Foucault, Michel. 1997. "The Ethics of the Concern of the Self as a Practice of Freedom." In *Ethics: Subjectivity and Truth*, edited by Paul Rabinow, 1: 281–301. The Essential Works of Michel Foucault 1954–1984. New York: The New Press.

2008. *The Birth of Biopolitics: Lectures at the College de France, 1978–1979*, edited by Michel Senellart, Francois Ewald, and Alessandro Fontana. Translated by Graham Burchell. Basingstoke, UK: Palgrave Macmillan.

Fregoso, Rosa Linda. 2003. *meXicana Encounters: The Making of Social Identities on the Borderlands*. Berkeley: University of California Press.

Fukumura, Yoko, and Martha Matsuoka. 2002. "Redefining Security: Okinawa Women's Resistance to U.S. Militarism." In *Women's Activism and Globalization: Linking Local Struggles and Global Politics*, edited by Nancy Naples and Manisha Desai, 239–66. New York: Routledge.

Gandhi, Mohandas. 1940. *Harijan*, October 13.

Gerlach, Luther P., and Virginia H. Hine. 1970. *People, Power, Change: Movements of Social Transformation*. Indianapolis, IN: Bobbs-Merrill Company.

Ghaziani, Amin. 2008. *The Dividends of Dissent: How Conflict and Culture Work in Lesbian and Gay Marches on Washington*. Chicago, IL: University of Chicago Press.

Gill, Lesley. 2004. *The School of the Americas: Military Training and Political Violence in the Americas*. Durham, NC: Duke University Press Books.

Gilmore, Ruth Wilson. 1998. "Globalisation and US Prison Growth: From Military Keynesianism to Post-Keynesian Militarism." *Race & Class* 40 (2/3): 171–88.

Giroux, Henry A. 2008. *Against the Terror of Neoliberalism: Politics beyond the Age of Greed*. New York: Routledge.

Givoni, Michel. 2013. "The Ethics of Witnessing and the Politics of the Governed." *Theory, Culture & Society* 31 (1): 123–42.

Glucklich, Ariel. 2003. *Sacred Pain: Hurting the Body for the Sake of the Soul*. Oxford, UK: Oxford University Press.

Gómez-Barris, Macarena. 2010. "Witness Citizenship: The Place of Villa Grimaldi in Chilean Memory." *Sociological Forum* 25 (1): 27–46.

Gordon, Avery. 1997. *Ghostly Matters: Haunting and the Sociological Imagination*. Minneapolis: University of Minnesota Press.

2010. "The Prisoner's Curse." In *Toward a Sociology of the Trace*, edited by Herman Gray and Macarena Gómez-Barris, 17–65. Minneapolis: University of Minnesota Press.

Gould, Deborah B. 2009. *Moving Politics: Emotion and ACT UP's Fight against AIDS*. Chicago, IL: University of Chicago Press.

Grandin, Greg. 2006. *Empire's Workshop: Latin America, the United States, and the Rise of the New Imperialism*. Reprint edn. New York: Holt Paperbacks.

Greenberg, Karen, and Joshua Dratel, eds. 2005. *The Torture Papers: The Road to Abu Ghraib*. New York: Cambridge University Press.

Grele, Ronald J. 2011. "The Reminiscences of Jeremy Varon." The Guantánamo Bay Oral History Project. Columbia University, NY: Columbia Center for Oral History.

Griffin, Larry. 2004. "'Generations and Collective Memory' Revisited: Race, Region, and Memory of Civil Rights." *American Sociological Review* 69 (4): 544–57.

Grudzinski, Marcus. 2017. "Quakers Sail to Vietnam – Mulocalhistoryprojects." Accessed July 13. http://mulocalhistoryprojects.org/afsc/afscphoenix/

Hafetz, Jonathan, and Mark Denbeaux. 2009. *The Guantánamo Lawyers: Inside a Prison Outside the Law*. New York: New York University Press.

Halbwachs, Maurice. 1925. *On Collective Memory*. Translated by Lewis A. Coser. Chicago, IL: University of Chicago Press.

Hale, Charles, ed. 2008. *Engaging Contradictions: Theory, Politics, and Methods of Activist Scholarship.* Berkeley: University of California Press.

Hall, Stuart. 1986. "The Problem of Ideology-Marxism without Guarantees." *Journal of Communication Inquiry* 10 (2): 28–44.

    1996. "Race, Articulation, and Societies Structured in Dominance." In *Black British Cultural Studies: A Reader,* edited by Houston A. Baker Jr, Manthia Diawara, and Ruth H. Lindeborg. Chicago: University of Chicago Press.

    2011. "The Neoliberal Revolution." *Cultural Studies* 25 (6): 705–28.

Hardt, Michael, and Antonio Negri. 2011. "The Fight for 'Real Democracy' at the Heart of Occupy Wall Street." *Foreign Affairs* 11.

Hartman, Saidiya V. 1997. *Scenes of Subjection: Terror, Slavery, and Self-Making in Nineteenth-Century America.* New York: Oxford University Press.

Hartsock, Nancy. 1983. "The Feminist Standpoint: Developing the Ground for a Specifically Feminist Historical Materialism." In *Discovering Reality: Feminist Perspectives on Epistemology, Metaphysics, Methodology, and Philosophy of Science,* edited by Sandra Harding and Merrill B. Hintikka, 283–310. Dordrecht: Springer Netherlands.

Harvey, David. 2005. *A Brief History of Neoliberalism.* Oxford, UK: Oxford University Press.

Haugerud, Angelique. 2013. *No Billionaire Left Behind: Satirical Activism in America.* Stanford, CA: Stanford University Press.

Hernandez, David M. 2005. "Undue Process: Immigrant Detention, Due Process, and Lesser Citizenship." ISSI Fellows Working Papers. Institute for the Study of Social Change. University of California, Berkeley.

Hernandez, Kelly Lytle. 2010. *Migra!: A History of the U.S. Border Patrol.* Berkeley: University of California Press.

Hobbes, Thomas. 1651. "Equality in the State of Nature." In *Equality: Selected Readings,* edited by Louis P. Pojman and Robert Westmoreland, 26–36. New York: Oxford University Press.

hooks, bell. 1984. *Feminist Theory: From Margin to Center.* Boston, MA: South End Press.

Horton, Scott. 2010. "The Guantánamo 'Suicides': A Camp Delta Sergeant Blows the Whistle." *Harper's Magazine,* March. http://harpers.org/archive/2010/03/the-guantanamo-suicides/

INCITE! Women of Color against Violence. 2009. *The Revolution Will Not Be Funded: Beyond the Non-Profit Industrial Complex.* Cambridge, MA: South End Press.

Ioanide, Paula. 2015. *The Emotional Politics of Racism: How Feelings Trump Facts in an Era of Colorblindness.* Stanford, CA: Stanford University Press.

Jaggar, Alison. 1989. "Love and Knowledge: Emotion in Feminist Epistemology." *Inquiry* 32 (2): 151–76.

Jasper, James M. 1997. *The Art of Moral Protest: Culture, Biography, and Creativity in Social Movements.* Chicago, IL: University of Chicago Press.

Jenkins, J. Craig. 1983. "Resource Mobilization Theory and the Study of Social Movements." *Annual Review of Sociology* 9: 527–53.

Joseph, Miranda. 2002. *Against the Romance of Community.* Minneapolis: University of Minnesota Press.

Joseph, Peniel E. 2007. *Waiting 'Til the Midnight Hour: A Narrative History of Black Power in America*. New York: Holt Paperbacks.

Kaplan, Amy. 2005. "Where Is Guantánamo?" *American Quarterly* 57 (3): 831–58.

King, Martin Luther. 1953. "An Experiment in Love." In *A Testament of Hope: The Essential Writings and Speeches of Martin Luther King, Jr.*, edited by James M. Washington, 16–20. New York: HarperCollins.

Klatch, Rebecca. 2002. "The Development of Individual Identity and Consciousness among Movements of the Left and Right." In *Social Movements: Identity, Culture, and the State*, edited by David S. Meyer, Nancy Whittier, and Belinda Robnett, 185–201. New York: Oxford University Press.

Kogelmann, Brian. 2013. "What's So Bad about Guantanamo?" *Libertarianism.org*. May 15, 2013. www.libertarianism.org/blog/whats-so-bad-about-guantanamo.

Koopman, Sara. 2008. "Cutting Through Topologies: Crossing Lines at the School of the Americas." *Antipode* 40 (5): 825–47.

Kosek, Joseph Kip. 2011. *Acts of Conscience: Christian Nonviolence and Modern American Democracy*. New York: Columbia University Press.

Kraemer, Kelly. 2007. "Solidarity in Action: Exploring the Work of Allies in Social Movements." *Peace & Change* 32 (1): 20–38.

Kriesi, Hanspeter. 1996. "The Organizational Structure of New Social Movements in a Political Context." In *Comparative Perspective on Social Movements: Political Opportunities, Mobilizing Structures, and Cultural Framing*, edited by Doug McAdam, John McCarthy, and Mayer N. Zald, 152–84. New York: Cambridge University Press.

Kurasawa, Fuyuki. 2007. *The Work of Global Justice: Human Rights as Practices*. Cambridge, UK: Cambridge University Press.

——— . 2009. "A Message in a Bottle: Bearing Witness as a Mode of Transnational Practice." *Theory, Culture & Society* 26 (1): 92–111.

Levinas, Emmanuel. 1969. *Totality and Infinity: An Essay on Exteriority*. Translated by Alphonso Lingis. Pittsburgh, PA: Duquesne University Press.

Lichtenstein, Nelson. 2003. *State of the Union: A Century of American Labor*. Princeton, NJ: Princeton University Press.

Lincoln, Patrick. 2003. "Prisoner of Conscience Court Statements." www.soaw.org/about-us/pocs/153-court-statements/598

Lipsitz, George. 2008. "Walleye Warriors and White Identities: Native Americans' Treaty Rights, Composite Identities and Social Movements." *Ethnic and Racial Studies* 31 (1): 101–22.

——— . 2011a. *How Racism Takes Place*. Philadelphia, PA: Temple University Press.

——— . 2011b. "Constituted by a Series of Contestations: Critical Race Theory as a Social Movement." *Connecticut Law Review* 43 (5): 1459–78.

Lipsitz, George, and Russell Rodríguez. 2012. "Turning Hegemony on Its Head: The Insurgent Knowledge of Américo Paredes." *Journal of American Folklore* 125 (495): 111–25.

Lofland, John. 1996: *Social Movement Organizations*. New York: Aldine de Gruyter.

López Vigil, María. 2000. *Oscar Romero: Memories in Mosaic*. Washington, DC: Epica Task Force.

Lorde, Audre. 1984. *Sister Outsider: Essays and Speeches*. Berkeley, CA: Crossing Press.

Luff, Donna. 1999. "Dialogue across the Divides: 'Moments of Rapport' and Power in Feminist Research with Anti-Feminist Women." *Sociology* 33 (4): 687–703.

Magaña, Rocio. 2008. "*Bodies on the Line: Life, Death, and Authority on the Arizona-Mexico Border.*" University of Chicago: Unpublished Dissertation.

Margulies, Joseph. 2013. *What Changed When Everything Changed: 9/11 and the Making of National Identity.* New Haven, CT: Yale University Press.

Marsh, Charles. 2004. *The Beloved Community: How Faith Shapes Social Justice, from the Civil Rights Movement to Today.* New York: Basic Books.

Martin-Baron, Michelle. 2014. "(Hyper/in)visibility and the Military Corps(e)." In *Social Justice: Queer Necropolitics*, edited by Jin Haritaworn, Adi Kuntsman, and Silvia Posocco, 51–70. Florence, KY: Taylor & Francis.

Martínez, Daniel, Robin Reineke, Raquel Rubio-Goldsmith, and Bruce Parks. 2014. "Structural Violence and Migrant Deaths in Southern Arizona: Data from the Pima County Office of the Medical Examiner, 1990–2013." *Journal on Migration and Human Security* 2 (4): 257–86.

Marx, Gary, and Michael Useem. 1971. "Majority Involvement in Minority Movements: Civil Rights, Abolition, Untouchability." *Journal of Social Issues* 27 (1): 81–104.

Marx, Karl, and Friedrich Engels. 1845. *The German Ideology, Including Theses on Feuerbach.* Amherst, NY: Prometheus Books.

Massey, Douglas S., Jorge Durand, and Nolan J. Malone. 2002. *Beyond Smoke and Mirrors: Mexican Immigration in an Era of Economic Integration.* New York: Russell Sage Foundation.

Mbembe, Achille. 2001. *On the Postcolony.* Berkeley; CA: University of California Press.

McAdam, Doug. 1982. *Political Process and the Development of Black Insurgency, 1930–1970.* Chicago, IL: University of Chicago Press.

———. 1986. "Recruitment to High-Risk Activism: The Case of Freedom Summer." *American Journal of Sociology* 92 (1): 64–90.

———. 1988. *Freedom Summer.* New York: Oxford University Press.

McAdam, Doug, Sidney Tarrow, and Charles Tilly. 2001. *Dynamics of Contention.* New York: Cambridge University Press.

McCarthy, John D., and Mayer N. Zald. 1977. "Resource Mobilization and Social Movements: A Partial Theory." *The American Journal of Sociology* 82 (6): 1212–41.

McDonald, Kevin. 2002. "From Solidarity to Fluidarity: Social Movements Beyond 'Collective Identity' – The Case of Globalization Conflicts." *Social Movement Studies.* 1(2): 109–28.

Meyer, David S. 2003. "How Social Movements Matter." *Contexts* 2 (4): 30–35.

Miles, Margaret R. 1981. *Fullness of Life: Historical Foundations for a New Asceticism.* Louisville, KY: Westminster John Knox Press.

Mills, C. Wright. 1956. *The Power Elite.* New York: Oxford University Press.

———. 1959. *The Sociological Imagination.* 40th anniversary edn. Oxford, UK: Oxford University Press.

Mitchel, Timothy. 2011. *Carbon Democracy: Political Power in the Age of Oil.* London: Verso.

Munkres, Susan. 2008. "Being 'Sisters' to Salvadoran Peasants: Deep Identification and Its Limits." In *Identity Work in Social Movements*, edited by Jo Reger, Daniel J. Myers, and Rachel L. Einwohner, 189–212. Minneapolis, MN: University of Minnesota Press.

Musto, David F. 1999. *The American Disease: Origins of Narcotic Control.* 3rd edn. New York: Oxford University Press.

Myers, Daniel J. 2008. "Ally Identity: The Politically Gay." In *Identity Work in Social Movements*, edited by Jo Reger, Daniel J. Myers, and Rachel L. Einwohner, 167–88. Minneapolis: University of Minnesota Press.

Nagel, Joane. 1996. *American Indian Ethnic Renewal: Red Power and the Resurgence of Identity and Culture*. New York: Oxford University Press.

Nelson, Diane. 1999. *A Finger in the Wound: Body Politics in Quincentennial Guatemala*. Berkeley: University of California Press.

———. 2009. *Reckoning: The Ends of War in Guatemala*. Durham, NC: Duke University Press Books.

Nepstad, Sharon Erickson. 2000. "School of the Americas Watch." *Peace Review* 12 (1): 67–72.

———. 2004. *Convictions of the Soul: Religion, Culture, and Agency in the Central America Solidarity Movement*. New York: Oxford University Press.

———. 2007. "Oppositional Consciousness among the Privileged: Remaking Religion in the Central America Solidarity Movement." *Critical Sociology* 33 (4): 661–88.

———. 2008. *Religion and War Resistance in the Plowshares Movement*. New York: Cambridge University Press.

Nevins, Joseph. 2010. *Operation Gatekeeper and Beyond: The War on "Illegals" and the Remaking of the U.S.-Mexico Boundary*. 2nd edn. New York: Routledge.

Ngai, Mae M. 2004. *Impossible Subjects: Illegal Aliens and the Making of Modern America*. Princeton, NJ: Princeton University Press.

Nixon, Rob. 2006. "Slow Violence, Gender and the Environmentalism of the Poor." *Journal of Commonwealth and Postcolonial Studies* 13.2–14.1 (July): 14–37.

Norris, Rebecca Sachs. 2009. "The Paradox of Healing Pain." *Religion* 39 (1): 22–33.

Notes from Nowhere, ed. 2003. *We Are Everywhere: The Irresistible Rise of Global Anti-Capitalism*. New York: Verso.

Novick, Peter. 1999. *The Holocaust in American Life*. Boston, MA: Houghton Mifflin Company.

Olick, Jeffrey K. 2007. *The Politics of Regret: On Collective Memory and Historical Responsibility*. New York: Routledge.

Oliver, Kelly. 2004. "Witnessing and Testimony." *Parallax* 10 (1): 78–87.

Omi, Michael, and Howard Winant. 2015. *Racial Formation in the United States*. 3rd edn. New York: Routledge.

Paik, A. Naomi. 2010. "Testifying to Rightlessness: Haitian Refugees Speaking from Guantánamo." *Social Text* 28 (3): 39–65.

Palmer, Bruce. 1980. *"Man Over Money": The Southern Populist Critique of American Capitalism*. Chapel Hill: The University of North Carolina Press.

Pasulka, Nicole. 2016. "How a Modest Wooden Boat Became an International Icon During the Vietnam War, Then Disappeared." *Atlas Obscura*. October 11. www.atlasobscura.com/articles/the-american-boat-that-sailed-to-vietnam-during-the-warthen-disappeared

Payne, Charles. 1995. *I've Got the Light of Freedom: The Organizing Tradition and the Mississippi Freedom Struggle*. Berkeley: University of California Press.

Pease, Donald E. 2009. *The New American Exceptionalism*. Minneapolis: University of Minnesota Press.

Pedwell, Carolyn. 2012. "Affective (self-) Transformations: Empathy, Neoliberalism and International Development." *Feminist Theory* 13 (2): 163–79.

Pfaff, Steven, and Guobin Yang. 2001. "Double-Edged Rituals and the Symbolic Resources of Collective Action: Political Commemorations and the Mobilization of Protest in 1989." *Theory and Society* 30 (4): 539–89.

Pilkington, Ed. 2015. "US Activists to Launch Guantánamo Protest along Camp's Perimeter." *The Guardian*, November 25. US news. www.theguardian.com/us-news/2015/nov/25/guantanamo-bay-protest-thanksgiving-fast

Polletta, Francesca. 1999. "'Free Spaces' in Collective Action." *Theory and Society*. 28(1): 1–38.

———. 2002. *Freedom Is an Endless Meeting: Democracy in American Social Movements.* Chicago, IL: University of Chicago Press.

Ratner, Michael, and Ellen Ray. 2004. *Guantánamo: What the World Should Know.* White River Junction, VT: Chelsea Green Publishing.

Reissiger, Andrew. 2006. "World Tour Radio Presents: The Sounds of Protest at the School of the Americas." *Public Radio Exchange.* November 1.

Risen, James, and Tim Golden. 2006. "3 Prisoners Commit Suicide at Guantánamo." *The New York Times*, June 11, sec. National. www.nytimes.com/2006/06/11/us/11gitmo.html

Robinson, Cedric. 1983. *Black Marxism: The Making of the Black Radical Tradition.* London, UK: Zed Books.

Robinson, William I. 2004. *A Theory of Global Capitalism: Production, Class, and State in a Transnational World.* Baltimore, MD: Johns Hopkins University Press.

Robinson, William, and Mario Barrera. 2011. "Global Capitalism and Twenty-First Century Fascism: A US Case Study." *Race & Class* 53 (3): 4–29.

Rodriguez, Dylan. 2006. *Forced Passages: Imprisoned Radical Intellectuals and the U.S. Prison Regime.* Minneapolis: University of Minnesota Press.

Roseneil, Sasha. 1995. *Disarming Patriarchy: Feminism and Political Action at Greenham.* Buckingham, UK: Open University Press.

Rupp, Leila, and Verta Taylor. 2003. *Drag Queens at the 801 Cabaret.* Chicago, IL: University of Chicago Press.

Russo, Chandra. 2014. "Allies Forging Collective Identity: Embodiment and Emotions on the Migrant Trail." *Mobilization: An International Quarterly* 19 (1): 67–82.

Said, Edward. 1992. *The Question of Palestine.* New York: Vintage Books.

Sanchez, George J. 1993. *Becoming Mexican American: Ethnicity, Culture and Identity in Chicano Los Angeles, 1900–1945.* New York: Oxford University Press.

Santino, Jack. 2004. "Performance Commemoratives, the Personal, and the Public: Spontaneous Shrines, Emergent Ritual, and the Field of Folklore (AFS Presidential Plenary Address, 2003)." *Journal of American Folklore* 117 (466): 363–72.

Scarry, Elaine. 1985. *The Body in Pain: The Making and Unmaking of the World.* New York: Oxford University Press.

Schacht, Steven, and Doris Ewing. 2001. "Feminist Women and (Pro)Feminist Men: Moving from an Uneasy to a Radical Alliance." In *Forging Radical Alliances across Difference*, edited by Steven Schacht and Jill M. Bystydzienki, 191–204. London, UK: Rowman and Littlefield Publishers.

Scheff, Thomas. 1979. *Catharsis in Healing, Ritual, and Drama.* Berkeley: University of California Press.

Scheper-Hughes, Nancy. 1995. "The Primacy of Ethical: Proposition of a Militant Ethnography." *Current Anthropology* 36 (3): 409–20.

Schwartz, Barry. 1982. "The Social Context of Commemoration: A Study in Collective Memory." *Social Forces* 61 (2): 374–402.

Scott, James C. 1977. "Protest and Profanation: Agrarian Revolt and the Little Tradition, Part I." *Theory and Society* 4 (1): 1–38.

———. 1987. *Weapons of the Weak: Everyday Forms of Peasant Resistance*. Princeton, NJ: Yale University Press.

Severson, Kim. 2010. "School of Americas Protesters Arrested at Fort Benning." *The New York Times*, November 21. www.nytimes.com/2010/11/22/us/politics/22protest.html

Sloan, Cliff. 2015. "The Path to Closing Guantánamo." *The New York Times*, January 5. www.nytimes.com/2015/01/06/opinion/the-path-to-closing-guantanamo.html

Smith, Christian. 1991. *The Emergence of Liberation Theology: Radical Religion and Social Movement Theory*. Chicago, IL: University of Chicago Press.

———. 1996. *Resisting Reagan: The U.S. Central America Peace Movement*. Chicago, IL: University of Chicago Press.

Smith, Donte. 2006. "SOA: On Crossing the Line and Life on the Otherside." www.soaw.org/about-us/pocs/153-court-statements/1255

Smith, Linda Tuhiwai. 1999. *Decolonizing Methodologies: Research and Indigenous Peoples*. London, UK: Zed Books.

Solis, Gabriel Daniel. 2012. "The Reminiscences of Matthew Daloisio, Session Two." *The Guantánamo Bay Oral History Project*. Columbia University, NY: Columbia Center for Oral History.

Solnit, Rebecca. 2000. *Wanderlust: A History of Walking*. New York: Penguin Books.

Spivak, Gayatri Chakravorty. 1988. "Can the Subaltern Speak?" In *Marxism and the Interpretation of Culture*, edited by Cary Nelson and Lawrence Grossberg, 271–313. London, UK: Macmillan Education UK.

Staggenborg, Suzanne, and Amy Lang. 2007. "Culture and Ritual in the Montreal Women's Movement." *Social Movement Studies* 6 (2): 177–94.

Sturken, Marita. 1997. *Tangled Memories: The Vietnam War, the AIDS Epidemic, and the Politics of Remembering*. Berkeley: University of California Press. www.ucpress.edu/book.php?isbn=9780520206205

Summers Effler, Erika. 2010. *Laughing Saints and Righteous Heroes: Emotional Rhythms in Social Movement Groups*. Chicago, IL: University of Chicago Press.

Sundberg, Juanita. 2007. "Reconfiguring North–South Solidarity: Critical Reflections on Experiences of Transnational Resistance." *Antipode* 39 (1): 144–66.

Sutton, Barbara. 2007. "Poner El Cuerpo: Women's Embodiment and Political Resistance in Argentina." *Latin American Politics and Society* 49 (3): 129–62.

Taft, Jessica K. 2011. *Rebel Girls: Youth Activism and Social Change across the Americas*. New York: New York University Press.

Taussig, Michael. 1999. *Defacement: Public Secrecy and the Labor of the Negative*. Stanford, CA: Stanford University Press.

Taylor, Diana. 1997. *Disappearing Acts: Spectacles of Gender and Nationalism in Argentina's "Dirty War."* Durham, NC: Duke University Press.

Taylor, Keeanga-Yamahtta. 2016. *From #BlackLivesMatter to Black Liberation*. Chicago, IL: Haymarket Books.

Taylor, Lawrence J. 2007. "Centre and Edge: Pilgrimage and the Moral Geography of the US/Mexico Border." *Mobilities* 2 (3): 383–93.

Taylor, Verta, Katrina Kimport, Nella Van Dyke, and Ellen Ann Andersen. 2009. "Culture and Mobilization: Tactical Repertoires, Same-Sex Weddings, and the Impact on Gay Activism." *American Sociological Review* 74 (6): 865–90.

Tharoor, Ishaan. 2003. "Viewpoint: Why Was the Biggest Protest in World History Ignored?" *Time*, February 15. http://world.time.com/2013/02/15/viewpoint-why-was-the-biggest-protest-in-world-history-ignored/.

Tilly, Charles. 1978. *From Mobilization to Revolution*. Reading, MA: Addison-Wesley. 2004. *Social Movements, 1768–2004*. Boulder, CO: Routledge.

Thomas, Merton. 1985. *The Hidden Ground of Love: Letters, edited by Thomas Shannon*. New York: Farrar, Strauss, Giroux.

Tomlinson, Barbara, and George Lipsitz. 2013. "American Studies as Accompaniment." *American Quarterly* 65 (1): 1–30.

Turner, Bryan S. 2006. *Vulnerability and Human Rights*. University Park, PA: Pennsylvania State University Press.

Turner, Bryan. 2007. "The Enclave Society: Towards a Sociology of Immobility." *European Journal of Social Theory* 10 (2): 287–304.

Turner, Victor. 1973. "The Center Out There: Pilgrim's Goal." *History of Religions* 12 (3): 191–230.

Tyler, Imogen. 2013. *Revolting Subjects: Social Abjection and Resistance in Neoliberal Britain*. London, UK: Zed Books.

Valantasis, Richard. 2008. *The Making of the Self: Ancient and Modern Asceticism*. Eugene, OR: Wipf and Stock Publishers.

Van Ham, Lane. 2011. *A Common Humanity Ritual, Religion, and Immigrant Advocacy in Tucson, Arizona*. Tucson: University of Arizona Press.

Verheyden-Hilliard, Mara. 2015. "Exposed: FBI Surveillance of School of the Americas Watch." *Partnership for Civil Justice Fund*. www.justiceonline.org/soaw

Volpp, Leti. 2002. "The Citizen and the Terrorist." *UCLA Law Review* 49: 1575–1600.

Voss, Kim, and Irene Bloemraad, eds. 2011. *Rallying for Immigrant Rights: The Fight for Inclusion in 21st Century America*. Berkeley: University of California Press.

Wacquant, Loïc. 2009. *Punishing the Poor: The Neoliberal Government of Social Insecurity*. Durham, NC: Duke University Press.

Walgrave, Stefaan, and Dieter Rucht, eds. 2010. *The World Says No to War: Demonstrations against the War on Iraq*. Minneapolis: University of Minnesota Press.

Wallerstein, Immanuel. 2008. "Remembering Andre Gunder Frank While Thinking about the Future." *Monthly Review* 60 (2).

Watkins, Mary. 2015. "Accompaniment: Psychosocial, Environmental, Trans-Species, Earth." *Journal of Social and Political Psychology* 3 (1): 325–41.

Weber, Max. 1904. *The Protestant Ethic and the Spirit of Capitalism*. Translated by Talcott Parsons. 2nd edn. London, UK: Routledge.
    1919. "Politics as Vocation." In *From Max Weber: Essays in Sociology*, edited by Hans Gerth and C. Wright Mills. New York: Oxford University Press.

White, Hayden. 2004. "Figural Realism in Witness Literature." *Parallax* 10 (1): 113–24.

Winant, Howard. 2004. *The New Politics of Race: Globalism, Difference, Justice*. Minneapolis: University of Minnesota Press.

Wittner, Lawrence. 1984. *Rebels against War: The American Peace Movement, 1933–1983*. Philadelphia, PA: Temple University Press.

Worthington, Andy. 2007. *The Guantanamo Files: The Stories of the 774 Detainees in America's Illegal Prison.* London, UK: Pluto Press.

2015. "The Path to Closing Guantánamo." *Closeguantanamo.org.* June 17.

Zelizer, Barbie. 1998. *Remembering to Forget: Holocaust Memory Through the Camera's Eye.* Chicago, IL: University of Chicago Press.

Zola, Irving Kenneth. 1993. "Self, Identity and the Naming Question: Reflections on the Language of Disability." *Social Science & Medicine* 36 (2): 167–73.

Index